AF597798

Europäische Schriften
zu Staat und Wirtschaft

edited by Prof. Dr. Klaus-Dirk Henke
Technische Universität Berlin
Fakultät Wirtschaft und Management

Volume 42

Marion Cornelia Schwärzler

The Multiregional Health Account

A Multiregional Analysis of the Health Economy in Germany

Nomos

Der Druck dieser wissenschaftlichen Arbeit wurde gefördert von:

Promotionsort:	Bremen
Termin des Prüfungskolloquiums:	18.10.2018
Erste Gutachterin:	Frau Prof. Dr. Jutta Günther
Zweiter Gutachter:	Herr Prof. Dr. Tobias Kronenberg

The Deutsche Nationalbibliothek lists this publication in the Deutsche Nationalbibliografie; detailed bibliographic data are available on the Internet at http://dnb.d-nb.de

a.t.: Bremen, Univ., Diss., 2018

ISBN 978-3-8487-5655-1 (Print)
978-3-8452-9734-7 (ePDF)

British Library Cataloguing-in-Publication Data
A catalogue record for this book is available from the British Library.

ISBN 978-3-8487-5655-1 (Print)
978-3-8452-9734-7 (ePDF)

Library of Congress Cataloging-in-Publication Data
Schwärzler, Marion Cornelia
The Multiregional Health Account
A Multiregional Analysis of the Health Economy in Germany
Marion Cornelia Schwärzler
227 p.
Includes bibliographic references.

ISBN 978-3-8487-5655-1 (Print)
978-3-8452-9734-7 (ePDF)

1st Edition 2019

Acknowledgements

The dissertation at hand is the result of four years of research I do not want to miss. I look at it proudly since it means something special to me, accompanying me for such a long time through both happy and rough times. Over these years, I let it grew with hard work and endurance so it became a piece of work I link to many experiences, which finally characterize both my dissertation and my person. Throughout those years, I have met several people, who had great influence to both my life and my dissertation, to whom I would like to express my particular thanks:

First, I want to thank the two people, who made it even possible for me to present this research output as a dissertation at this point. Both my supervisors, Prof. Dr. Jutta Günther and Prof. Dr. Tobias Kronenberg, have provided me with the feeling that my research is interesting and worth discussing. This feeling supported me to believe in what I am doing also in hard times. It felt like true and honest support I received from both of them. I feel absolutely honored to be supervised by two such professional researchers in this field.

I would also like to extend my thanks to the German Federal Ministry for Economic Affairs and Energy, represented by Dr. Rüdiger Leidner, Jochen Puth-Weißenfels and Dr. Toni Glaser, for their interest in this research field. Without their support, I would not have been able to conduct the present and earlier research regarding the economic contribution of the German health economy to this extent.

In this context, of course, my former employer, WifOR, played an essential role. Therefore, I would like to thank WifOR, represented by Dr. Dennis Ostwald and Benno Legler, for supporting this direction of research, so I was able to apply my research findings in several projects.

I will never forget the contribution of earlier project partners, Dr. Markus Schneider and Thomas Krauss from the research institute BASYS, who challenged my approaches especially in the first years of research with their critical queries. I am grateful they did so, since it further ignited my ambitions, at the same time knowing that competition and friendship can be closely allied.

This and further research regarding the German health economy could not have been accomplished to this extent without the support of the Federal Statistical Office, represented by Angela Höh. She did not only act as a representative of the Federal Statistical Office in providing an essential database for this research, but also spent much time to patiently listen and reply to my questions, for which I am very grateful.

A particular mention is worthwhile for Johannes Többen, who acted as a trailblazer for this research. Even in times he had not yet finished his own dissertation at Rijksuniversiteit Groningen, he was always keen to supply me with helpful information, encouraged me to participate at conferences and hinted towards papers, which might be helpful in the context of my research.

Thanks to Benno, the most important person in my life during the last years. He had the challenging role of being my direct superior at WifOR, my partner and my best friend at the same time. Therefore, he had always had my interests in the context of my dissertation as my direct superior in mind, yet much more was a wonderful partner, who reassured and comforted me, providing me with sufficient space so I could focus on my dissertation. At the same time, he was my most critical friend, who incited me to deliver top performances with his support and input. I know, this time has been challenging and I thank Benno for his patience and understanding.

Finally yet importantly, thanks to my beloved family, who supported me throughout the whole time and helped me restore the necessary easiness in times of concerns and powerlessness. At the same time, they provided me with feedback in times outside opinion was necessary in order to focus on the essential further steps. It was a wonderful experience to know that I can count on your support despite quite a geographical distance between us.

Table of Contents

List of figures

List of tables

Abbreviations

AFLQ	*Augmented Flegg's location quotient*
CHARM	*Cross-Hauling Adjusted Regionalization Method*
CN	*Combined Nomenclature*
CPA	*Classification of Products by Activity*
EGW	*Warengruppen der Ernährungswirtschaft und der Gewerblichen Wirtschaft (Classification by Commodity Groups and Subgroups of the Food Industry and Trade and Industry)*
ESA	*European system of accounts*
EU	*European Union*
EVS	*Einkommens- und Verbrauchsstichprobe (Income and Consumption Survey)*
FLQ	*Flegg's location quotient*
GDP	*Gross domestic product*
GP	*Güterverzeichnis für Produktionsstatistiken (Product Classification for Production Statistics)*
GVA	*Gross Value Added*
HIOT	*Health Input-Output Table*
HSA	*Health Satellite Account*
MR	*Multiregional*
MRHA	*Multiregional Health Account*
NACE	*Nomenclature statistique des activités économiques dans la Communauté européenne*
NHA	*National Health Account*
R&D	*Research and Development*
RoC	*Rest of Country*
SHA	*System of Health Accounts*
SNA	*System of National Accounts*
SUT	*Supply and Use Table*
TLS	*Taxes less subsidies*
WA	*Warenverzeichnis für die Außenhandelsstatistik (Commodity Classification for Foreign Trade Statistics)*

Country codes

BW	*Baden-Württemberg*
BY	*Bavaria*
BE	*Berlin*
BB	*Brandenburg*
HB	*Bremen*
HH	*Hamburg*
HE	*Hesse*
MV	*Mecklenburg-Western Pomerania*
NI	*Lower Saxony*
NW	*North Rhine Westphalia*
RP	*Rhineland Palatinate*
SL	*Saarland*
SN	*Saxony*
ST	*Saxony-Anhalt*
SH	*Schleswig-Holstein*
TH	*Thuringia*

1. Introduction

1.1. *Background and motivation*

Health economics and health policy is a growing field of interest throughout the recent decades. This is due to several contributing factors such as a higher awareness for health itself, demographic change and, associated therewith, the challenges of a shift towards an older population with increased needs for health care supply, medical innovations and last but not least increased data availability. Increased interest in health policy also led to applying typical policy analysis instruments in this area, input-output analysis among them. However, such analyses are still rare compared to other fields of interests, such as energy and climate policy.

Reasons for this are various. On the one hand, a thorough analysis of the health economy is not possible from available input-output tables, since the health economy, as defined in this context, comprises not only health services but also the production of medicine and medical products and hence calls for a satellite account approach for further analyses. On the other hand, it is due to the initiatives of the German Federal Ministry for Economic Affairs and Energy, that the health economy is not only perceived as a cost factor but as an important contributor to economy. However, this perception, even if applied in Germany, is still rare in the rest of the world.

Hence, this dissertation aims to contribute to research in the field of health economics in terms of the economic effects the health economy has on German gross value added, employment and trade. Existing research focuses on the key figures for overall Germany. That research, however, led to the finding that the German health economy is characterized by various different influencing factors and therefore request more differentiated analyses. Further research suggested that the various influencing factors do not only arise from the different categories of the health economy but also from the characteristics of German regions.

Hence, the compilation of the Multiregional Health Account for the German federal states, as a further enhancement of the National Health Account, is in the center of this dissertation (chapter 3). Its foundations are based on the National Health Account. Its underlying principles and compilation steps are therefore presented at the beginning (chapter 2). Chapter

4 and 5 review the established Multiregional Health Account and aim to verify its basic results. Since the model refers to multiregional supply, use and input-output tables and is therefore applicable to answer specific questions in the context of German health policy, we apply it in the context of lagging investments in German hospitals in Chapter 6. Chapter 7 concludes.

1.2. Outline of the following chapters

Chapter 2 presents the background of the to-be developed Multiregional Health Account, the National Health Account (NHA) for Germany. The latter is a satellite account for the health economy, based on the foundations of the national accounting framework. It therefore consists of supply, use and input-output tables. The National Health Account quantifies the economic contribution of the health economy to national GVA, employment and international trade. Input-output analysis enables to calculate spillover effects.

The principles of the National Health Account for Germany were elaborated within several projects commissioned by the Federal Ministry for Economic Affairs and Energy since 2010. The availability of international standards favor the validity of results. Those international standards involve the national accounting framework on the one hand and the health expenditure survey on the other hand. The latter is the foundation for the definition and the subsequent quantification of the health economy. It acts as a secondary database in this context and assures validity of the results by matching health expenditures with private and public final demand from the use table. The National Health Account also provides key figures for several years, even if the underlying main database, a special evaluation on national supply and use tables, is only available for the years 2010 and 2011. We solve this challenge by applying the SUT-RAS algorithm to this very detailed level of data referring to the statistical standards of NACE 2008 and ESA 2010.

Chapter 3 is the centerpiece of this dissertation as it describes the elaborated methodology of the Multiregional Health Account (MRHA) for the German federal states. This methodological enhancement of the National Health Account consists of multiregional supply, use and input-output tables. The same principles developed for the national case apply for the multiregional case. This setting ensures consistency in definitions, methodology and results of the National Health Account and the Multiregional

Health Account. However, since there are no official multiregional supply and use tables available for the German federal states, the latter have to be compiled first.

The corresponding approach is based on the SUT-RAS algorithm developed by Temurshoev & Timmer (2011) and is adapted for the multiregional case. The main advantages of the approach are that initial tables of supply and use are consistently updated to given industry-specific information by assuring accounting balances to hold and simultaneously taking into account defined cell-specific information. The approach therefore relies on a rather mathematical approach, where the economic cycle of supply and use determine interregional trade.

Chapter 4 deals with an assessment of the basic results of the Multiregional Health Account for Germany. It therefore aims to validate the model before it is applied to answer concrete policy questions. This chapter focuses on the direct effects of the health economy in the federal states of Germany. This is essential, since the underlying satellite account pursues a product specific approach. Therefore, the corresponding results already refer to modelled information.

This chapter provides an overview of the results in terms of GVA, employment and international trade of the health economy in order to supply the reader with a first assessment of the characteristics federal states show in this context. This applies for both, one year in specific, which is 2011, and the time series of 2006 to 2015. The latter can be critically scrutinized from a methodological point of view, but reveals the power of the approach for a thorough assessment. Next to a general overview of basic results, the chapter also focuses on specific characteristics. This includes different production structures, such as the amount of manufacturing, trade and R&D for 2011 on the one hand, but also an assessment of dynamics medication supply shows in certain federal states. Available company data reveals similarities between modelled and observed dynamics.

Chapter 5 takes a further step in the assessment of the developed model. By applying input-output analysis, it evaluates the indirect effects of the Multiregional Health Account for Germany. This includes the evaluation of interindustry and interregional effects. Results are presented for specific areas of the health economy and are compared to actual observations.

Chapter 6 concerns the application of the Multiregional Health Account for Germany. It focusses on the current challenge of lagging investments in German hospitals. The dualistic framework of hospital financing in Germany obligates the federal states to finance the latter, while health insurance companies come up for current costs of health care supply. There is evidence that federal states do not fulfill their obligations, which implies severe challenges for German hospitals both in terms of quality and financing. This chapter investigates certain existent redistribution mechanism in order to figure out whether observable differences in regions are considered within those in order to supply needs-based health care, which, turns out, do not exist.

Consequently, this chapter established a redistribution mechanism of finances based on the Multiregional Health Account. The underlying idea is that federal states, which profit from health care supply in other federal states, since they supply necessary inputs such as energy or medication, should therefore be obligated to contribute to a certain earmarked fund to a higher amount. In a further step, the chapter also summarizes effects from actual investments taken in the health economy in order to establish a fundamental understanding for advantages of interregional support.

Chapter 7 concludes on the contribution of this dissertation. It therefore focuses on three main aspects. First, it describes the contribution of this dissertation to multiregional input-output analyses. Second, it focuses on achieved research in the field of the German regional health economy, including its characteristics and dynamics. Third, it describes the contribution this dissertation has on German health policy in the context of lagging investments in German hospitals.

2. Methodology of the National Health Account for Germany[1]

The National Health Account (NHA) for Germany quantifies the contribution of the health economy to gross value added, employment and trade. Its compilation methodology refers to satellite account standards based on supply and use tables of the national accounting system. Matching of official data on health expenditures with final consumption patterns of use tables represent an approach to identify the economic contribution of the health economy caused by the expenditures paid for health care. The framework of consistently processed supply and use tables allows us to compile a health input-output table. We calculate results for several years by making use of SUT-RAS to overcome the problem that we have at our disposal official supply and use tables for two years only. Definitions, concepts and methodology have been developed throughout several projects since 2010. This chapter describes foundations and methodology for the compilation of the NHA.

2.1. Introduction

Patient treatment has an impact on employment, economic performance and international trade. To quantify the role of the health economy, we have compiled the National Health Account (NHA) for Germany. This chapter describes the methodology underlying our compilation. The methodology is based on a satellite account approach by matching of health expenditures with the use side of national accounts.

To indicate the importance of the health economy, it follows from the latest NHA (Bundesministerium für Wirtschaft und Energie (BMWi) 2017) that the German health economy amounts to 12.0 percent of national GVA and contributes 16.1 percent to employment in 2016. The share of 8.2 percent of German exports indicates its relevance for manufacturing next to health care services. The indicators calculated for the period from 2006 until 2016 show an increasing importance of the health economy for the

1 This chapter is based on Schwärzler and Kronenberg (2016).

overall economy in terms of GVA, employment and international trade. Next to the direct effects of the German health economy, input-output analysis reveals indirect output multipliers of 1.54 (Schwärzler and Kronenberg 2016).

The NHA quantifies the economic contribution of the health economy by making use of the concepts, methodology and data of the national accounting framework. This focus enhances scientific research in the field of health economics next to analyses regarding the cost side of health care, which are still dominant in the political discussion (Organization for Economic Co-Operation and Development (OECD) 2015; Xu and Saksena 2011). Since health care costs impact on employment, economic performance and international trade, we derive the economic output of the health economy by matching health expenditures with the use side of national accounts.

In accordance to the categories of health expenditures, the health economy consists of a high number of heterogeneous products and services such as health care services, medication and medical technology. A broader definition also involves R&D, health tourism or e-health services and products among others. However, it is not possible to perform impact analyses on the economic significance of the health economy from available official data without making specific adjustments and calculations. Standard classifications (CPA and NACE) are in most cases too aggregated to specify health-specific product categories.

Industries characterized by a heterogeneous structure of involved contributors are called cross-section industries. Tourism, sports and education are further prominent examples (Ahlert and An der Heiden 2015; DIW Econ 2012; Haan and Rooijen-Horsten 2003; Helmenstein, Kleissner and Moser 2006; Instituto Nacional de Estatística Portugal 2016; Laimer, Ehn-Fragner and Smeral 2014; Steeg, van de 2009). To name one example in detail next to health, the tourism account of Aruba involves several different contributing industries in its concepts. Those range from activities of restaurants and hotels to real estate and construction activities, also including health services for the case when treatment is the purpose of traveling (Steeg, van de 2009). In order to evaluate the economic contribution of these industries as an integrated part of the overall economy, a satellite account approach has been applied in all these cases.

The aim of this chapter is to document the methodological approaches applied to compile the NHA. The concepts described are based on supply and use tables referring to the statistical standards of NACE 2008 and ESA 2010. Earlier work on this topic was based on different statistical databases and standards (Essig and Reich 1988; Geigant, Holub and Schnabl 1986; Henke et al. 2010; Ostwald, Henke, et al. 2014; Sarrazin 1992; Schneider et al. 2016). Methodological concepts have not been discussed extensively within these contributions especially in recent times, but have emphasized the description of results. The author of the present contribution joined the research activities in 2013 and performed the calculations and methodological advancements for the main key indicators of the NHA of the latest reports (Bundesministerium für Wirtschaft und Energie (BMWi) 2017 & 2016 & 2015; Schneider et al. 2016).

This chapter proceeds as follows: Section 2.2 describes the historical background and the paradigm shift concerning health care. That section is followed by a description of the main methodological background concerning international standards, satellite accounts, database and principles of the NHA. Section 2.4 focusses on the compilation methodology. Section 2.5 concludes and gives insight in further research areas.

2.2. Historical background and paradigm shift concerning health care

First attempts to calculate the economic contribution of health as part of national accounts arose in Germany as early as 1986 referring to the official input-output table of 1975 (Geigant et al. 1986). They did not conduct input-output analysis, since the calculated interrelationships with the overall economy could not be integrated consistently into the overall framework.

A combined approach involving national accounts on the one hand and health expenditure on the other hand, which is still the basic principle of calculation today, was developed in the late 1980s (Essig and Reich 1988). The authors stressed the necessity of characterizing the heterogeneity of health care, which goes in hand with the later definition of 'health economy' as a cross-section industry, consisting not only of health care services but also of additional services and products such as health tourism or pharmaceuticals.

The work of Essig and Reich (1988) referred to a conceptual framework only. First attempts to model a health satellite account according to their work were conducted a few years later in (Sarrazin 1992). This work was not only the first implementation of a health satellite account in association with health expenditures, but also involved a high number of conceptual ideas and validity checks. However, it did not include information on intermediate use. Consequently, input-output analysis was not possible.

From mid-1990 on, a paradigm shift has shaped the perception of the health economy within the political context (Goldschmidt and Hilbert 2009). This paradigm shift implied the focus on the cost side to turn into a focus on the economic impacts of health on the one hand and the perceived number of involved agents and contributors to health to increase on the other hand.

On a national level, the economic significance of health care first found substantial consideration within the special report of the Advisory Council on the Assessment of Developments in the Health Care System in 1997 (Sachverständigenrat zur Begutachtung der Entwicklung im Gesundheitswesen 1998). It named health care as a decisive element of the overall economy and its respective dynamics. Accordingly, its effects on GDP and employment were deemed to be important, in addition to its contribution to maintaining, restoring and promoting health of the population.

While this section of the special report exclusively emphasized the service-oriented part of health, the health economy was defined in a broader way as '[...] the production and marketing of goods and services, which serve for prevention as well as for the provision of health and for rehabilitation.' a few years later (Kuratorium Gesundheitswirtschaft 2005).

Therefore, the paradigm shift in the context of health is twofold: first, the supply of health care is not only service-oriented, it also consists of the production of goods, e.g. medicine or medical technology. Second, politicians now started to perceive the health economy as a contributor to economic output, employment and international trade. Previously, economists and politicians perceived the costs of health care supply as a major handicap for economic growth (Hilbert, Fretschner and Dülberg 2002). Especially in combination with demographic change, the topic was mainly discussed as a burden.

For Goldschmidt and Hilbert (2009) it is undeniable that the German health economy can only develop properly, if quality, efficiency and equity are of great importance within the industry. From a scientific point of view, however, they say a lot remains to be done in that field today, in order to identify the next steps enabling a proper future development of the health economy.

The research activities initiated by the Federal Ministry of Economic Affairs and Energy a few years ago followed Goldschmidt & Hilbert's statements. The first Health Satellite Account for Germany was published for the year 2005 (Henke et al. 2010). Both this and its updated version (Ostwald, Henke, et al. 2014), which reviewed the economic impact of the health economy for 2006 to 2008, based on the concepts and methods according to ESA 1995 (Eurostat 1996) and the classifications of industries according to NACE 2003 (Eurostat 2002). Underlying basic data, provided by the Federal Statistical Office, consisted of an input-output table and a supply table, both in a rectangular shape with 3,118 categories on the product side but with 120 industries in the input-output table and 221 industries in the supply table and hence a different number of categories on the industry side due to aggregation in the input-output table. From this statistical segmentation of the whole economy into 3,118 products, detailed information on 524 selected products with relevance to health were available for the calculations. Restricted data on the non-health related parts of the economy was available on an aggregated level only.

While calculations conducted in Henke et al. (2010) concentrated on the year 2005 and two additional projections on future values in 2020 and 2030, Ostwald et al. (2014) focused on annual data points for 2006 until 2008. In order to conclude on dynamics up to the current period, Ostwald et al. (2014) projected key indicators by making use of a forecast model based on evaluated drivers of future dynamics. In this project, input-output analysis was conducted for the first time. At that point of research, the initial name of the project changed from 'Health Satellite Account" (HSA) into 'National Health Account' (NHA).

Extensive revisions in the compilation of national accounts and the reclassification from NACE 2003 to NACE 2008 required adjustments in the existing methodology in 2015 (Schneider et al. 2016). Underlying basic data did not longer refer to input-output tables, but consisted of supply and use tables in the dimension of 2,643 products and 64 industries for the overall economy. These tables were available for the years 2008 to 2010. The number of 888 partially or fully health-related product groups were available for the calculations. Schneider et al. (2016) derived input-output tables from calculated health specific supply and use tables. This change of available basic data, which was not longer a detailed input-output and supply table but detailed supply and use tables, led to a revised way in computation and projection of key indicators. Schneider et al. (2016) applied the SUT-RAS method (Temurshoev and Timmer 2011) to update the detailed supply and use tables for the overall period of 2000 until 2014. This way, it became possible to extract the health economy from the overall economy consistently for a longer period for the first time.

The statistical standard ESA 1995 was replaced by ESA 2010 at the end of 2014 (Destatis 2014). This made straightforward updating of previous databases on national accounts impossible again (Bundesministerium für Wirtschaft und Energie (BMWi) 2016). Detailed data of supply and use tables were now available for 930 out of 2,643 product categories for the years 2010 and 2011. Based on this, health specific supply, use and input-output tables were calculated for the period 2000 until 2015.

The following sections focus on the current compilation methodology, which is based on supply and use tables, the calculation of the health input-output table based on the latter two tables and the projection of the underlying database by applying SUT-RAS.

2.3. Methodological background

This section aims to describe the methodological background for the compilation of the NHA. We present this in order to facilitate a better understanding of section 2.4. Basic principles of the NHA described have been implemented in earlier works already (Bundesministerium für Wirtschaft und Energie (BMWi) 2017 & 2016 & 2015; Henke et al. 2010; Ostwald et al. 2014; Schneider et al. 2016) and do not refer to our contribution exclusively. The remainder of this section is structured as follows: First, subsection 2.3.1 is dedicated to presenting official standards on the international level, which promote the concepts of the NHA. Secondly, the underlying database is portrayed in 2.3.2. Subsection 2.3.3 supplements with information on the principles of the NHA, which have to be considered during the compilation.

2.3.1. International standards

In order to develop the NHA, two basic principles are of main concern – the concept of satellite accounts on the one hand and the consideration of the health expenditure survey as part of the approach on the other hand. We will discuss those two basic principles in the remainder of this section. At this point, it is important to mention that the centerpiece of this work is to match national accounts with expenditures on health in order to obtain a satellite account enabling analyses concerning this cross-section industry. Both the compilation of satellite accounts and the health expenditure survey underlie specific international standards, which we will discuss in the following.

The System of National Accounts (SNA) defines satellite accounts as follows:

> 'Satellite accounts or systems generally stress the need to expand the analytical capacity of national accounting for selected areas of social concern in a flexible manner, without overburdening or disrupting the central system.'
> (European Commission et al. 2009)

National accounts contain a high amount of information about economic relationships and conceptual interconnectedness of industries. However, satellite accounts allow deeper analyses in the context of national accounts, focusing on certain fields or aspects of interest, which rely on information official data does not reveal. The objective of satellite accounts is therefore to quantify components of national accounts that are hidden or shown only to a minor extent (European Commission et al. 2009). Special evaluations of national accounts, like they are available in our case in the form of detailed supply and use tables, promote the deep analysis of goods and services of the economy, in order to shape areas of interest and to reveal relationships, which cannot be captured from the official framework.

In general, satellite accounts may involve some methodological differences from national accounts, i.e. regarding the treatment of auxiliary production or the disaggregation of industries (European Commission et al. 2009). Basic concepts of national accounts, however, have to remain in order to prevent the disruption of the central system.

Moreover, satellite accounts can concentrate on patterns of e.g. consumption, investment or intermediate use. This is also the case for the NHA, which refers to the final consumption patterns from official data on health expenditures. By matching this additional database with final consumption patterns of the use table we assure the exclusive focus on human health, which represents a main goal of the NHA. This way, we exclude health care services or medicine that do not promote better human health. For example, plastic surgery or illegal drug consumption would both be part of the health satellite account, if we were not able to match national accounts with data on health expenditures. The latter focusses exclusively on human health and follows international standards like national accounts.

Hence, official data on health expenditure from the Federal Statistical Office in Germany contributes to the validity of the NHA to a great extent. Next to national accounts, it therefore serves as the second main database to quantify the economic performance of the health economy. Guidelines for the compilation of the health expenditure survey are described in the following.

The System of Health Accounts (SHA), published in its recent edition in Organisation for Economic Co-operation and Development (OECD) et al. (2011) aims to serve as an international guideline for the definition and accounting mechanisms of health expenditures. It enables internationally harmonized comparisons across countries and time in order to obtain analyses and monitoring of health systems and related expenditures. The conceptual framework of health care and long-term care expenditure is tri-axial and therefore examines expenditures from the three perspectives of consumption, provision and financing. The health expenditure survey consequently answers the following questions and provides the corresponding information on expenditures (Organisation for Economic Co-operation and Development (OECD) et al. 2011):

- What kind of health care goods and services are consumed?
- Which health care providers deliver these goods and services?
- Which financing schemes pays for these goods and services?

Regarding the incurred costs of health care it is essential to provide a clear definition of which services and goods are considered within the health expenditure survey, so the database allows the wanted comparability between countries. The health expenditure survey from the Federal Statistical Office of Germany follows the guidelines of the SHA. Therefore, the definition of the NHA is directly linked to the definition of health care expenditures obtained from the SHA and hence of great importance for the compilation of the NHA.

According to the guideline of the SHA, all services and products, which have the primary goal to improve and preserve health or prevent from illness, are considered as being related to health and are consequently considered within the health expenditure survey. Hence, the concept follows a functional approach only. Questions of responsibility in terms of provision or funding do not decide upon the fact whether or not the amount spent on a certain service or good is considered within the health expenditure survey. For example, even if the statutory health insurance does not pay for a specific health care service, it is still considered within the health expenditure survey – and consequently the NHA - , as long as it serves the primary goal to improve and preserve health or prevent form illness.

The publication of the SHA contributed to an increasing number of studies on the economic impact of health on international grounds (Czypionka et al. 2014; Dunn, Rittmueller and Whitmire 2015; Instituto Brasileiro de Geografia e Estatística (IBGE) 2008; Instituto Nacional de Estatística Portugal 2015; Orosz and Morgan 2004). The approaches applied in the just mentioned literature differ from the approach of the current NHA for Germany in aspects such as they focus on health services only or relate health expenditure to GDP, the interrelations of the economy being left unconsidered.

2.3.2. Underlying database

The two main underlying databases of the NHA are the national accounts and the health expenditure survey. The Federal Statistical Office of Germany produces both statistics on an annual basis. The former provides the macroeconomic statistical framework for the satellite account. The intention of the latter database is to assure validity, acting as the statistical special evaluation in the field of health.

Data on health expenditures are currently available for the period 1992 until 2015 divided into the categories of function, providers and funding (Destatis 2017c; Destatis 2017d). Each of those is again divided into subsections.

The eight main functional categories are: investments; health prevention and public health services; medical services; nursing and therapeutic services; food and lodging; health care goods; patient transport; administrative services. Most categories provide further detail, e.g. pharmaceuticals, dentures, or therapeutic appliances in the category health care goods.

The eight main types of providers are separated into public health, outpatient facilities, inpatient facilities, ambulance services, administration, other providers/private households, rest of the world and investments. The latter is a fictional category, which was introduced to make a clear distinction between current costs and overall costs (Destatis 2011). Outpatient and inpatient care are both subdivided into further categories. They include information on medical practices, dental practices, other health care practices, pharmacies, health trade professions and ambulatory care on the one hand and hospitals, preventive care, rehabilitation clinics and stationary/semi-stationary care facilities on the other hand.

The third axis, sources of funding, is subdivided into a total of eight categories: general government excluding social security funds; statutory health insurance; social long-term care insurance; statutory pension insurance; statutory accident insurance; private health insurance; employers; private households/private non-profit organizations.

Expenditures on education and training of health personnel, research and development in health, health-related social services as well as health-related cash-benefits are shown in a separate area, but are not part of the overall amount of health expenditures.

Figure 1: Simplified supply and use framework in the dimension of available data.

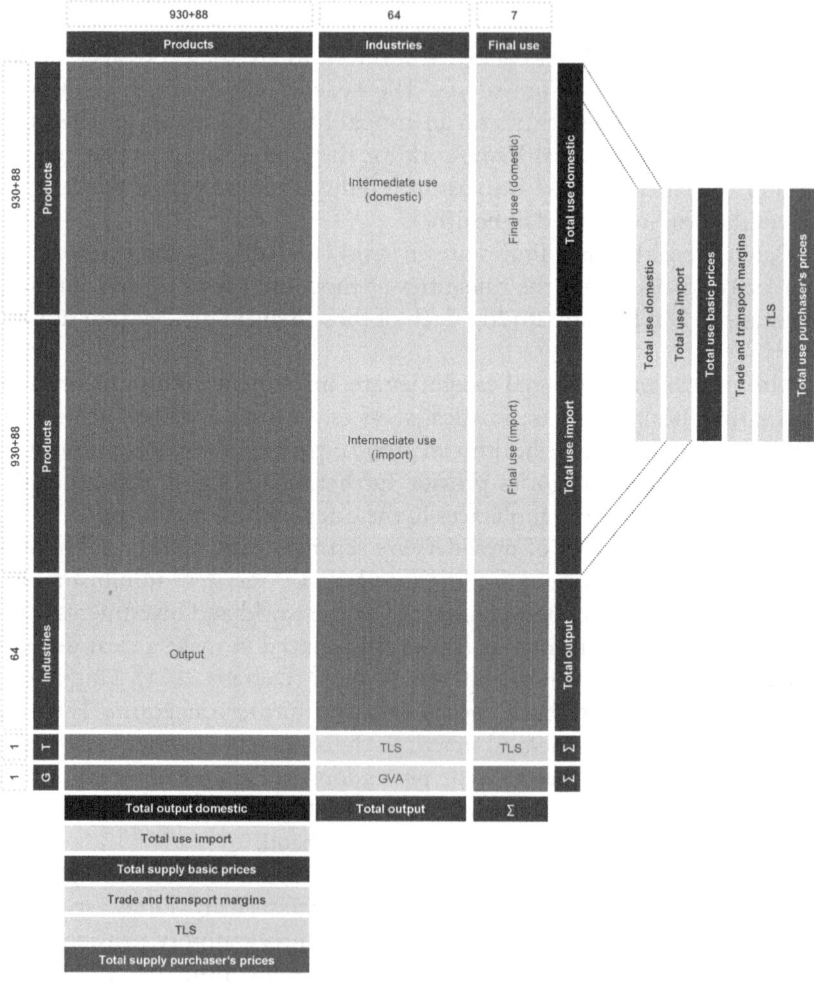

T = TLS = Taxes Less Subsidies G = GVA = Gross Value Added
Source: Own illustration based on (Eurostat 2008a), page 22.

The main underlying database for the compilation of the NHA is the special evaluation of national accounts, which corresponds to unpublished detailed data on supply and use tables. Its dimension corresponds to 64 industries and 2,643 product groups, from which 930 were assigned of being completely or partly health-related and therefore available for our calculations. We have full information for the 930 product groups in the supply and use tables for domestically produced as well as for imported goods and services. The remaining 1,713 product groups are blanked and therefore ignored in the further compilation. However, we have aggregated supply and use tables for the overall economy with full information in the dimension of 88 products groups and 64 industries. Therefore we are able to compile residual product groups, which are made up by the residual sums of the aggregated tables with full information on the overall economy subtracted by the corresponding available information from the special evaluation. Combing the residual product groups in the dimension of 88 product groups on the non-health area and the special evaluation corresponding to 930 product groups related to health, gets us our final database to compile the NHA. It covers the overall economy and exhibits detailed data on health-related areas and aggregated information on non-health areas.

Figure 1 shows the supply and use framework and hence main dependencies, shape and scope of available data. It includes all three main tables: supply, domestic use and import use, whereas the latter two contain information on intermediate and final use. Moreover, it shows the dependencies between tables, which is the balance between supply and use in both basic and purchasers' prices, whereas the latter differs from the prior by assigning trade margins and taxes less subsidies directly on products. Information from aggregated tables of supply and use in the dimension of 88 product groups and 64 industries is already considered in the figure in terms of residual product groups. Hence, in order to reflect the overall economy in Figure 1, the product dimension refers to 930 + 88 products, the latter representing the residuals of each aggregated product group. Note for the further sections and corresponding notations that the dimension of the supply is transposed compared to the use table. Hence, it has industries in rows and products in columns, whereas the use tables behave contrary.

International guidelines applying for both statistics, national accounts and health expenditures, aim to enable consistency over time and countries, but also to enhance compatibility among economic and social statistics. Since the System of Health Accounts (SHA) includes definitions and concepts from national accounts, the information recorded in the SHA is also included in national accounts, which is final and intermediate consumption of health care services and products (Organisation for Economic Co-operation and Development (OECD) et al. 2011). However, comparability between the two statistics is not always possible to the whole extent. In the following, we describe differences between the concepts according to Organisation for Economic Co-operation and Development (OECD) et al. (2011), which imply exceptions from straight away matching of health expenditures with the use side of national accounts. In order to get a thorough understanding of the NHA and its compilation, it is essential to consider these differences, also for a proper interpretation of NHA results.

First, and from a broader perspective, the aim of the two statistics differ from each other. National accounts focus on the supply and use of products next to the generation and distribution of income of the whole economy. Hence, it corresponds to a macroeconomic picture, involving monetary circulation flows. Health expenditures focus on the consumption, provision and financing patterns of health products and services exclusively, by aggregating partially micro-based data. This leads to a meso-economic accounting principle.

Another main underlying difference between the two databases is the domestic concept characterizing national accounts, opposed by the national concept, referring to the health expenditure survey. Correspondingly, focus of use and supply tables lies on domestically used and supplied products, whereas health expenditures relate to residents of Germany exclusively, treated within the country or abroad. Therefore, expenditures from non-residents within Germany are not included in the survey, whereas 'exported' money to other countries are part of the statistics. Impacts on the calculations result in underestimated results for i.e. GVA of the health economy, since expenditures for non-residents within Germany are not included in the health expenditure survey and therefore not considered within the NHA. The fact that it is not possible to include given information on health expenditures for patients treated abroad does not have any impact on the results of the NHA, since it does not involve any domestic health care output.

Another difference is the price concept of statistics. Supply and use tables refer to basic prices, whereas health expenditures are reflected in purchasers' prices. This conceptual difference has no impacts on results of the NHA, as available data on supply and use tables enable a conversion into purchasers' prices. The difference between the two concepts is that basic prices refer to the price realized by the producer, whereas purchasers' prices refer to the price the consumer pays for the specific produced product. In between those two concepts lie taxes less subsidies and the trade and transport margin the consumer has to pay and of which the producer is not the recipient (Eurostat 2008a).

Next, costs borne by dependency allowances for services of households to care for persons with severe functional mobility or cognitive handicap are considered within health expenditures, whereas they are not part of final consumption in the use table of national accounts. The same holds for household production. Social transfers for taking care of dependents are included in the health expenditure survey, but not considered within national accounts. Impact on key indicators is small, but existent.

As an exemption to main concepts, certain parts of expenditures on health prevention and expenditures of employers for occupational health services are recorded as intermediate use in national accounts instead of final consumption. The amount of expenditures is considered within the satellite account nevertheless, since the conceptual difference is only a matter of compilation.

2.3.3. Principles of the National Health Account

We concentrated on international standards and the databases used within the previous subsections. This section focuses on the general principles of the NHA, which have been developed throughout a number of projects conducted so far in this context (Bundesministerium für Wirtschaft und Energie (BMWi) 2017 & 2016 & 2015; Henke et al. 2010; Ostwald et al. 2014; Schneider et al. 2016).

The NHA follows a product-specific definition of the health economy rather than an industry-specific one. There are two main reasons for this specific approach. First, the functional approach of the health expenditure survey, to include all *goods and services*, which promote and preserve health as well as prevent from poor health conditions, supports this procedure in terms of the intended consistency with this secondary database and its definition of health. Second, from a national accounting framework, an industry-specific selection would ignore the existence of auxiliary production of industries. For example, defining the pharmaceutical industry as a part of the health economy, would suggest including auxiliary production like veterinary medicine or possible financial activities some companies might undertake as a part of the health economy. Conversely, defining the health economy from the product-specific side ensures to include all products and services related to health, irrespective of the industry producing it. The special evaluation on supply and use tables provided by the Federal Statistical office favors this product-specific approach, as the amount of data available on the product side is very detailed.

The product specific approach aims to separate the overall economy into a non-health related area, a core area and an extended area of health. All balancing conditions and interdependencies of the national accounting framework are maintained in order to obtain a consistent picture of this cross-section industry within the German economy. It can be argued that this disaggregation into non-health related and health related areas has already been conducted by selecting 930 out of 2,643 product categories of the overall economy. This is true to some extent, but ignores the fact that substantial shares of these product categories refers to human health only to a minor extent in the sense it is defined within the concepts of the SHA (Organisation for Economic Co-operation and Development (OECD) et al. 2011) or the NHA. One example is plastic surgery, which is part of services within hospitals, but is not defined as being health-related. Another example is pharmaceuticals used for other purposes than to promote and preserve health or prevent from illness, e.g. anabolic agents.

Reasons for the distinction between a core health area and an extended area of health derive from the definition of health expenditures according to the SHA. We quantify output of each good and service, which is an integrated part of the health expenditure survey, consistently in the core area of health. Products related to health beyond this definition refer to the extended area of health of the NHA. Basically, each good and service, which we do not consider in the core health area, but demonstrates health benefits and is consumed with a conscious personal decision for better health, is considered within the extended area of health. Furthermore, we quantify output of goods and services, which play a decisive role for operations of the health economy in the extended are of health. Examples are consultancy for health facilities, R&D and expenditures for education of health professionals.

2.4. Compilation methodology

Sections 2.2 and 2.3 have focused on the historical and methodological background of the NHA. This section concentrates on the compilation approach of the NHA. Subsections 2.4.1 and 2.4.2 describe the compilation of the health-specific supply and use tables at basic and purchaser's prices. Subsection 2.4.3 focuses on key indicators such as employment and components of GVA. Subsection 2.4.4 indicates towards concepts to calculation input-output tables from supply and use tables. While preceding steps describe the calculation for one year, section 2.4.5 targets the compilation of time series data.

2.4.1. Compilation of health-specific supply and use tables at basic prices

In this section, we concentrate on the compilation of health-specific supply and use tables at basic prices. We demonstrate conversion into purchasers' prices in subsection 2.4.2, even though it is already part of the final accounting framework pictured in Figure 2. This figure depicts the objective function of our intention and thus represents the final NHA. Figure 2 therefore shows a direct connection to Figure 1 with the only difference that the prior already specifies health industries and products in the green shaded areas, whereas the latter represents the starting point of compilation and therefore the original database.

Over here, we give a short overview of the compilation steps, which are described in more detail in the following subsections of 2.4.1.

In order to compile the NHA, we split up products as well as industries first in order to obtain the three main areas, non-health related, core health area and extended area of health. Splitting of products is necessary since the available products of the special evaluation cannot be directly assigned to either the non-health, the core health or the extended are of health. We split industries accordingly in the next step, in order to obtain industry-specific information on the producing industries of health products and services. Subsequently, we define tangible health-specific categories and aggregate the product side of health-specific areas correspondingly. Furthermore, we adjust input structures before we align the industry-specific information in accordance to the previously defined classifications of health on the product side. This complete procedure results in square supply and use tables, consisting of 64 non-health, 14 core health and 18 extended health related product and industry categories. We describe the compilation steps just summarized in detail in the following subsections.

Figure 2: Final accounting framework of the NHA

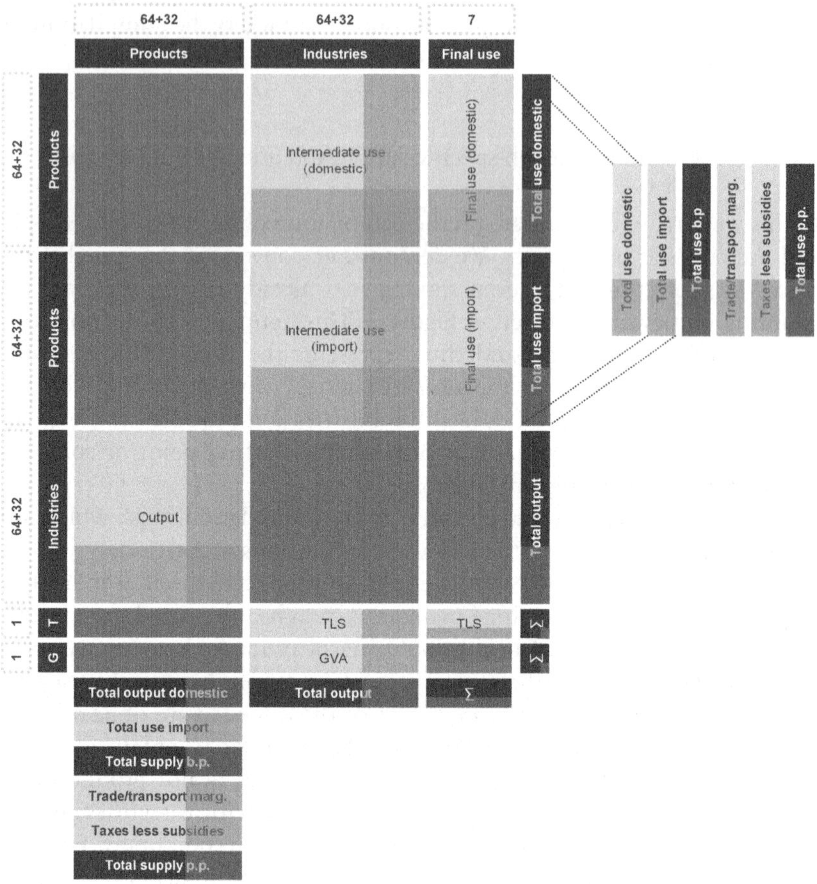

Source: Own illustration.

2.4.1.1. Product specific splitting with respect to health areas

For compiling supply and use tables with emphasis on health in the overall economic setting, we conduct a product-specific splitting of tables first. By applying shares on available data of supply and use tables for (930+88) product groups, 64 industries and the components of final use, we split the product-specific information into the non-health related area, the core area and the extended area of health. This procedure is necessary since the products defined in the special evaluation cannot be directly assigned to either the non-health, the core health or the extended area of health. One example, which shows this fact very clearly, is the product group referring to the classification of products activity (CPA) of national accounts of "325050200 – Preparation in the form of gels, used in human or veterinary medicine as lubricant for body parts in surgeries, medical examinations or as a coupling agent between body and medical instruments". It is obvious that its use in veterinary medicine refers to the non-health area, since we exclusively focus on human health in the NHA. Accordingly, this product is also not considered in the health expenditure survey. Making use of the product in the context of human medicine, however, is health related. We assign it to the core health area by calculating shares, corresponding to the given information in the health expenditure survey, which is our prior database for the definition of health. However, we assign some share of the product to the extended area of health as well, in cases it is used for a medical-cosmetic purpose, which goes beyond the definition of the health expenditure of the SHA but is to some extent related to health nevertheless according to the NHA.

The following equations reflect the concept of applying shares on the special evaluation of national accounts in order to conduct a product-specific splitting of tables.

$$\mathrm{V}_{ij} = V_{ij}*\left(1 - K_{ij}^{VC} - K_{ij}^{VE}\right) + V_{ij}*K_{ij}^{VC} + V_{ij}*K_{ij}^{VE} \quad (1)$$

$$\mathrm{U}_{jl} = U_{jl}*\left(1 - K_{jl}^{UC} - K_{jl}^{UE}\right) + U_{jl}*K_{jl}^{UC} + U_{jl}*K_{jl}^{UE} \quad (2)$$

$$\text{for } \mathrm{K}_{ij}^{VC} + K_{ij}^{VE} \leq 1\, and\, K_{jl}^{UC} + K_{jl}^{UE} \leq 1$$
$$and\, K_{ij}^{VC},\ K_{ij}^{VC},\ K_{jl}^{UC},\ K_{jl}^{UE} > 0$$

Where ⍰ denotes the supply table and U the use table. Consequently, V_{ij} and U_{jl} correspond to the elements of the supply and the use table. j indicates the (930+88) product groups, which are the same for supply and use tables. i corresponds to the 64 industries, whereas l indicates the number of industries plus the seven components of final use within the use table and therefore 71. ⍰ indicates the share matrix and the letters V and U in superscript form denote the corresponding tables. Indexes refer to the respective elements. C and ⍰ indicate the core area and the extended area of health.

After applying the shares on the supply and use tables to define the non-health, the core health and the extended area of health each and by arranging one under the other we arrive at:

$$\dot{V}' = \begin{pmatrix} V^N \\ V^C \\ V^E \end{pmatrix}', \tag{3}$$

$$\dot{U} = \begin{pmatrix} U^N \\ U^C \\ U^E \end{pmatrix} \tag{4}$$

For the core area of health, we calculate respective shares, which aim to match the health expenditure survey with the final use components of the use tables of national accounts. These shares indicate the degree to which use of a product can be considered as health-related. In order to do so, we reconcile household and government consumption with private and public expenditure on health. In addition, we adjust intermediate use of industries with respect to products in consideration. For example, we do not assume pharmaceutical products, which are used in agriculture, to have any positive effect on human health and weight them with zero. This procedure is straight forward but time consuming, given the extent of information provided by the health expenditure survey and the special evaluation of national accounts. The most challenging step is to consider existing differences in price concepts, which will be discussed next.

Price concepts differ between the health expenditure survey and the use table at this stage of calculation. Consequently, these differences in prices, which consist in trade margins and taxes, are considered during the compilation of shares. Data on taxes are available at an aggregated level only, which makes a proportional allocation into the detailed level of data of the use table at basic prices necessary. Trade margins for wholesale and retail trade are available at a very detailed level, explicitly indicating the product group they refers to. Consequently, it becomes possible to consistently match health expenditure data at purchasers' prices and the use table at basic prices by considering the product-specific information on trade margins and the proportionally allocated taxes when calculating share matrices.

We compile shares for the supply table with respect to balancing conditions in accordance with just weighted use tables. In some cases, however, e.g. R&D, the supply table serves as a starting point of compilation, as it reveals superior information on corresponding activities conducted by industries according to ESA 2010.

In order to obtain the extended area of health, we compile shares for supply and use tables similarly to the previously described procedure of the last three paragraphs for the core health area, but with respect to various secondary data. The secondary data we use refers to additional statistical material from the Federal Statistical Office, i.e. in the case of construction investments or expenditures on education of health specialists. This is different in the case of products and services for e-health, health tourism, organic food or literature. In those cases, we consult supplementing literature which does not originate from the statistical office. Calculated shares for this area can be critically scrutinized, just like the underlying definition of the extended area of health itself. This is the crucial reason for us to distinct between a core area and an extended area of health, as the former refers to officially and internationally standardized data and the second one relies on additionally introduced classifications and databases. The detailed derivation of share matrices and the underlying secondary databases used are beyond the scope of this contribution and therefore not discussed in more detail.

2.4.1.2. Industry-specific splitting with respect to health areas

This compilation step aims to obtain industry-specific information on the producing entities of the products and services of the health economy, which we defined product-wise beforehand. Industry-specific information includes e.g. intermediate use, GVA, employment or compensation of employees. The supply table in its three-area shape – non-, core area and extended area of the health economy according to 2.4.1.1 - acts as the starting point for the splitting of genuine industries.

The underlying assumption is that health-specific products are exclusively supplied by health industries, whereas non-health related products are exclusively supplied by non-health related industries. Clearly, this assumption cannot be observed from reality, since industries normally produce more than just one product, as can be obtained from the supply table in general. Accordingly, it is just as unnatural that health-specific industries exclusively produce products and services related to health. However, this assumption is necessary, since we explicitly want to determine industry-specific information such as GVA, which is obtained from producing health products and services. Consequently, we split the supply table obtained from 2.4.1.1 industry-wise by arranging the non-, core and extended area of health in the design of a block diagonal matrix. Industries still carry out auxiliary production, but only within their area.

$\hat{V}'$ represents the block diagonal matrix of the dimension (3x(930+88)) X 3x64, with V'^{N}, V'^{C} and V'^{E} indicating the non-health related area, the core health area and the extended area of the health economy.

$$\hat{V}' = \begin{pmatrix} V'^{N} & 0 & 0 \\ 0 & V'^{C} & 0 \\ 0 & 0 & V'^{E} \end{pmatrix} \tag{5}$$

In order to maintain the industry-specific input quota, we split up the input structures of the 64 industries of the use table by applying the output share of the industry in consideration, gathered from the block-diagonal shaped supply table $\hat{V}'$. The mentioned output share refers to the share of each industry occurring in the non-, core and extended area of the health economy.

The notation for industry-specific splitting of use tables is shown in the following:

Let x be the vector of industry-specific output and let $\tilde{x}'$ be its 3x64 element row vector in which industry-specific output is arranged next to each other threefold in the way that:

$$\tilde{x}' = (x', x', x') \tag{6}$$

$\hat{v}_j$ indicates the industry-wise sums of the block diagonal matrix:

$$\hat{v}_i = \sum_{j=1}^{3x(930+88)} \hat{v}'_{ij} \tag{7}$$

Output shares are then calculated as follows:

$$m_i = \frac{\hat{v}_i}{\tilde{x}} \; for \; i = 1, \ldots, 3 \, x \, 64 \tag{8}$$

The information on m is used to split the use table industry-specific in the following, where $\dot{U}$ corresponds to 2.4.1.1 and denotes the already product-specific split use tables for both domestically produced and imported goods for the non-health, the core health and the extended area of the health economy.

In order to obtain the industry-wise disaggregation of the use table, we calculate the following:

$$\dot{U}_{ji} = \widetilde{U}_{ji} * m_i + \widetilde{U}_{j,i+64} * m_{i+64} + \widetilde{U}_{j,i+64+64} * m_{i+64+64} \tag{9}$$

where j = 1, …, 3x(930 + 88)
and i = 1, …, 64
and $m_i + m_{i+64} + m_{i+64+64} = 1$
and $\widetilde{U}_{ji} = \left(\dot{U}_{ji}, \dot{U}_{ji}, \dot{U}_{ji}\right)$

Note that $\widetilde{U}_{ji}$ corresponds to intermediate use only, since the industry dimension is i compared to l from equation 2.4.1.1. At the end of this procedure, supply and use tables exhibit the most disaggregated dimensions during the compilation of the NHA. The supply table corresponds to 2.4.1.2 and the use table to

$$\ddot{U} = \begin{pmatrix} U^{NN} & U^{NC} & U^{NE} & U_f^N \\ U^{CN} & U^{CC} & U^{CE} & U_f^C \\ U^{EN} & U^{EC} & U^{EE} & U_f^C \end{pmatrix}. \tag{10}$$

The entries of $\ddot{U}$ correspond to single matrices, each of them in the dimension of (930+88) X 64, and the final demand matrices, U_f^N, U_f^C and U_f^E, which obtain the dimension of $l - i$, which is 71 – 64 = 7. For $\ddot{U}$ it holds that the first entry of the superscript refers to the product-specific splitting and hence the weighted products, belonging to the non-health, the core health or the extended are of health. The second entry of the superscript however refers to the industry-specific splitting of tables and therefore the receiving industry. For example, U^{EC} refers to the matrix of products from the extended area of health, which are used as intermediate consumption in industries of the core health area.

From this procedure we see that the industry-wise splitting of use tables depends on the output of selected and weighted products in order to differentiate between the non-health related area, the core area and the extended area of health. As a result we obtain supply and use tables, which consist of 3 x (930+88) product groups and 3 x 64 industries plus seven categories of final demand for the use table. However, the relative input structure of each of the basic 64 industries is available threefold now, but differs in absolute terms in accordance to the output share. We reconcile the input-structure at a later point of compilation (see sub-subsection 2.4.1.4 for more details). Figure 3 depicts the approach of disaggregating product groups and industries in a supply-use framework. Numbers indicate the sequential steps of the procedure.

Figure 3: Product- and industry-specific separation of supply and use table with respect to health

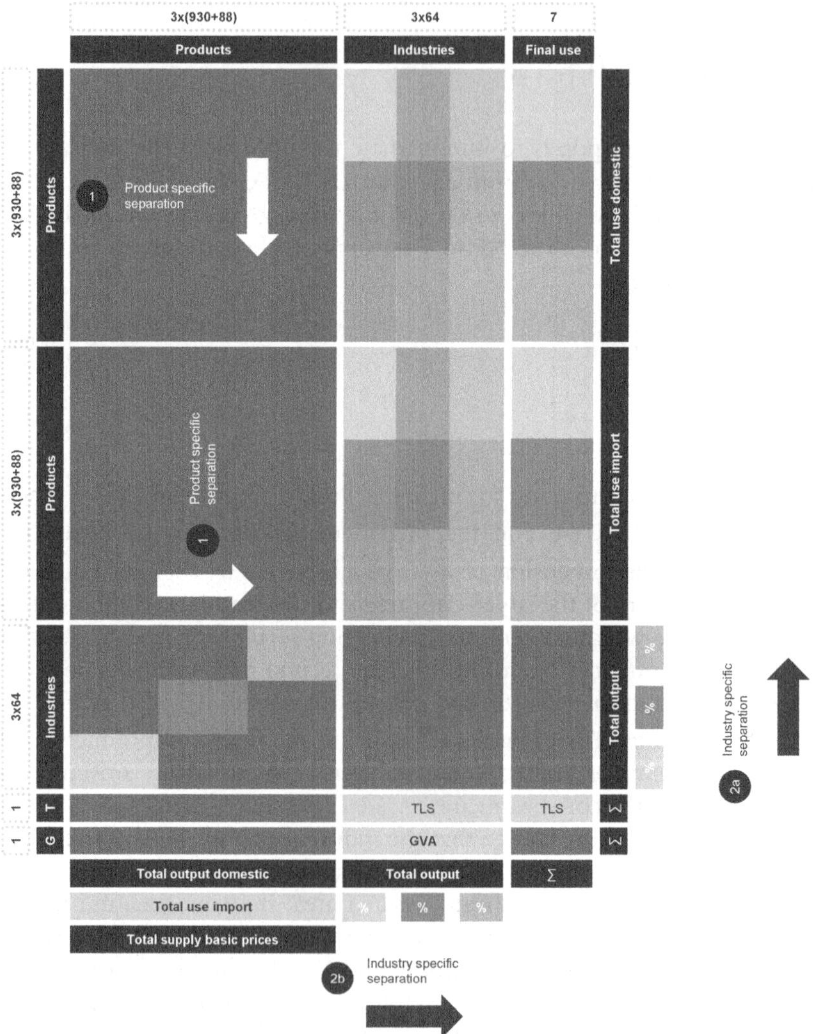

Source: Own illustration.

2.4.1.3. Product specific aggregation

It is our goal to determine industry-specific information such as GVA, employment or intermediate use, which results from supplying health products and services. Therefore, we define tangible health-specific product groups by fields of interest, which allow deeper analyses. The core health area, which is consistent with the health expenditure survey with regard to defined areas and quantities of final consumption patterns, is classified into 14 different categories. The extended area of health is more diverse in terms of composing structure, as a various number of different, but in monetary quantity and importance smaller, groups characterize this field. This leads to a differentiation of the extended area of the health economy into 18 categories.

The detailed table of categories, which define the health economy in the core and the extended area of health, is shown in Table 1. The classification of health categories follows a product specific definition. Consequently, the aggregation of the 930 products in the core area and the extended area of the health economy each, is a straightforward procedure. At this point, we also aggregate the non-health are with respect to its product dimension. For this procedure, we choose the level of 88 product groups, which is also the dimension official aggregated tables on supply and use refer to. By doing so, we do not lose any precious information in the non-health area since the information on purely non-health related products and services was blanked in the special evaluation on supply and use anyway before we completed it by calculating residual product groups from aggregated tables corresponding to 88 product groups. We refer to the supply and use tables with aggregated product categories according to $\widetilde{V}$ and $\widetilde{U}$ in the following.

Table 1: Definition of the health economy with respect to product groups and industries

Area	Code	Product group / industry
Core area of health economy	**H1**	**Medication**
	H11	Pharmaceuticals products
	H12	Chemical products
	H2	**Medical devices**
	H21	Medical technology products
	H22	Wheelchairs
	H23	Digital medical technology products
	H3	**Retail trade services of the core area**
	H31	Retail trade services for medication
	H32	Retail trade services for medical devices
	H4	**Health insurance**
	H41	Social health insurance and public administration
	H42	Private health insurance
	H5	**Services of inpatient facilities**
	H6	**Services of non-inpatient facilities**
	H7	**Wholesale trade services of the core area**
	H71	Wholesale trade services for medication
	H72	Wholesale trade services for medical devices
	H73	Commission trade services for the core area
Extended area of health economy	**E1**	**Products for self-contained health care**
	E11	Products for personal hygiene, nutritional supplements
	E12	Organic food
	E13	Anti-allergenic clothing
	E14	Literature for health and medical science
	E15	Sports equipment
	E2	**Services for sports, wellness and tourism**
	E21	Services for sports
	E22	Services for wellness and tourism
	E3	**Other services of the health economy**
	E31	Consultancy for health care facilities
	E32	Other services of health care facilities
	E33	Advocacy and information services of the health economy
	E34	Trade services of the extended area
	E4	**Investment**
	E41	Education of health professionals
	E42	Research and development of the health economy
	E43	Construction of health care facilities
	E44	Architectural services for the construction of health care facilities
	E5	**E-Health**
	E51	Appliances of telecommunication technology and data processing for the health care sector
	E52	Services of information technology within the health care sector
	E53	Services of data processing within the health care sector

Source: Own illustration, based on Schneider et al. (2016)

2.4.1.4. Reconciliation of input structure

At this point of compilation, supply and use tables obtain the dimension of 88 non-health related and 32 health-related product categories. On the industry side, the tables consist of 3 x 64 industries since we separated each of the genuine 64 industries into a non-health, a core health and an extended area of health. Next, we reconcile the input structure of use tables before we align industries with respect to defined health categories.

The necessity for such adjustments arises from the assumptions taken during the industry-specific disaggregation of use tables in accordance to m, which is an identical input structures for each of the triplet of industries in relative terms. However, we do not want this assumption to remain since we expect the industry triplets to differ from each other with respect to what they produce. Hence, we assume that for example the pharmaceutical industry has a different relative input structure with respect to its output, which either refers to the non-health area, the core health area or the extended area of health. To adjust the input structure of industry triplets we evaluate each product consumed by the industry triplet and check whether it needs a certain adjustment.

One example is the health product category "E14 Literature for health and medical science" and the industry corresponding to the category "NACE 85 Education". We observe that health-specific literature is used not only in the education industry specified as being health related but to an absolute large amount also in the non-health area due to the underlying assumption on m. This observation differs from our intention, which is that this health-related literature is used for education of health professionals. It seems straight forward to just reassign the health-related books as input from the non-health area to the health area. However, this simple procedure would result in an adjusted GVA rate of this industry, measured by GVA per output, due to a changed sum of intermediate consumption. However, we have no legitimization for adjusting the GVA rate. Hence, we make use of an algorithm, which restores original row and column sums after we have made adjustments to specific inputs.

In a first step, we obtain the shares of the product – i.e. of "E14 Literature for health and medical science" - referring to the shares by which it is currently consumed by the triplet of industries, which is the education industry in this case.
Figure 4 shows this initial situation with shares of

$$\mathrm{r}_{ji} + r_{j(i+64)} + r_{j(i+64+64)} = 1 \qquad for\ i = 1,\ \ldots, 64\ and\ r \leq 1 \tag{11}$$

And with

$$\bar{u}_i = \sum_{j=1}^{88+32} \tilde{u}_{ji} \tag{12}$$

indicating the industry-specific sums of intermediate consumption and

$$u_j = \sum_{i=1}^{3 \times 64} \tilde{u}_{ji} \tag{13}$$

indicating the product-specific sums of intermediate consumption.

Figure 4: Initial situation with identical relative input structures of disaggregated industries

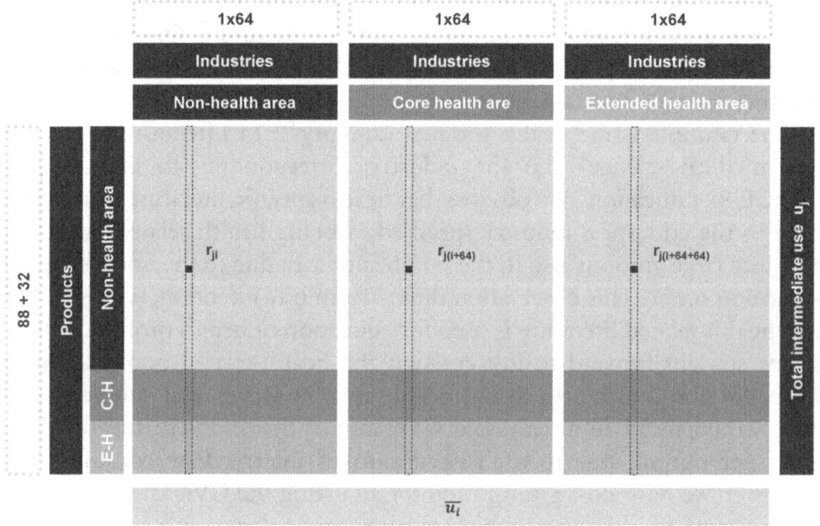

Source: Own illustration.

Based on this initial situation, we adjust shares in consideration of secondary data or knowledge upon the specific intention assigned to the respective good or service. For r^* indicating the adjusted shares, the following applies, which assures consistency in row sums:

$$r^*_{ji} + r^*_{j(i+64)} + r^*_{j(i+64+64)} = 1 \tag{14}$$

Following our example, we adjusted the shares to which health-specific literature is consumed in the non-health, the core health and the extended area of health. However, as a consequence, the column sums cannot be maintained by definition, as soon as adjusted shares are applied. Adjustments in the overall sum of inputs of single industries impact on the amount of GVA, since the supply table obtains fixed output. This, however, is not the intention of this procedure. Consequently, we use the GRAS algorithm in order to obtain the initial value of column sums again (Lenzen, Wood and Gallego 2007). The GRAS algorithm can be applied to adjust matrices in accordance to given row and column sums.[2]

Figure 5: Adjustment of input structures and consolidation with GRAS algorithm

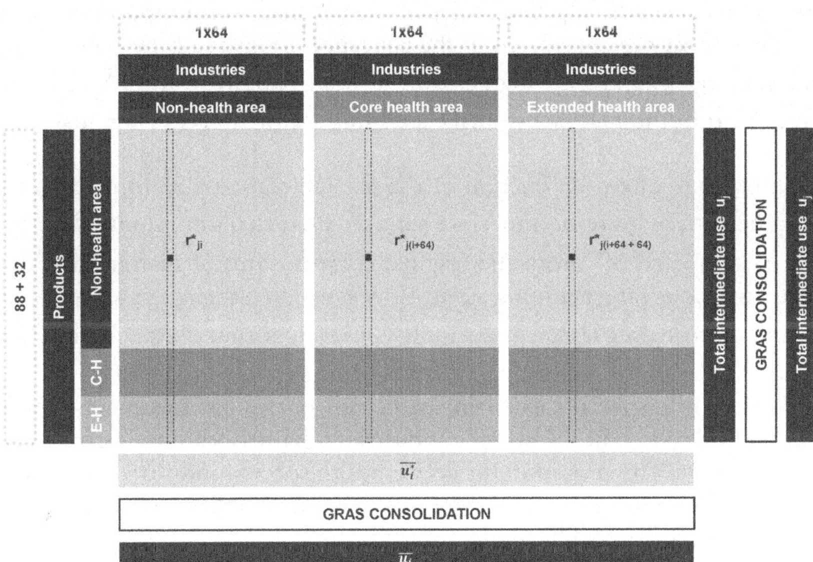

Source: Own illustration.

2 The GRAS algorithm differs from the RAS algorithm in the respect that it allows for negative values in the matrix, whereas the latter does not. Since all entries of the matrix are positive, it would be sufficient to use RAS. However, there are a few single entries in the current matrix, which are in theory positive but in the compilation negative with very low numbers in the eighth or higher decimal place. These very little negative numbers are caused by rounding errors from subtracting tables with the statistical software R.

By adjusting input structures, we proceed industry-wise one after the other. Let us assume we focus on industry z, which represents the input structure of, for example, the education industry. Therefore, when we adjust input structures, we consider the matrix of corresponding industry triplets and hence

$Z = (z_i \; z_{i+64} \; z_{i+64+64})$ where $i \leq 64$. Consequently, Z corresponds to a (88+32) X 3 matrix.

We have defined one or more products and services, which need adjustment in their amount of consumption by the non-health, the core health and the extended area of health. Let us define a submatrix of Z by Y, which corresponds to health-specific literature and i.e. medical products. In a next step, Y obtains adjusted shares of intermediate consumption for each product or service considered in the education industry of the non-health, the core health and the extended area of health and turns into Y^*. We extract Y^* from the matrix Z to make sure this adjusted part of the matrix is fixed.

In order to align the fraction of the use table, matrix Z, to its original column sums with respect to Y^* we subtract y_i^*, the column sums of the adjusted submatrix Y^*, from the original column sums of matrix Z and define this as our target column sums. Row sums do not change, since r_{ji} and r_{ji}^* sum up to 1. In a last step, we apply GRAS algorithm on the matrix Z by ignoring the entries referring to Y^*, which are supposed to be fixed.

There is the special case of inpatient and outpatient treatment, which correspond to two health-specific industries obtained from industry-specific alignment. The procedure to derive health-specific industries is subject of the next sub-subsection. However, since we apply input reconciliation in this special case, we address it here already.

Inpatient and outpatient treatment is a special case because it represents the centerpiece of the health economy by contributing more than 50 percent to the overall cross-section industry in terms of i.e. GVA or employment. However, both inpatient and outpatient treatment descend to high amounts from the genuine industry "NACE 86 – Health services". Hence, the overall input structure of the totals of inpatient and outpatient treatment correspond to a great extend to this genuine industry, especially since the latter exhibits only minor amounts of auxiliary production. However, the relative input structure of inpatient and outpatient care is very similar to each other and does not show great specifics due to its common origin.

Accordingly, we reconcile the input structure of inpatient and outpatient treatment, according to the described procedure and additional data sources. This includes cost data of hospitals (Destatis 2017b), cost structure survey of doctors', dentists' and psychotherapists' practices (Destatis 2017a) and cost structure survey of facilities from health services (Destatis 2016d). GVA is allowed to adjust in this field of interest, reflecting the specifics of inpatient and outpatient care, but only within the overall sum of the two industries in concern.

2.4.1.5. Industry-specific alignment

In a further step, we align industries to obtain health-specific industries corresponding to the health categories we previously defined on the product side. Consequently, we derive key indicators such as intermediate use, GVA or employment for each of the categories listed in Table 1. In other words, we derive industry-specific key indicators, which result from producing the defined health products and services. Since we defined a total of 32 health categories on the product side, we accordingly derive 32 industry-specific key indicators in the following. If we had chosen any other amount of health categories on the product side with respect to areas of interest and validity, the number of health-specific industries would accordingly correspond to the equal amount of categories.

The industry-specific alignment indicates an input-output framework for the health economy as we follow a product-specific approach without auxiliary production. The newly defined health industries comprise of shares of different industries. Those different shares of industries occur in cases when a health product or service is produced in different industries. Figure 5 shows the initial situation and first steps of compiling health-specific industries.

Figure 6: Initial situation of industries before alignment into health categories

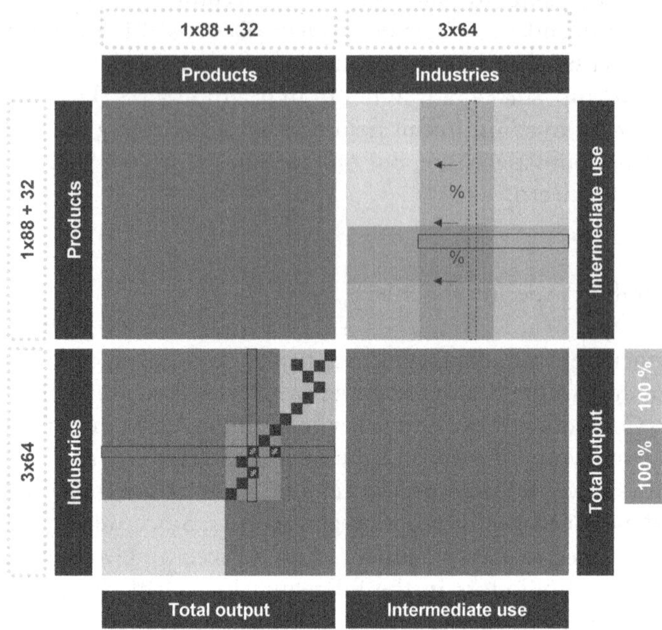

Source: Own illustration.

The following equations correspond to the alignment of health industries in the supply and use table, where the procedure applied on the use table is based on information gathered from the supply table.

$$\dddot{V} = \widetilde{V}_{ij} \, for \; i = 65, \; \ldots, \; 192 \text{ and } j = 89, \; \ldots, \; 120 \tag{15}$$

$$\dddot{U} = \widetilde{U}_{ji} \, for \; j = 1, \; \ldots, \; 120 \, and \; i = 65, \; \ldots, \; 192 \tag{16}$$

$\dddot{V}$ and $\dddot{U}$ define specific areas of the supply and use tables at the current state of compilation $\widetilde{V}$ and $\widetilde{U}$. The corresponding defined supply table is restricted to health industries and health product categories, while the use tables are defined by the former restriction only.

$\dddot{v}_i$ indicates the industry-specific sums of the selected area. Furthermore, $\overline{\overline{V}}$ is defined as a matrix containing information on shares of the restricted supply table on the calculated industry-specific sums. Consequently, these shares correspond to the distribution of industry output among the respective product portfolio. For example, we obtain from $\overline{\overline{V}}$ that about 91 percent of output of the pharmaceutical industry of the core health area is caused by the production of medication (category H1 from Table 1), 6 percent by the production of medical products (category H2 from Table 1) and 3 percent by retail trade with medication (category H31 from Table 1).

$$\dddot{v}_i = \sum_{j=1}^{32} \dddot{v}_{ij} \tag{17}$$

$$\bar{\bar{V}} = \frac{\dddot{v}_{i.}}{\dddot{v}_i} \tag{18}$$

In order to align industries according to health classifications, we arrange output values of the supply table in a diagonal matrix. Consequently, product-specific output of health categories equals industry-specific output of health categories. Hence, we have already derived the first industry-specific key indicator for the classifications of health, which is industry-specific output.

In a next step, we adjust industries in the use table by applying the information derived from the supply table in order to calculate intermediate consumption of health categories. Since we focus on health industries exclusively we get the following equations for these areas $\check{V}$ and $\check{U}$:

$$\check{V} = \hat{\ddot{v}}_j \tag{19}$$

$$\check{U} = \bar{\bar{V}} * \dddot{U} \tag{20}$$

This procedure corresponds to the industry technology assumption from compiling input-output tables. It implies that the input structures of the newly defined health industries are a combination of weighted genuine industries in accordance to the place and amount of production of the category in consideration. For example, medicine is produced by different genuine industries, which is the food industry, the chemical industry and the pharmaceutical industry among others to the amount of 0.2 percent, 5.8 percent, 93.3 percent and so on. The input-structure of the health industry "H1 – Medicine" now corresponds to a weighted combination of these contributing genuine industries.

Figure 7: Final situation of industry alignment into health groups

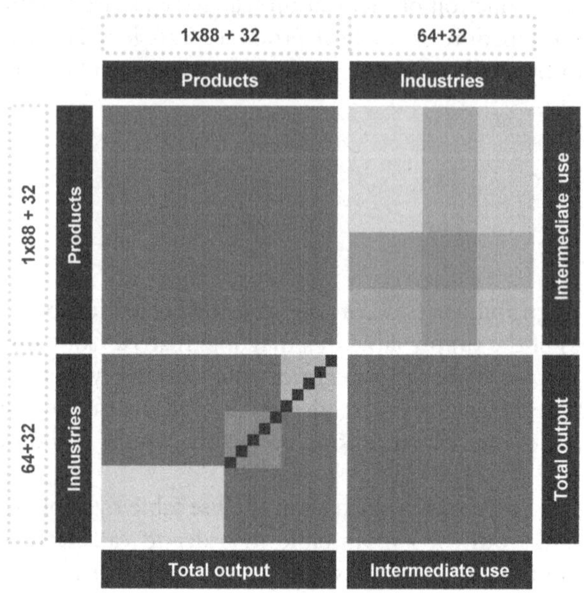

Source: Own illustration.

At the end of this procedure, we obtain supply and use tables from domestic production and imports with 32 health categories each. Health-specific industries do not obtain auxiliary production, since the assignment of product categories to a specific calculated composition of generic industries involved in production is conducted by applying industry technology.

In order to obtain a square structure of tables for input-output analysis, we aggregate the existing 88 product categories from the non-health related area consistently to the structure of industries. Apart from conversion into purchasers' prices, the resulting tables are shown in Figure 2 on page 40.

2.4.2. Compilation of health-specific supply and use tables at purchasers' prices

Conversion of health-specific supply and use tables to purchasers' prices is necessary so we can match the health expenditure survey with final consumption patterns of use tables. We calculated shares for tables at basic prices already with respect to trade margins and taxes less subsidies. Consequently, no additional adjustment of the share matrices is necessary.

Detailed data on wholesale and retail trade are provided as part of the special evaluation on national accounts. These tables classify the 2,643 product categories of the economy at a 9-digits level. On overall, 254 of the 2,643 product categories refer to wholesale and retail trade. The 9-digits level of this trade data refers to its corresponding product at the 3-digits level. Hence, we can compile tables for wholesale and retail trade each by transferring trade margins to the referring goods and subtract the counter entries at their original position in use tables at basic prices.

Available data on taxes and subsidies refer to the aggregated 88 product categories only. Consequently, we distribute this information over the non-health, the core health and the extended area of health with respect to the elementwise shares of the product in consideration on the product in its generic appearance. By adding tables of wholesale, retail trade and taxes less subsidies to already compiled use table at basic prices for the different areas of health, we obtain the use table for the sum of imported and domestically produced goods and services at purchasers' prices.

The remaining procedure is familiar. We adjust the input-structure, align health-specific industries to categories of health and merge the non-health product groups into 64 areas. Conversion to purchasers' prices for the supply table is straightforward, as we sum up trade margins, respective counter-entries and taxes less subsidies by rows and attach them to the existing health-specific supply table at basic prices.

2.4.3. Employees and composition of gross value added

Key indicators on employees and the composition of GVA, including compensation of employees, net taxes on production, consumption of fixed capital and net operating surplus, are of interest for further analyses regarding the health economy in Germany.

Detailed information on indicators with emphasis on health are only available for the area of health care services. Hence, the procedure for all areas apart from inpatient and outpatient health care is straightforward. From equation 2.4.1.2) we know output shares of industry triplets. We apply those shares on the number of employees and on the four components of GVA. Within the next step, we align the health-specific industries according to the procedure described in sub-subsection 2.4.1.5. This procedure ensures consistency with already calculated tables.

We use secondary data to improve data on inpatient and outpatient industries. Employees refer to data from health personnel survey (Destatis 2017e; Destatis 2017f). Moreover, we reconcile the composition of GVA by including information from cost data of hospitals (Destatis 2017b), cost structure survey of doctors', dentists' and psychotherapists' practices (Destatis 2017a) and cost structure survey of facilities from health services (Destatis 2016d). However, we obtain reconciliation by making use of these indicators as guide values only, since conceptual differences appear, i.e. in the case of employees from national accounts compared to the definition of workforce from health personnel survey.

2.4.4. Calculation of the Health-Input-Output Table

In order to conduct input-output analysis of the health economy, we have to compile an input-output table from derived health-specific supply and use tables. This procedure refers to the commodity technology assumption, which leads to the challenge of negative values appearing during the calculation. We chose the commodity assumption for the greatest possible agreement with official input-output tables for Germany, which are compiled based on the same assumption (Eurostat 2017a). In order to cope with occurring negative values we apply the industry technology assumption in specific cases according to Raa, ten and Rueda-Cantuche (2013) and Armstrong (1975). Since the overall procedure follows existing principles of commodity and industry assumption, the corresponding derivations are beyond the scope of this contribution. Further information on the exact approach can however be found in the underlying discussion paper (Schwärzler and Kronenberg 2016).

2.4.5. Compilation of time series data

In the previous subsections we concentrated on the compilation of health-specific supply and use tables for one year and gave a short introduction to the compilation of the corresponding input-output table. However, as it is one main objective to compile tables for approximately ten years, we want to project the underlying special evaluation on supply and use tables for the periods before and after the point of time, to which the database actually refers. Due to statistical revisions and costs involved, the special evaluation on national accounts is only available for the years 2010 and 2011 according to the ESA 2010 standard at the current point of time. The second main underlying database, the health expenditure survey, is available for a sufficient period of time.

We aim to apply the identical methodology to compile health-specific tables as described so far, in order to assure consistency of the approach over all the years being analyzed. To enable this, we make use of the SUT-RAS Algorithm (Temurshoev and Timmer 2011) to project the supply and use tables of the special evaluation for the required years. This way, we can match data on health expenditures with projected tables of national accounts accordingly to the described procedure of this chapter, which enables us to quantify the contribution of the health economy for respective years consistently.

In order to update and project available supply and use tables in accordance to SUT-RAS, we need information on industries and components of final use. Subject-matter series 18, series 1.4 provides this information on output, intermediary use in purchasers' prices and gross value added for the 64 sectors of the economy for several years (Destatis 2017g). Moreover, totals of the components of final use (final consumption expenditure by households, non-profit institutions serving household and governments, gross capital formation and exports) are available. We update use tables for domestic production and imports separately, hence we need data on the overall sum of imports from the corresponding subject-matter series in addition. Furthermore, we want to maintain the concept of basic prices for the projected supply and use tables on 930+88 product categories and 64 industries. In order to apply the SUT-RAS algorithm based on available data on intermediate use of industries referring to purchasers' prices, we obtain additional data on the overall sum of taxes less subsidies from the same database. Concluding, the provided information is already sufficient to apply the SUT-RAS algorithm on supply and use tables for domestically produced and imported data.

However, we use additional data to improve the quality of projected tables. Product specific information on exports and imports is provided for 88 product categories within the same database. Consequently, this information is used in an adjusted version of SUT-RAS as suggested in Temurshoev and Timmer (2011). In order to do so, however, information on exports and imports has to be disaggregated into the (930+88) available product groups by making use of the respective shares of the original table. Moreover, we separate exports with respect to their place of origin, domestic or import by applying again information from the original table. The compilation mechanism of the SUT-RAS algorithm with respect to product specific information on exports and imports is presented in the corresponding discussion paper (Schwärzler and Kronenberg 2016).

2.5. Concluding remarks

The present contribution describes the methodology of compiling the NHA. The latter represents a satellite system of supply, use and input-output tables of the national accounting system, which aims to match macroeconomic data with the health expenditure survey in a consistent way, without disrupting the overall economic system. Moreover, it refers to international standards in compiling satellite systems with respect to health and includes present standards of statistical accounting in terms of NACE 2008 and ESA 2010.

Based on the present state of methodology, further research should be conducted in order to carry out advanced analyses of particular fields of health services such as hospitals, nursing and practicing doctors among others. This, however, still needs an even more precise matching between the health expenditure survey and national accounts. Our close cooperation with both the national accounts division and the health expenditure survey division of the Federal Statistical Office reveal inconsistencies between the two main databases when more detailed aspects of the health economy are considered. Given that reported inconsistencies are going to be considered within further revisions of national accounts and the health expenditure survey, improving the quality of data of the Federal Statistical Office could be seen as a further contribution to scientific research.

Moreover, detailed data on the health economy show a high heterogeneity among the different components of the industry in terms of the respective contribution to GVA, employment or international trade. Embedding a regional aspect within the calculations brings additional facets to the analyses. In the special case of Germany, which has been divided for several decades, a high heterogeneity of economic performance and respective dynamics among federal states can be recognized. As demand and supply of health services and products are influenced by regional characteristics and embedded interrelationships within and between federal states, a Multiregional Health Account for Germany could bring up additional insights into the dynamics of this industry.

3. Methodology of the Multiregional Health Account for Germany[3]

The Multiregional Health Account is a methodological enhancement of the National Health Account for Germany. The latter represents an established and annually updated satellite account quantifying the economic contribution of the health economy in terms of gross value added, employment and international trade (e.g. Schneider et al. 2016). Its methodological enhancement to a multiregional framework for the 16 federal states of Germany is represented by multiregional supply and use tables. This setting allows to compile a multiregional health input-output table and subsequently to carry out input-output analysis. Hence, we are able to quantify the direct and indirect economic impacts of the health economy to analyze interdependencies between industries and federal states. For the purpose of compiling the Multiregional Health Account, we elaborate a new approach based on the SUT-RAS algorithm (Temurshoev and Timmer 2011), which we adapt for the multiregional framework. We call it the MR-SUT-RAS algorithm. The methodology and its application in the context of the health economy is the subject of this contribution.

3.1. Introduction

First approaches to compile a German satellite account for health were implemented already from the late 1980s on (Geigant et al. 1986; Essig and Reich 1988; Sarrazin 1992; Henke et al. 2010; Ostwald, Henke, et al. 2014; Schneider et al. 2016). Those differed partially significantly in the definition of the health economy, the underlying database, the approach or the statistical standards compared to what is called the National Health Account for Germany (NHA) nowadays (Bundesministerium für Wirtschaft und Energie (BMWi) 2016 & 2017; Schwärzler and Legler 2017).

The purpose of the NHA is to elute the health economy from the overall economy without disrupting or overburdening the overall national accounting system. The underlying database refers to supply and use tables

3 This chapter is based on Schwärzler and Kronenberg (2017d).

from national accounts. This way, the NHA demonstrates the contribution of the health economy to gross value added (GVA), employment and international trade. From 2010 on, several related research activities were conducted with the purpose of pointing out the economic relevance of the health economy (Henke et al. 2010; Ostwald et al. 2014; Bundesministerium für Wirtschaft und Energie (BMWi) 2016 & 2017; Schneider et al. 2016). This enforced the ongoing paradigm shift, which promotes the supply of health as an important driver of economic growth, employment and trade and does not focus exclusively on the cost perspective of healthcare.

The most recent results confirm the importance of the health economy for the overall economical dynamics (Bundesministerium für Wirtschaft und Energie (BMWi) 2017). In 2016, the health economy contributes 12.0 percent of overall GVA, 16.1 percent of German employment and 8.2 percent of exports. Therefore, GVA generated by the German health economy approximately equals Austrian overall GVA, employs 7 million people and is the third most important export industry of Germany. The significance of the industry has increased throughout the years from 2005 on and it acted as a stabilizer of the economy in times of the crisis (Bundesministerium für Wirtschaft und Energie (BMWi) 2017; Hesse 2013). The results also show the high heterogeneity that characterizes the health economy, which is caused by the composition of this cross-section industry. It does not only comprise health services but also the manufacturing of medicine and medical technology next to a number of further products involved in healthcare. Therefore, the overall characteristic and development of the sector is influenced by various economic factors. The established NHA allows to track and analyze the impacts different subsectors of the health economy have on GVA, employment and trade.

Moreover, first evaluations indicated towards a high heterogeneity regarding regions and the federal states of Germany (Ostwald, Legler, Schwärzler, Plaul, et al. 2015; Ostwald, Legler, Schwärzler and Tetzner 2015a; Ostwald, Legler and Schwärzler 2014; Ostwald and Schwärzler 2015; Ranscht 2009; AG GGRdL 2016; Schneider 2013; Schneider et al. 2003; Schneider, Biene-Dietrich and Hofmann 2000a; Schneider, Biene-Dietrich and Hofmann 2000b; Schneider et al. 1998; Schneider et al. 2002; BASYS and GÖZ 2012). These studies, however, did not aim to apply the methodology derived for the compilation of the NHA. The rationale for this is that official statistical institutions of Germany do not provide regional supply and use tables, which is a basic prerequisite for an equivalent compilation. Only regional supply and use tables in the same level of detail as used for the national calculations enable applying the same methodology for the federal states as established in the national context.

The high heterogeneity of the health economy in federal states observed within the aforementioned named studies calls for a deeper analysis in this context. In order to provide consistent results with the NHA, we first compile multiregional supply and use tables for the 16 federal states of Germany based on the same special evaluation of national accounts, which has also been used to calculate the NHA. In a second step we compile a satellite account with emphases on health from established multiregional supply and use tables following the approach developed for the national level.

The choice to compile one multiregional supply and use table each instead of 16 single regional supply and use tables is motivated by methodological considerations. The multiregional framework provides the possibility to compile 16 supply and use tables within one harmonized framework, and therefore considers all given information at the same time. This way, it is less likely to obtain contradicting results between the overall German table and the sum over all regional tables. We believe that this approach enhances the validity of results. Moreover, compiling the regional tables in an overall multiregional framework reveals the modelled individual interconnectedness of federal states to each other. This enables input-output analysis with respect to the dependencies between individual federal states. The underlying compilation approach of multiregional supply and use tables is in the center of this contribution.

In order to multiregionalize supply and use tables of the German economy we elaborate a methodology based on the concept of SUT-RAS by Temurshoev and Timmer (2011). This approach was in its origins devised for updating supply and use tables at the national level. We develop this approach further to make use of the concepts in a multiregional context. The iterative calculations assure balancing conditions of supply and use to be held by taking into account regional industry and product-specific information. Since it is closely related to the SUT-RAS algorithm, we call it the MR-SUT-RAS algorithm.

The MR-SUT-RAS has already been applied once in order to evaluate the direct effects of the health economy in Ostwald et al. (2017). The respective study evaluated the product-sided defined health economy of the 16 German federal states for the time horizon of 2006 until 2015 having available only two sets of national supply and use tables for 2010 and 2011. The reasonability of results over temporal progression and regional characteristics are evaluated in chapter 4. In chapter 5 we calculate the multiregional health input-output table in order to analyze dependencies within and among federal states with the main goal to implement results in political decision making, which is conducted in chapter 6. Focus of the present chapter is, however, the methodology of the Multiregional Health Account for Germany.

The remainder of this chapter is structured as follows: In section 3.2 we describe the motivation to compile the MRHA. This includes the background of the heterogeneous characteristic of the regional health economy in Germany and one possible field of application of the MRHA. Section 3.3 focusses on the methodological background of the approach. It describes specifics of the satellite account approach, points out differences to existing regionalization methodology and introduces the reader to the basic multiregional context. In section 3.4 we discuss the methodological approach itself before we draw conclusions in section 3.5.

3.2. Motivation

The established NHA shows heterogenetic results with regard to national GVA, employment and international trade among the different categories of the health economy (e.g. Bundesministerium für Wirtschaft und Energie (BMWi) 2017). Previous studies for different regions found a high degree of specifics among the federal states under review as well (Ostwald, Legler, Schwärzler, Plaul, et al. 2015; Ostwald, Legler, Schwärzler and Tetzner 2015a; Ostwald, Legler, et al. 2014; Ostwald and Schwärzler 2015; Ranscht 2009; AG GGRdL 2016; Schneider 2013; Schneider et al. 2003; Schneider et al. 2000a; Schneider et al. 2000b; Schneider et al. 1998; Schneider et al. 2002; BASYS and GÖZ 2012). The established MRHA confirms the high heterogeneity among regions concerning the direct effects of the health economy on GVA, employment and international trade for the first time in Ostwald et al. (2017). The approach applied over there relies on the methodology developed for the national level, which is described in this chapter. In this section, we focus on historical and political reasons causing the differences in results between federal states and making an in-depth analysis of the regional health economy necessary. In addition, we describe one field of application, in which the MRHA could prove as a useful analysis tool.

Care structures have a high impact on the characteristics of the health economy within a federal state. These structures of inpatient and outpatient care supply have developed historically in Germany. In East Germany, outpatient care was mainly characterized by public and operational organized supply within polyclinics and outpatient clinics before the Unification of Germany in 1989. As of that year, outpatient care was adapted to health care supply provided by private suppliers in terms of resident doctors. (Prütz et al. 2014)

Moreover, there are significant differences between federal states in terms of their supply density of health care. Supply density of health care in terms of doctors per inhabitant is highest for the city states Berlin, Bremen and Hamburg. To some extent, this is certainly promoted by health care supply for the population in the catchment area of these city states. But also Bavaria and Saarland exhibit considerably above average values of doctors per inhabitant, while federal states from the Eastern part of Germany and Lower Saxony show the lowest rates. Yet, the new Länder of Germany exhibit the highest increase of this indicator since 1991. (Klose and Rehbein 2015)

Next to disparities caused by geographical circumstances, the availability of a skilled workforce and financial resources influences the development and structure of the health economy. Certain occupational groups of the health economy, such as medical doctors, certified nurses, medical engineers, orthopedic and rehabilitation technicians exhibit a significant and partly region-specific growing scarcity of skilled workforce already today. (Bundesagentur für Arbeit (BA) 2016a; Ostwald et al. 2016)

Furthermore, there happens to be a heterogeneity concerning the availability of financial resources, which impacts on inpatient facilities. Recent and past funding programs such as been implemented by the Health Care Structure Act (*Article 14 of Gesundheitsstrukturgesetz*), promoted a modernization of hospitals in Eastern Germany after the Unification of Germany. Regional differences appear with respect to investments made (Deutsche Krankenhausgesellschaft (DKG) 2015) and investments necessary (Rheinisch-Westfälisches Institut für Wirtschaftsforschung (RWI) 2014).

The necessity for investments to be undertaken in hospitals is linked to the demographic development in the respective federal state. Increasing age leads to a rise of health problems in terms of the number of people affected and the complexity of diseases (Böhm, Tesch-Römer and Ziese 2009). This leads to an increase in the demand for health services and health-related products (Kronenberg 2009 & 2011). Demographic change therefore requires an efficient health system (Augurzky et al. 2015). Yet, federal states are affected in different ways in this matter: Senior citizens make up 6.4 percent of the population in most sub-regions of Saxony, whereas they make up only 4.8 percent in large parts of Bavaria (IEGUS and Rheinisch-Westfälisches Institut für Wirtschaftsforschung (RWI) 2015).

Increased needs for health care supply caused by demographic change affect the regional distribution of doctors as well. A demographic factor was recently introduced into the distribution mechanism of doctors carrying out outpatient treatment in order to react on regional differences concerning the number of elderly people (Kassenärztliche Bundesvereinigung (KBV) 2016; Gemeinsamer Bundesausschuss (G-BA) 2016). The effects of regionally differentiated demographic change has been studied with input-output techniques in earlier work (Kronenberg and Engel 2008; Kronenberg, Kühntopf and Tivig 2010). However, these studies relied on individual input-output tables for single regions and were therefore unable to account for interregional spillover effects. This shortcoming is one of the motivations for the multiregional approach developed in the present contribution.

Moreover, industrial specializations of the health economy are distributed in a heterogeneous way across Germany similarly to the overall industrial structure. This causes differences in international and national openness of federal states, which impacts on dependencies and economic spill-over effects.

The MRHA provides a consistent data base, which quantifies the health economy of German federal states within one model, thereby using the same methodology to establish this satellite account that was used for the national calculations described in chapter 2. Therefore, it becomes possible to analyze existing heterogeneities among the federal states in the context of the contribution to GVA, employment and trade of the respective health economy. In the following, we describe one field of application of the MRHA, which points out the political relevance of the established tool.

Due to the dualistic financing framework of the health system in Germany regulated in the Hospital Finance Act (*§ 4 Krankenhausfinanzierungsgesetz*), both health insurance companies and federal states have to bear costs caused by health care supply. While the former are responsible for current expenditures, the latter institutions have to come up for the costs of building, maintaining and equipping hospitals with medical technology.

This framework of health care financing leads to challenges for federal states and results in a cumulated investment bottleneck in hospitals said to amount between 14.6 Bn. € (Augurzky et al. 2014) and 50 Bn. € (Deutsche Krankenhausgesellschaft (DKG) 2009a), depending on the author of the specific study and the definitions used.

This significant investment bottleneck and a regional heterogeneity of actual investments taken represent severe challenges in the light of ensuring equal standards regarding the equipment with medical technology and consequently needs-based health care supply. Future challenges, such as demographic change, the debt brake (Sachverständigenrat zur Begutachtung der gesamtwirtschaftlichen Entwicklung and Statistisches Bundesamt 2014) and the end of the investment program for hospitals in Eastern Germany's federal states at the beginning of 2015, determined by the Health Care Structure Act (*Article 14 of Gesundheitsstrukturgesetz*), may toughen the already existing challenge. The relevance of the topic and its political awareness are illustrated by its addressing within the recently published revision of the Hospital Finance Act (*§ 12 Krankenhausfinanzierungsgesetz*). Numerous statements however stress the inadequacy of incorporated approaches (Bundesärztekammer 2015; Verband der Ersatzkassen (vdek) 2015; Dachverband Deutsche Hochschulmedizin e.V. 2015).

Up to now, there is no compensation mechanism between federal states, which addresses this challenge. While the morbidity-oriented risk structure compensation focusses on current expenses borne by health insurance companies solely, the German Federal Financial Equalization System (*Länderfinanzausgleich*) does not consider factors such as demographic composition or status of health (Ulrich and Wille 2014; GKV-Spitzenverband 2015; Wissenschaftlicher Beirat beim Bundesministerium der Finanzen 2013; Rürup et al. 2008).

Due to existing interdependencies between federal states, we hypothesize that some regions even profit from a higher demand for health care in cases they supply the rest of the country with products and services necessary for patient treatment. Interdependencies among regions hence result from the production and provision of medication, medical products and other goods and services – produced in one region and consumed in another region.

In the course of the application of the MRHA in chapter 6, we conduct input-output analysis to reveal the interconnectedness of federal states caused by patient treatment. Based thereon, we derive federal-specific contribution amounts to a fund for the specific purpose to cope with lagging hospital investments. The individual contribution to the fund is derived from federal states' profits from patient treatment in the rest of the country.

3.3. Methodological background

Within this section, we describe the methodological background of the MRHA in order to facilitate a better understanding of section 3.4. Attention should be paid on the fact that the presented methodology concentrates on a general multiregionalization of a set of supply and use tables of national accounts, but superior emphases are put on the health economy in selected cases. The subsequent step - the compilation of a multiregional health satellite account from an overall economic multiregional account - follows national standards and is therefore consistent with chapter 2. The remainder of this section is structured as follows:

Subsection 3.3.1 describes the principles and specifics of the NHA and therefore the MRHA. In subsection 3.3.2, we address the characteristics of our approach and compare it to existing methodology on (multi)regionalization. Subsection 3.3.3 focusses on the general multiregional framework.

3.3.1. Principles of the multiregional and national health account

Within this subsection, we describe the basic principles of the NHA, which were developed throughout the several projects on the national level. As we apply the same methodology to calculate the MRHA, the principles described in the following count for the MRHA as well. In order to facilitate a better understanding of the explanatory power of the NHA and MRHA, a short overview of principles and the approach is given over here.

The health economy in the context of the NHA is defined as '[…] the production and marketing of goods and services, which serve for prevention as well as for the provision of health and for rehabilitation.' (Kuratorium Gesundheitswirtschaft 2005). At this point it is essential to note the focus on goods and services related to health in contrast to involved agents. Consequently, one good or service is part of the health economy, if it serves a better status of health or prevents its deterioration, regardless of who produced and financed it. This makes clear why the set of supply and use tables is essential for the calculations of the NHA and the MRHA. Supply and use tables provide data on the product-side as well, while most key indicators of national accounts such as GVA and employment refer to the industry side exclusively.

The health expenditure survey serves as a main secondary data base to quantify the so-called 'core area' of the health economy. It also follows a product-specific approach in accordance with the international standard called the "System of Health Accounts" by Organisation for Economic Co-operation and Development (OECD) et al. (2011). In order to quantify the economic output of the product-sided defined health economy, we match private and public consumption of the use table with product-sided defined expenditures from the health expenditure survey. The 'extended area' of the health economy, however, does not refer to any comparable secondary data base or international standard but comprises products and services, which are of main concern to the health economy beyond the definition of the health expenditure survey, i.e. E-Health services and products, R&D or health tourism.

Special evaluations of national supply and use tables, provided by the Federal Statistical Office, serve as the basis for the NHA and accordingly the MRHA. Its uniqueness lies in the detailed dimension of tables, representing 930 partly or fully health related goods out of 2.643 products and services, which make up the overall economy in German national accounts. For the current calculations we have available supply and use tables in this detail for the years 2010 and 2011. Tables refer to domestic production and imports separately at basic prices. Most recent statistical standards such as the classification of industries according to NACE 2008 (Eurostat 2008b) and concepts and methods according to ESA 2010 (Eurostat 2013) apply.

3.3.2. Differences to existing methodology for the regionalization of national accounts

Throughout the last years there has been an increasing interest in regional input-output tables for scientific research. In matters of compilation and data availability it is essential to differentiate between regional tables involving several nations in contrast to input-output tables on the subnational level.

Usually, poor data availability of the regions in consideration poses a central challenge to the compilation of the latter. Consequently, survey based input-output tables on the subnational level are hardly available, as high expenses result from the collection and processing of data (Jensen, Mandeville and Karunaratne 2017). Scarcity of data especially occur with regard to interregional trade flows, information on production technology and resulting input-output coefficients.

However, there are several non-survey techniques available to compile regional input-output tables, though many of these show obvious inadequacies (Brucker, Hastings and Latham III 1987; Brucker, Hastings and Latham III 1990). To overcome the difficulties resulting from the absence of survey-based regional input-output tables and low the quality of non-survey tables, it is suggested to compile input-output tables based on hybrid approaches, which combine non-survey techniques with superior data (Lahr 1993). This facilitates insights into macroeconomic characteristics of economic activities of subnational regions.

The most common approach to regionalize IO tables are locations quotients, from which FLQ and AFLQ perform best (Bonfiglio and Chelli 2008). Those approaches are most suitable for type B tables (Kronenberg 2012).[4] Even if those approaches show reasonable results for single regional tables, FLQ and AFLQ depend on a variable parameter, which has to be chosen for the calculation and has high impacts on the results. Literature also shows that neglecting the existence of cross hauling leads to unsatisfactory results (Többen and Kronenberg 2015) and consequently overestimated input-coefficients.

Cross-hauling is considered by the methodological approach of CHARM (Kronenberg 2009a). This approach is most suitable for type E tables.[5] However, especially in the case of small regions the approach does not always produce reasonable results due to assumptions made in association with national patterns (Flegg, Huang and Tohmo 2015). CHARM has also been extended to multiregional applications (Többen and Kronenberg 2015).

Schröder and Zimmermann (2014) used both CHARM and location quotients for calculating intraregional output multipliers for a German region. Differences between results are considerably high. This fact stresses the challenge to derive realistic regional input-output tables especially in cases when no survey based tables are available to evaluate their accuracy.

From a traditional point of view, input-output tables have been used as a starting point for regional or interregional impact analysis instead of supply and use tables. However, recent literature shows that the framework of supply and use tables is preferable over input-output tables. There are a number of reasons for that. For example, supply and use tables are based on the methods used by the statistical offices to compile national accounts and therefore refer directly to the collected data (Madsen and Jensen-Butler

4 Type B tables focus on national demand and production and involve international imports only as necessary supplement at the edge of tables.

5 Type E tables represent supply and use as the sum of domestically produced and imported goods.

1999). Consequently, supply and use tables are not affected by technology assumptions applied to derive input-output tables.

A further advantage of this concept is the classification of tables with respect to both categories of industries and products, which enhances incorporating additional information significantly (Lenzen and Rueda-Cantuche 2012). Furthermore, the square format of input-output tables is considered with an essential loss of information, as the rectangular shape of supply and use tables has to be aggregated first in order to compile a square input-output table.

Moreover, data availability makes the set of supply and use tables to be the preferable database for regionalization in the special case of German federal states. Information on GVA, output and employment refer to categories of industries and represent important information for the supply and use framework (e.g. Statistische Ämter des Bundes und der Länder 2017). This information is not available in categories of products, referring to the German input-output framework (Destatis 2010). Consequently, available fundamental data cannot be integrated into the input-output concept without making further assumptions. We consider this as a critical argument against the regionalization of German input-output tables, as assumptions concerning the most fundamental database used can have high impacts on the results. This circumstance can be avoided by making use of the supply and use framework.

One challenge, however, comes along with applying regionalization approaches on supply and use tables. Balancing conditions of supply and use have to be contained or at least restored. Similar problems arise when implementing hybrid approaches to regionalize input-output tables. The common way to calculate hybrid subnational multiregional input-output tables is to model the necessary set of single region tables by making use of non-survey methods. In a further step, they are linked to each other by including estimates on interregional trade (Többen and Kronenberg 2015; Boero, Edwards and Rivera 2017). Adjustments become necessary in order to include external information or to assure accounting identities. Mostly, optimization techniques are performed in order to minimize the differences between the non-survey table and the final table. Conversely, this means that the input-output table and hence multipliers are likely to be affected by the specific non-survey technique used (Bonfiglio and Chelli 2008).

As a result from the previous description, we devise a new approach to calculate regionalized input-output tables and call it MR-SUT-RAS. The procedure is based on the known concept of SUT-RAS (Temurshoev and

Timmer 2011), which had in its origins been developed for simultaneously updating national supply and use tables by assuring accounting identities without necessarily specifying any information on the product side. In those matters it behaves unlike RAS and its relatives. This iterative algorithm considers secondary information already during compilation, which makes additional balancing obsolete. We developed the concept of SUT-RAS further to make it suitable for the multiregional framework. This extension is essential in order to maintain consistency with the national supply and use tables as it preserves the row and column sums of the national table. To be more specific, in an n-regional framework, the row sum of each n-fold available good equals the row sum of the national table. The same applies for industry-specific information or information on final consumption patterns. The possibility of cross-hauling is explicitly accounted for within the approach. A multiregional input-output table is then calculated from compiled multiregional supply and use tables by applying the product technology assumption.

Similar approaches such as RAS have already been applied to regionalize input-output tables. According to Miernyk (1976) however, results lack on accuracy. This rather mechanical approach misses economic logic, he says. We do not disagree at this point. Moreover, the mechanical approach - the logic of the economic cycle within a multiregional system of a number of supply and use tables - is exactly what our approach relies on. Goods and services, produced by one federal state, are made available for the global economy, where either the region itself, the world outside of the nation or other federal states require especially this product or service. Hence, we accomplish to balance the multiregional supply and use tables for each product of each federal state taking into account interregional trade flows. The latter are hence predetermined by what federal states produce and what they need. These interregional trade flows can be modelled with a higher accuracy if we implement available data on the use of products and services, such as international trade statistics of federal states. Since our approach balances the multiregional supply and use table it becomes obsolete to define row sums, which are hardly available and are a prerequisite to apply the conventional RAS. This circumstance counters another of Miernyk's concerns regarding regional input-output tables. He explicitly points out the challenges in changes which may arise from a reconciliation procedure. Also Miller and Blair (2009) point out the challenges that come with partially high differences when comparing RAS-estimated coefficients with the values, which entered the iteration. Wiebe and Lenzen (2016) address the special case of using balancing techniques when obtaining multiregional input-output tables. However, they do not find a clear answer to the contribution or non-contribution of the RAS-balancing approach to the validity of the examined multiregional table, since – as in most cases concerning this matter – there is not enough available and validated data to decide upon the most 'correct' table (Tukker and Dietzenbacher 2013).

Often, tables lack detailed information in cases a specific research question is applied. Under these circumstances, available data on national accounts have to be disaggregated first (Wenz et al. 2015). This is not necessary in the context of our approach due to a special evaluation on national supply and use tables provided by the Federal Statistical Office. Information on supply and use tables is available for 930 health-related products and services from an overall amount of 2.643 goods, which make up the German economy. Non-health related information is available in an aggregated manner. In order to make use of this maximum of information, we compile the multiregional satellite account for the health economy on the basis of the detailed set of national supply and use tables.

In total, we are well aware of the fact that this hybrid approach cannot in any way contest a survey based multiregional table. The MR-SUT-RAS algorithm is rather seen as a new approach, which makes implementation of additional data and assumptions easily possible once the setup is programmed and addresses some weaknesses of earlier approaches.

However, implementing additional information does not always lead to better results of the model in cases the assumptions applied to make this information suitable violate the macroeconomic picture. At this point one must decide upon the goal of the model. Especially in the case of our developed approach, the concept of holistic accuracy (Jensen 1980) is preferable. This does not reflect accuracy in each cell of the table, but it serves a 'mathematical portrait' interpretation of the table.

During compilation, we have experienced the difference and impact of partitive accuracy in contrast to holistic accuracy in the case of consumption patterns. The Income and Consumption Survey (EVS) corresponds to a sample survey on German household consumption conducted on behalf of the Federal Statistical office with a periodicity of five years (Destatis 2005). Data corresponds to purchasers prices from the overall amount of domestic production and imports. Consequently, several assumptions have to be incorporated in order to implement this specific information cell-wise into the multiregional use tables at basic prices for domestic production and imports separately. This implies that data has to be transferred into basic prices and assumptions concerning the amount of international imports and imports from other federal states have to be made. Moreover, the concept of EVS corresponds to the resident in contrast to the domestic concept, whereas the latter is applicable for national accounts.

In the context of the MR-SUT-RAS we must decide particularly careful which additional secondary data we implement. On the one hand, i.e. EVS data proofs challenging, since we have to make several assumptions in order to apply it to our framework. Moreover, we lack on assumptions to adjust the deviating concept it refers to. On the other hand, the MR-SUT-RAS is an iterative algorithm, which considers additional information not only as a suggestions but takes it as completely given. Since household consumption accounts for big shares of the use side in some cases, the implementation of highly uncertain data - due to the several assumptions taken and the different concept applying – can cause the algorithm to develop into unrealistic directions.

In our case we tried to implement EVS data but it turned out it took the algorithm many more iterations to converge, which led to highly unreasonable results in the end. Consequently, we used this data for plausibility checks only. It turned out that consumption patterns of our final resulting tables show reasonable similarities to EVS data. Temurshoev and Timmer (2011) also address the circumstance of additional information not always improving resulting estimates. However, they do not dwell any further upon this matter at this point.

Summarized, data scarcity and the fact no subnational tables are produced in general due to high costs involved, make it is hard to investigate research in this field. Consequently, we see the application on health in a multiregional context as an opportunity to develop a proper assessment on the quality of results and the developed approach. This way, we can concentrate on the dynamics of the regional health economy and profit from our profound knowledge in this field resulting from several years of research.

3.3.3. The multiregional context

In this subsection we want to proclaim the fundamental dimensions and interrelationships of multiregional supply and use tables. In order to facilitate a better understanding, the following concentrates on a three region economy. However, a multiregional table for the 16 federal states of Germany consists of a 16 x 16 framework.

Figure 8: Multiregional use table in a 3 regional economy

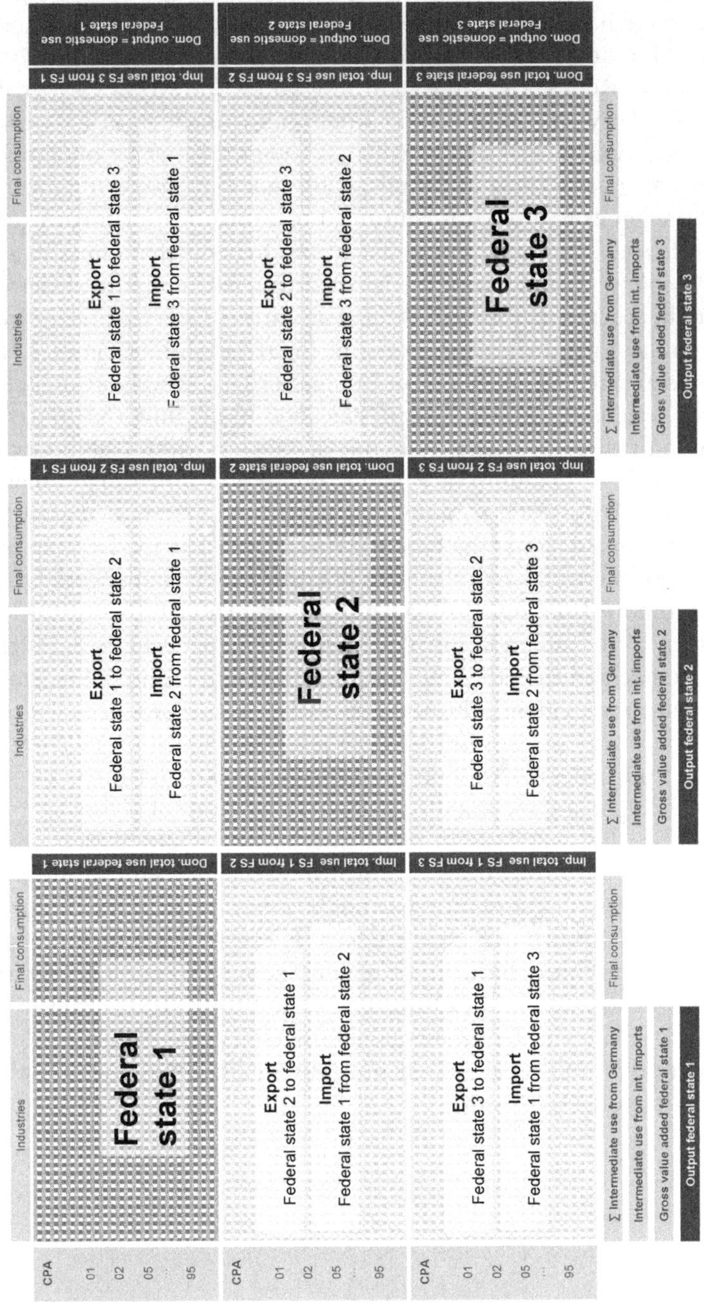

Source: Own illustration.

The multiregional use table shown in Figure 8 pictures the interrelationships of the economy. Federal state one produces output by making use of intermediate inputs from international, regional (i.e. federal state one) or 'national but not regional' grounds (i.e. federal state two and three or 'Rest of Country' (RoC)). The same counts for goods and services for final consumption. They are either bought from international areas, are produced by the very same federal state in which it is consumed or are obtained from federal state two or three in a three region economy. Following this framework, the goods and services consumed or demanded for further production in federal state one can originate from four different areas in a three region economy, from which the latter three refer to imports: federal state one itself, federal state two, federal state three or international grounds. This results in national macroeconomic interrelationships between federal state one and the three regions of product origins as well as inter-sectoral interconnectedness within federal state one itself. Imports from federal state two or three to federal state one are shown within the bottom two squares in the left column of Figure 8, the sum of nine squares representing the overall domestic economy. Imports from international grounds are recorded within a row at the bottom. This is caused by the fact that national interdependencies are in the focus of tables but the framework is incomplete if imports from international grounds are ignored.

In turn to the situation just described, interdependencies between federal state one and the other regions also arise from exports of federal state one to the other regions. This is the case when goods produced within one federal state are not consumed by the resident population or enterprises. Exports from federal state one to federal state two and three are shown within the right and the middle square of the top row of Figure 8.

Described linkages lead to interdependencies of production and consumption between federal states, which are shown within the multiregional use table. This circumstance may not be mixed up with the multiregional supply table shown in Figure 9, which reflects multiregional production structures. This figure shows three regional supply tables for a three region economy, embedded in a 3x3 multiregional setting. This means a fundamental difference to the multiregional use table from Figure 8 exhibiting information on multiregional relationships in all of the nine sub-tables of the multiregional framework.

Figure 9: Multiregional supply table in a 3 regional economy

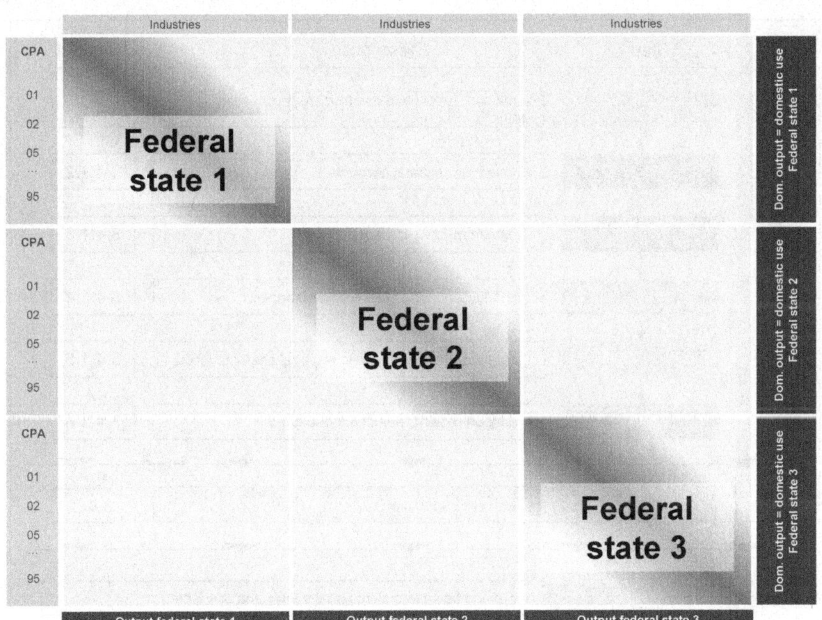

Source: Own illustration.

The regional supply tables of the multiregional model are arranged in the shape of a block diagonal matrix. There are only entries of zeroes in the off-block-diagonal areas since the allocation of regional economic key indicators such as output, GVA or employment refer to the local unit of enterprises rather than its technical unit in the case of multiregional operating companies.

Consequently, products and services produced within one federal state are always generated by regional enterprises and hence by employees working in this federal state. This circumstance is represented by the block-diagonal shape of Figure 9, representing the multiregional supply table for the overall economy.

Figure 10: Steps of compilation

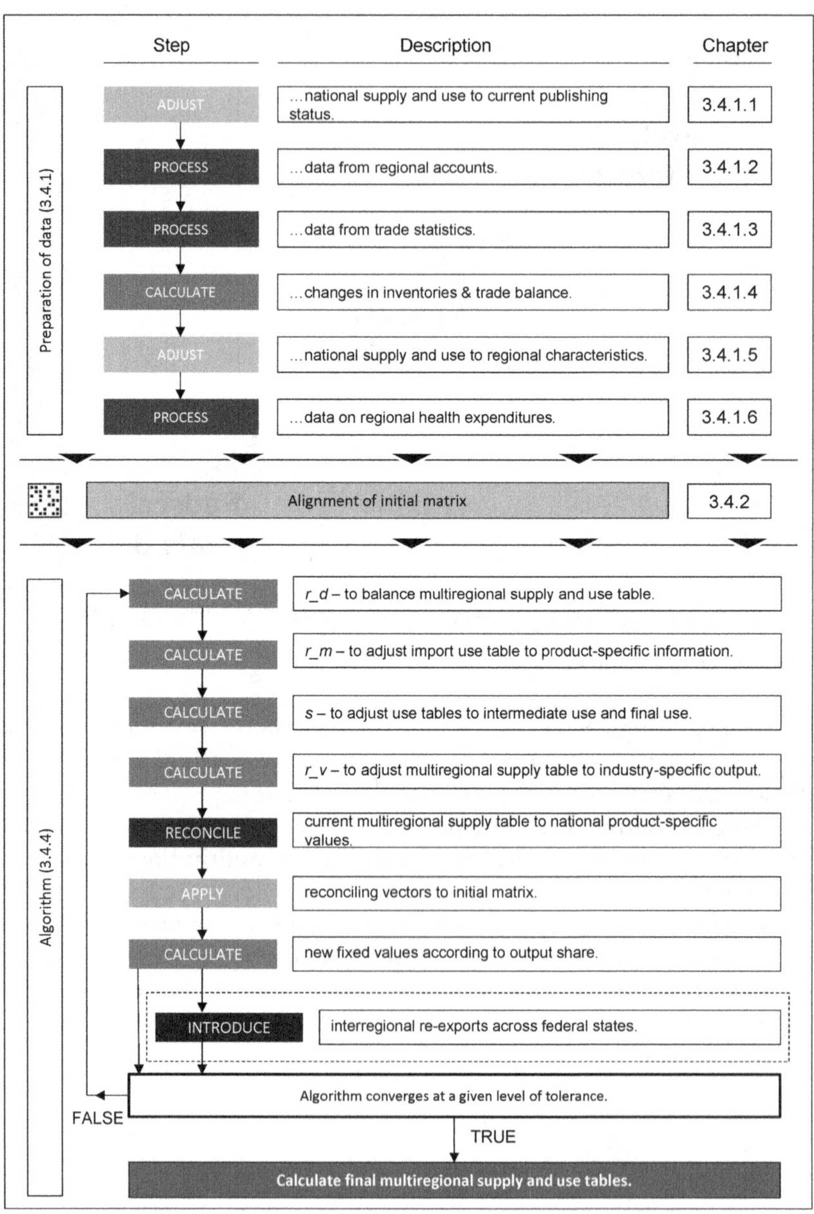

Source: Own illustration.

3.4. Compilation methodology

The motivation and the methodological background of the MRHA have been described in sections 3.2 and 3.3. The main contribution of this chapter, the compilation approach of the MRHA, is discussed within this section. Subsection 3.4.1 focusses on used data and its preparation. In subsection 3.4.2 we describe the preparation and design of the starting point before applying the iterative algorithm to it. Subsection 3.4.3 focuses on the known concept of SUT-RAS, which is further developed to the multiregional framework in subsection 3.4.4. Subsection 3.4.5 comprises of a short description of results from applying the MR-SUT-RAS and opposes it with initial tables. In a final step, we describe the way of compiling the satellite account from the calculated set of multiregional supply and use tables in subsection 3.4.6. In Figure 10, the steps of compilation are summarized.

3.4.1. Preparation of data

The selection and preparation of data used for the compilation of the MRHA are an essential part of the overall calculation. There are numerous different data bases, which play a decisive role during the compilation: The special evaluation of supply and use tables represents a particular feature of the application as it comprises of very detailed and non-official information and represents the main underlying data base for the MRHA. Available data on regional accounts goes also beyond published data but needs further processing in order to be suitable for the compilation. Trade statistics on international export and import of federal states is a further essential source of information. In order to use a maximum of available data in this matter, we consulted two different data sources with different categorization and matched them. Data on changes in inventories and the overall amount of interregional trade are not available from official data. The derivation can however be conducted with regard to the missing amounts to close the economic circle. Data on health expenditure refer to private and public expenditure for health care services and products. Several assumptions needed to be made in order to implement this product-specific information. The summarized steps in compilation are discussed in further detail in the following.

3.4.1.1. Special evaluation of supply and use tables

The special evaluation of supply and use tables, provided by the Federal Statistical Office, comprises detailed information on the goods and services related to the health economy. Consequently, we have information on domestic use, domestic supply and import use at basic prices for 930 out of overall 2.643 products, which make up the German economy according to the national accounting framework. For the selected goods we have complete information. This amounts to information on 930 goods for 64 industries and seven categories of final consumption. Moreover, aggregated tables for supply and use are available, which enables us to calculate the aggregated values of missing data of the special evaluation. This way we have full information on the overall economy with selected areas of detailed information, referring to goods and services partially or fully related to the health economy. We have two sets of supply and use tables available, referring to the years 2010 and 2011. Statistical standards correspond to NACE 2008 and ESA 2010.

Substantial additional adaptations of this data base are not necessary as it represents the main fundament for calculating the MRHA. In fact, it is all other data that must fit this data base. However, in order to assure consistency of the present tables of national accounts with secondary data regarding regional accounts, it is essential to refer to the same date of publishing. The set of tables on supply and use were published in 2015, whereas the secondary data on regional accounts used are from 2016. We do not have available the set of data on regional accounts from an earlier publication date. Consequently, we update the available supply and use tables for the German economy in accordance to revised data published in 2016 making use of the original SUT-RAS algorithm (Temurshoev and Timmer 2011). Data for this procedure refers to (Destatis 2017g). For more information concerning this procedure see Schwärzler and Kronenberg (2016). The resulting slightly adjusted supply and use tables now fit the data of regional accounts, i.e. result in the same overall amount for the German economy.

3.4.1.2. Regional accounts

We use official but partially unpublished data of regional accounts on GVA, employment, intermediate consumption, compensation of employees and total amounts of the several categories of final use (Statistische Ämter des Bundes und der Länder 2017). As mentioned, we aim to compile the MRHA based on the special evaluation on national supply and use tables. Consequently, regional industry-specific information has to equal the level of aggregation on the national level, which is 64 industries and seven categories of final use. However, data available on regional GVA and employment refer to 38 aggregates of industries and five categories of final demand. The latter includes the sum of household final consumption expenditure (households and non-profit organizations serving households), government final consumption expenditure, investments in machinery, the sum of equipment and other products, and gross fixed capital formation in construction. Additionally, information on taxes less subsidies is available for the federal states of Germany. Intermediate consumption and compensation of employees refer to 21 aggregates of industries. In this section, we only concentrate on the derivation of GVA, output, intermediate consumption and compensation of employees into 64 aggregates.

We proceed this way, since data on the overall amounts of final consumption categories except for exports and change in inventories are available from regional accounts and only need minor adjustments in the case of household final consumption expenditure. We differentiate the latter into households and non-profit organizations serving households by applying the national distribution. Since non-profit organizations serving households account for only 2.8 percent of overall household consumption, we think that this unsophisticated approach is acceptable. Information on international trade does not refer to regional accounts but to trade statistics. Hence we focus on that field in subsection 3.4.1.3 and do not discuss it any further over here. We address the derivation of changes in inventories and the amount of interregional trade, for which no data is data available, in subsection 3.4.1.4.

Up to three federal states did not provide data on GVA, employment and intermediate consumption at the same level of disaggregation as the other federal states of Germany did. Consequently, we use data on employees subject to social security contribution (Bundesagentur für Arbeit (BA) 2016b) to derive missing information on employees from residual sums of regional accounts. Regarding GVA, we use available or calculated information on employees and weight this information with labor productivity in terms of GVA per employee from the next related aggregate in order to distribute the residual sum over the federal states of concern. We calculate missing data of intermediate consumption by applying national GVA quota in order to disaggregate the residual sum. We proceed accordingly, since no information on higher aggregates is available in this case. After each step of disaggregation we apply the GRAS algorithm (Lenzen et al. 2007)[6] on the resulting matrix of derived missing data in order to align the compiled matrix to given national values and available data of federal states at some given aggregate level.

The procedure to calculate missing data equals the approach to disaggregate available industry data of federal states at the level of 38 aggregates into 64 industries, which corresponds to the level of detail at the national level and hence the national supply and use table we want to multiregionalize. In order to facilitate a better understanding of this approach we use the disaggregation of employees from 38 aggregates into 64 aggregates as an exemplary field of application in accordance to Figure 11.

Likewise to the previous procedure we use information on employees subject to social security contribution to derive first estimates on employees within each of the aggregates. For example, we have available data on the overall sum of employees working in agriculture, forestry and fishing for each of the federal states but want to derive each single amount for each of the federal states. We hence derive a matrix of first estimates on the distribution over agriculture, forestry and fishing for each federal state. However, the sum over federal states of employees working in agriculture deviates from the national sum in cases we are not able to derive the absolute exact distribution key, which is in general the case. Since we know the sum of each of the industries on national level (indicated by the dark blue area in Figure 11) and the aggregate sum of agriculture, forestry and fishing for each of the federal states (indicated by "1. Σ R1", "1. Σ R2", "1. Σ R3" in Figure 11), we know the row sums and the column sums the matrix of first estimates is supposed to match. Consequently, we reconcile this matrix in accordance to these target values by making use of the GRAS algorithm. We proceed this way for each of the 38 aggregates (according to Figure 11) in the case of data on employees and GVA and for the 21 aggregates we have available for intermediate consumption and compensation of employees.

6 We use the GRAS algorithm instead of the RAS algorithm since it is capable to deal not only with positive but also with negative values and is therefore applicable to all occurring situations. In some very special cases it happens that i.e. GVA takes on negative values according to provided official data on federal states.

Figure 11: Consolidation of disaggregated regional accounts data

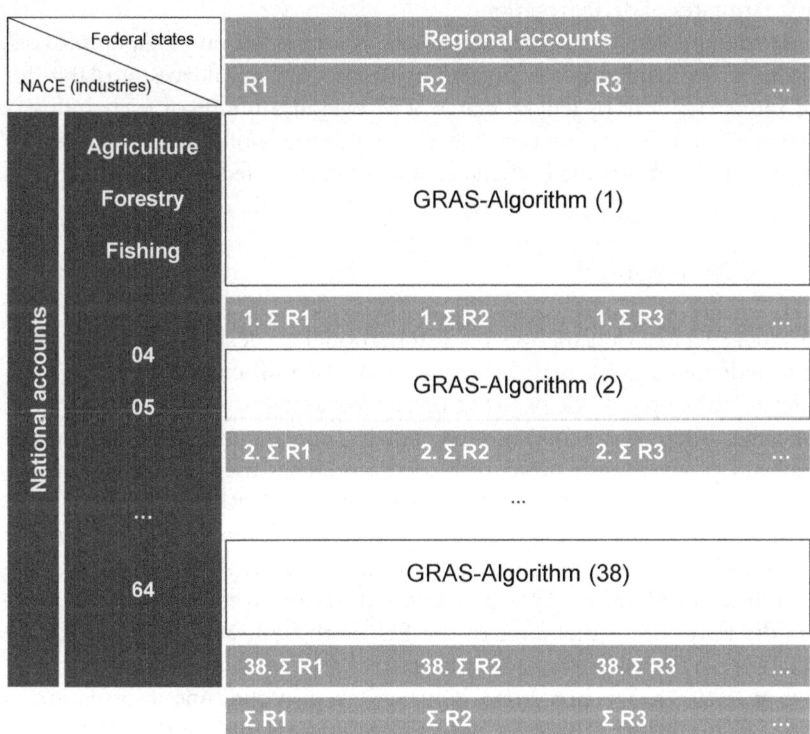

Source: R1, R2 and R3 refer to region one, region two and region three.

Source: Own illustration.

In order to derive first estimates for GVA, intermediate consumption and compensation of employees we use different approaches. As mentioned, we use information on employees subject to social contribution to derive a first estimation of employees. We disaggregate GVA in accordance to the employees derived, weighted with national values on labor productivity per industry. For a first estimate of intermediate consumption for 64 industries we apply the national GVA quota on existing 21 aggregates in order to obtain a first estimate on the disaggregation. Compensation of employees is available for 21 aggregates as well. As we know the national share of compensation of employees to GVA, we take this information in combination with calculated and consolidated data on GVA on the regional level.

Again, we apply the GRAS method on each of the matrices referring to first estimates of disaggregation.

At the end of this procedure we have information on GVA, employees, intermediate consumption and compensation of employees available for 64 industries and 16 federal states. The overall amount of each industry matches the values on national level and subtotals of federal states match aggregates from provided official economic data on federal states.

3.4.1.3. Trade statistics

Product-specific information on international trade is available for German federal states. Actually, there are even two official data bases, which refer to this topic, both showing certain advantages. In the following, we describe differences between trade statistics and national accounts in general and proceed with presenting the approaches used to implement the two different data bases on trade statistics into the MRHA.

In general, data on international export and import are based on the Commodity Classification for Foreign Trade Statistics (WA), which corresponds to the Combined Nomenclature (CN) and which in turn is a binding directive for all members of the EU. Both trade statistics used for the MRHA we describe below can be recoded to the WA classification (Destatis 2017h; Destatis 2018). This way, we can combine information of the different statistics and use both for the compilation of the MRHA. We proceed accordingly in order to obtain the maximum of information available, so we can actually profit even more from the detailed use tables we have available from the special evaluation on national supply and use tables.

It is essential to note that we use trade statistics to disaggregate the national export vectors and the product-specific information on imports into 16 vectors each, representing the number of German federal states. Therefore, we do not use any absolute values of trade statistics but merely its distribution among federal states. We proceed accordingly, since trade statistics and national accounts in fact both refer to international trade but show slight differences in methodology (United Nations 2013). In the following, we explain differences in order to point out the challenges and possible inaccuracies of international imports and exports of German federal states within the MRHA, which arise from differences in methodology.

One significant aspect is a different understanding of transferring of goods. While trade statistics record exports and imports with physical border crossing, national accounts refer to trade in accordance to a transfer of economic ownership since ESA 2010. To be more specific, in the case of bilateral contract processing, only the payment for manufacturing service is registered in national accounts, while export and import activities of the good to be processed is part of trade statistics (Destatis 2017i). There is no product-specific data available for the German federal states, which enables to conclude upon the respective amount of bilateral contract processing. Hence, we assume that the differences in methodology are product-specific and have therefore no impact on the distribution across federal states. However, we are aware that this must not apply i.e. specifically in the case of border states.

While national accounts differentiate between domestically produced and imported exports, the trade statistics in concern focus on domestically produced exports exclusively. The reverse conclusion is that imports from trade statistics do not consider re-exports, i.e. exports from imports (Braakmann and Goldhammer 2016). Consequently, we have to disaggregate the export vector of the import use table according to further assumptions. These re-exports make up about 18 percent of overall imports in Germany in the year 2011 (Destatis 2016f). We disaggregate this vector in accordance to the product-specific information regarding imports for domestic use of federal states since we assume that a certain – over federal states identical – share of imports stays within the importing region and hence shows a suitable approach for disaggregation. In cases in which no imports take place for a specific good, we use output as approximation.

Another methodological difference between trade statistics and national accounts relates to the concepts of 'special trade' and 'general trade' (Eurostat 2017b). For the federal states of Germany, exports from trade statistics refer to the first, while imports refer to the latter concept just as national accounts do. Consequently, international exports of federal states lack information concerning the amount of exports, which are received into customs warehouses without subsequently entering the country of receipt. Export in terms of general trade amounted to 1,066 Bn. € opposed to 1,061 Bn. € in terms of special trade in 2011 for overall Germany (Destatis 2016c). The difference, i.e. 5.2 Bn. € makes up around 0.5 percent of overall exports in terms of general trade. Consequently, we assume that this methodological difference does not essentially impact the relative importance of product-specific export among federal states, i.e. every federal state exports the same share into customs warehouses without having them subsequently entering the country of receipt.

Moreover, no information on imports and exports of services are available in trade statistics. With respect to the relatively small amount, which refers to this number on the national level, we disaggregate the national values with respect to regional output.

After we have explained the differences in methodology between national accounts and trade statistics and have described our approaches for disaggregation, we continue with introducing the specific trade statistics used for the MRHA.

The first trade statistic we implement into our model refers to the 'Product Classification for Production Statistics' (GP) (Destatis 2016a). It shows advantages especially in its reference to production statistics and consequently national accounts in terms of classification. Based on this fact we can easily transfer this information, available for all federal states, into our model. One main disadvantage, however, shows the fact that this data is only available for 30 aggregates of goods. When we disaggregate the available information and implement it into our framework of detailed use tables it leads to the circumstance that each of the federal state shows an identical distribution of goods among subcategories of aggregates. However, we can derive adjusted distributions for each federal state by considering the second available data base on international trade. In the case of the MRHA, which lays special emphases on the health economy, this fact is of major concern. Medical technology is a part of the economy, which is not consistently shown within only one classification compared to i.e. products of the pharmaceutical industry, which refer to Classification of Products by Activity (CPA) number 21. Medical products refers to CPA 26.6 and 32.5 and is hence part of subsections of the first trade statistic in concern. Therefore, it is essential to integrate more information on this matter in order to specify differences in trade between federal states. We proceed accordingly by implementing information from the second trade statistic.

The second data base we use refers to the 'Classification by Commodity Groups and Subgroups of the Food Industry and Trade and Industry' (EGW) (Destatis 2016b). It represents a traditional national classification of trade statistics. The information published arranges the goods with respect to the degree of processing. One main disadvantage of this information on international exports and imports of federal states is the fact that it does not refer to the categories of production statistics. As a consequence, it shows a classification very unlike to the one used in national accounts. Its major advantage, however, is the amount of available information on

211 categories. To use the example described above, one of these categories directly refers to medical products.

Consequently, we recode the EGW statistics to make it suitable the categorization of national accounts. This way we link both data bases. In order to recode the EGW statistics to the GP statistics, we need a recoding table. Unfortunately, no such table is available, establishing a direct link. However, recoding tables for both statistics are available in order to reconcile with the WA statistics mentioned before. We are hence able to merge data following a two-step procedure. We transfer international trade from the EGW statistics into the WA classification in a first step and reconcile the obtained data with the GP classification in a second step.

In order to implement this data into our model we proceed as follows. Trade from the GP classification still is our superior data base, as it represents a direct link to the categories of national accounts. Data from EGW statistics consist of information mostly reflecting very specific characteristics, representing only similarities to the product in concern from national accounts; one could also call it the 'closest reference value'. Consequently, we disaggregate the export vector from the domestic use table with respect to the distribution of the GP statistics among federal states in a first step.

In a second step we implement data from the EGW data base. When matching this data we obtain a situation similar to the one shown as an example in column three and four of Table 2. Some goods of the nine-digits-level of GP match more than one EGW category. Conversely, one EGW category matches more than one GP category. The main goal is to implement as much information as possible by keeping in mind that we do not implement the absolute values of data on export and import but their relative distribution over federal states in order to reach the national value.

In order to cope with that circumstance, we evaluate the lowest common GP-denominator to eliminate double entries within the EGW statistics. The highest aggregate evaluated refers to the three-digit-level since we leave the one- or two-digit-level unconsidered, as the GP trade statistics is our superior data base, referring to the two-digits-level already. It follows that, for example, EGW 109 refers to GP categories 014310000, 014512000, 014919999, 030069000, 0149110000, 014913000 and 014912000. The lowest common GP-denominator among GP categories is 014 on the one hand and 030069000 on the other hand. At this point we are able to aggregate the volumes of the respective exports and imports leaving out double entries of EGW information, which is $b + c$ for exports and $v + w$ for imports in the case of the GP aggregate "014" from the example shown in Table 2.

Within the next moves we proceed stepwise. We start with reconciling information consistently to a three-digits-level and sum up the information equaling to the same three digit level. From the example of Table 2 this procedure corresponds to calculate the sum of *a to f* for exports and *v to z* for the three digit level "014". In a next step, we apply the resulting federal state distribution on the national values of exports and imports corresponding to the CPA "014" at the three-digit level as well.

Within the further procedure we apply more information concerning the four- to eight-digits-level on the available data with respect to available information. That is "a" for exports and "y" for imports for the example of the four-digit level of "0143". We apply the resulting distribution over federal states to the national export and import values referring to the same four-digit level.

Within the final step, we apply the distribution of the available nine-digits-level over data. Keep in mind, that the amount of information implemented gets less with each step with respect to the lowest common GP-denominator.

Table 2: Matching of GP and EGW classifications on international trade

Export	Import	EGW	GP	Aggregates
a	y	101	014310000	014310000
b	v	109	014310000	014
c	w	102	014110000	014
c	w	102	014211000	014
c	w	102	014212000	014
d	x	103	014610000	014610000
e	y	105	014511000	014511000
b	v	109	014512000	014
f	z	107	014711000	01471
f	z	107	014712000	01471
f	z	107	014714000	01471
f	z	107	014713000	01471
b	v	109	014919000	014
b	v	109	030069000	030069000
b	v	109	014911000	014
b	v	109	014913000	014
b	v	109	014912000	014

Source: Own calculations.

Resulting estimates concerning the distribution of national trade from domestic production are reconciled within the next step by applying the

GRAS algorithm on subsections of the resulting matrix. Row sums refer to values of the national table, whereas the column sums in concern refer to the amounts of trade from the very first estimate resulting from pure GP data on each of the two-digits-level. This way we use superior data to define to volume of imports and exports on the two digits level, but obtain a variation of specialization within the three- to nine-digits level as we have implemented information from the EGW data base.

One special situation occurs during the procedure. Trade statistics refer to purchasers' prices while the use table on hand refers to basic prices. In turn, this means we asserted i.e. exports at basic prices according to information on trade at purchasers' prices. Consequently, we only distributed a part of trade statistics across federal states up until now. Hence, there is a positive gap between the overall amount of the trade statistic and the already distributed exports at basic prices for each federal state. We assume this gap refers to trade margins. Consequently, we distribute the national value of export trade margins according to federal-state-specific gaps.

3.4.1.4. Changes in inventories and amount of interregional trade

National accounts represent one consistent framework, in which the amount of goods and services supplied – produced and imported – equals the amount of goods and services used – within the country considered and exported to other countries. We have information on output from regional accounts - derived from information on GVA and intermediate consumption - and estimated the amount of international imports in the previous subsection. Consequently, the only information missing on the supply side is imports from other federal states. On the use side, we have information on intermediate consumption, final consumption of households and governments, investments and estimated international exports. Therefore, information missing on the use side represents changes in inventories and the amount of exports to other federal states.

Figure 12: Available and missing data

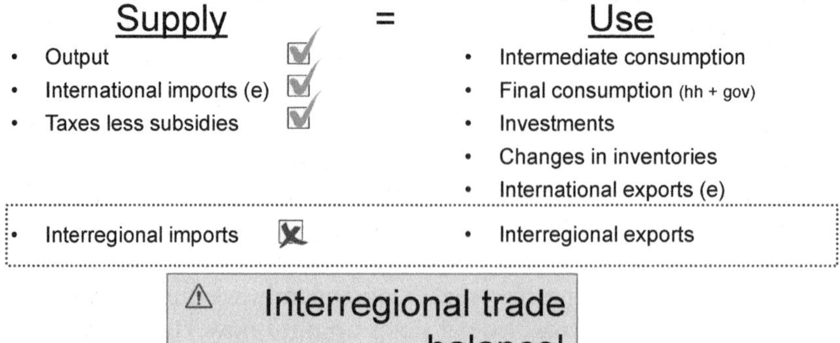

Source: Own illustration.

Table 3: Calculated interregional trade balances and data on international trade balances for 2011

	interregional trade balance (MRHA)*	internationale trade balance (Destatis, GP classification)**	total trade balance
Baden-Württemberg	-13,000	28,501	15,501
Bavaria	-6,000	14,339	8,339
Berlin	5,000	2,748	7,748
Brandenburg	-8,000	-4,617	-12,617
Bremen	3,000	1,245	4,245
Hamburg	37,000	-27,819	9,181
Hesse	42,000	-21,387	20,613
Mecklenburg Western Pomerania	-12,000	2,718	-9,282
Lower Saxony	-10,000	-7,854	-17,854
North Rhine-Westphalia	52,000	-27,682	24,318
Rhineland Palatinate	-24,000	13,345	-10,655
Saarland	-1,000	1,821	821
Saxony	-28,000	9,155	-18,845
Saxony-Anhalt	-9,000	-170	-9,170
Schleswig-Holstein	-12,000	-2,668	-14,668
Thuringia	-14,000	4,624	-9,376

Source: Own calculations, Destatis (2016a); *deviations from zero of the overall sum due to rounding; **calculation of the trade balance from official trade statistics on German federal states is methodologically incorrect, as exports refer to the concept of 'special trade', while imports refer to 'general trade' (see page 85 for more details). In order to get a rough feeling of the amount, however, the difference of international exports and imports is shown nevertheless.

Given the situation we knew about changes in inventories, we would be able to tell the interregional trade balance of each federal state. On the national level, changes in inventories represent about 0.2 percent of overall use, ignoring the amount changes in inventories itself. As this number is very little, we decided to apply this share to the already calculated amount of use for each of the federal states. The difference between supply and use, now calculated changes in inventories included, results in the interregional trade balance depicted in Table 3.

We do not explicitly add this information on interregional trade to our model. Moreover, it represents the remaining amount of products and services of federal states, which they lack or have in advance and therefore start trading with the other federal states. Consequently, by allowing interregional trade, the restriction of supply equaling use can be fulfilled. The iterative algorithm hence independently applies the trade balances for each of the federal states as a necessary condition to be met.

3.4.1.5. Employees subject to social security contribution

Data on employees subject to social security contribution are available for German federal states at the three-digit level, hence providing information for 272 industries each (Bundesagentur für Arbeit (BA) 2016b). This information is of high informational content in the case of the special evaluation on supply and use we are working with. This way, we can use this data to implement some characteristics of federal states into the initial tables already one step before the algorithm is applied onto it.

We discuss the preparation of the initial table in subsection 3.4.2 in detail. In order to understand the following procedure it is however useful to be aware of the fact that we start with multiple national supply and use tables arranged within one initial multiregional supply and use table. This initial supply and use tables are subsequently adjusted when the iterative algorithm is applied. In contrast to starting with 16 identical national supply tables, we now adjust those in advance by incorporating information on employees subject to social security contribution and apply the information gathered on the domestic use tables as well.

Before we describe this procedure we set an example in order to facilitate a better understanding of the approach. Products of medical technology refer to CPA 26.6 and 32.5. Hence, it is a primary product of industry aggregates NACE 26 "Computer, electronic and optical products" and NACE 31-32 "Furniture; other manufacturing goods" for which we have information on GVA, output and employment. As the names of industries suggest, the mentioned indicators refer to many more products of primary production than just medical technology. Hence, we want to add some regional characteristics on the product side of the 'to-be-adjusted' supply tables for the 16 federal states. This way, we honor information we have on federal state specialization (in terms of employees subject to social security contribution) within the industry aggregate at the two-digit level (i.e. 26 and 31-32) and apply this regional-specific distribution among the product side of the subcategories of aggregates. To be more concrete, this means a regional-specific distribution of output among the subcategories of i.e. CPA 26 "Computer, electronic and optical products" in accordance with information we have on employees subject to social security contribution instead of the national distribution. This information refers to eight subcategories of NACE 26, from 26.1 to 26.8. We do not concentrate on medical technology exclusively but apply this procedure on the overall table.

Figure 13: Imbalance between industry- and product-specific information in the supply table

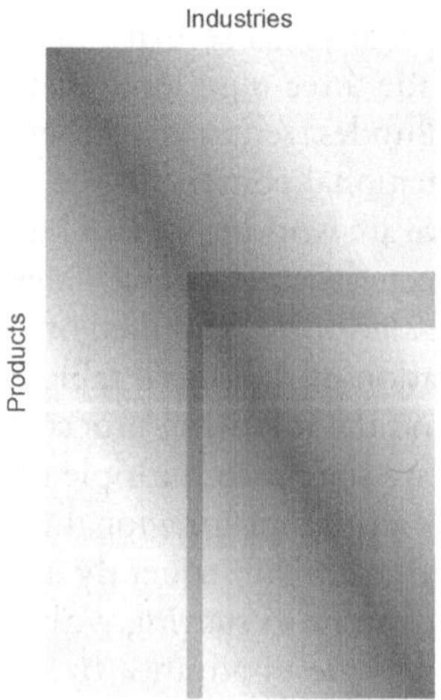

Source: Own illustration.

At this point it is essential to note that the sums of product aggregates at the two-digit level of each supply table remain consistent with the national table. We only adjust the subcategories of aggregates in their composition with respect to the information on employees subject to social security contribution.

The rectangular dimension of the special evaluation of supply and use tables is responsible for carrying out this adjustment. On the one hand, it is of high value for our model to have such detailed information on the product side of supply and use tables. On the other hand, however, for each federal state, available data on output for 64 industries is supposed to simulate product information of around 900 categories. This results in an imbalance between given and desired information we try to represent in Figure 13. Hence, it is likely the algorithm fails to implement certain characteristics on the product side that are not reflected by the given information on the industry side. This is the rationale to adjust subcategories of two-digits-level aggregates in accordance to information on employees subject to social security contribution. This way, we obtain 16 different supply tables in terms of specialization at the subcategories of the two-digit level.

We are well aware of the fact that we mix up information from the industry side with the product side by following this procedure. However, since information on structures of federal states are seldom at this level of detail we decided to ignore the fact of secondary production of industries and assume that a specialization of employment in a certain industry leads to a specialization of the corresponding production of goods or services. At this point we stress the fact that this procedure only puts regional characters into the model without further assumptions such as assuming any fixed numbers.

3.4.1.6. Health expenditure

One essential step of calculating the NHA and consequently the MRHA it to match household and government final demand with data from the health expenditure survey. The latter serves as a secondary data base, which provides information on expenditures for a better health status of the inhabitants. By matching both data bases, we obtain the core part of the health economy in terms of definition and quantification. At the national level, official data on health expenditure is available by categories of providers, function and financing. For the compilation of the MRHA, our colleagues from BASYS extended these national figures by a regional component.

Our colleagues conducted the calculations with respect to the concepts of national accounts, therefore referring to the domestic concept of health expenditures. This differs from the health expenditure survey provided by the Federal Statistical Office at the national level. The latter corresponds to the resident concept, consequently referring to health expenditures of German citizens only. The same overall amount of expenditures applies to the regional health expenditure survey our colleagues calculated. However, the difference lies in the treatment of patient migration among federal states. The resident concept registers expenses at the place of the patient's residence, while the domestic concepts asserts expenditures to the place of treatment. The latter applies for the MRHA, since expenditures at the place of treatment correspond the output of the respective federal state. Consequently, output of patient treatment is always recorded at the place of treatment, not at the place of the patient's residency. Hence, patient migration cannot be observed as import and export in the MRHA.

Categories of the health expenditure survey refer to inpatient treatment, outpatient treatment, medication, medical products and administrative expenditures of health insurance companies. This information is necessary in order to extract the health economy from the overall economy and hence calculate a satellite account from national and multiregional accounts. During the compilation of the NHA, matching of expenditures with final consumption of households and the government reveals some deviations of German national accounts from the health expenditure survey when there should be none. This is due to some differences in concepts, which are described in more detail in Schwärzler and Kronenberg (2016). However, deviations also arise due to inaccuracies of national accounts. To some point, this is justifiable since national accounts focus on the overall economy whereas the health expenditure survey evaluates more accurate information on its specific field. Conversely, it means we should implement data on health expenditures already at this point of compiling the MRHA in order to improve the quality of the multiregional supply and use tables. Hence, we use information from the regional health expenditure survey to distribute national values among federal states. By doing so, some additional assumptions have to be made, which are discussed within the next paragraphs.

Expenditures on inpatient and outpatient treatment as well as on administration of health insurance companies directly refer to domestic output of respective federal states. This is due to the domestic concept applicable to both regional accounts and regional health expenditures. Hence, we use the respective information from the regional health expenditure survey in order to distribute the corresponding values of the national use table among federal states.

Obviously, this assumption does not hold for medication and medical products as they show international and interregional export and import dynamics in contrast to inpatient and outpatient treatment. In this context, we assume perfect heterogeneity of the products in concern and hence argue there is no preference for regionally manufactured products. Moreover, transport costs are irrelevant in decision making. There are several reasons, which support these assumptions.

First of all, the kind of disease a patient suffers from is the greatest influencing factor on the sort of medication he or she receives. In this context, we assume an identical distribution of diseases patients suffer from across federal states. Hence, it is always x percent of patients, who suffer from cancer and y percent of patients, who suffer from cardiovascular disease in each of the federal states and so on. This implies an identical distribution of the need for the specific kind of medication, which treats the disease in concern.

Second, manufacturers of medication and medical products usually only have one site for the production of a certain kind of medication within a larger area, due to a high specificity of the manufacturing process. For example, the company Bayer AG produces the medication Aspirin at a site in Saxony-Anhalt. This site is one of the most important locations for the production of Aspirin worldwide (Bayer AG 2017b). There are other painkillers, which are produced in Germany, however. Yet, Aspirin is only produced in Saxony-Anhalt.

Third, the decision upon the kind of i.e. painkiller a patient consumes, does usually not depend on regional origin. Much more, it is a question of ingredients and patient's tolerability. Apart from that, around 87 percent of sales of medication obtained from the pharmacy refers to prescription drugs (Bundesverband der Arzneimittel-Hersteller e.V. 2017). In the case the doctor prescribed only the name of an active ingredient for treatment or does not specifically exclude replacement of the prescribed medication by another one, the so-called 'aut-idem ruling' applies (*Sozialgesetzbuch* SGB V, § 129). This obligates the pharmacy to hand over the cheapest available alternative medicine showing consistency in terms of ingredients, dosage form and package size. In the case a rebate contract exists between statutory health insurance funds and the manufacturer of the product for a suitable medication, the pharmacy is obligated to hand over no other than this medication (*Sozialgesetzbuch* SGB V, § 130a).

We hence argue that the assumption of perfect heterogeneity of products and irrelevance of transportation costs is given. Each site produces a completely individual medication in terms of ingredients, price and the existence of rebate contracts. This mixture of different health products manufactured distributes across all over Germany. However, the perfect solution would be to match production sites with data on prescribed drugs in order to evaluate interregional trade. This is not possible due to unavailability of data.

In order to introduce interregional trade of health products, we hence implement the assumption on perfect heterogeneity into our model. We distribute the national amount of international imports over federal states first and quantify the amount of interregional imports in a second step.

Figure 14: Assumptions on the origins of health goods for region 1

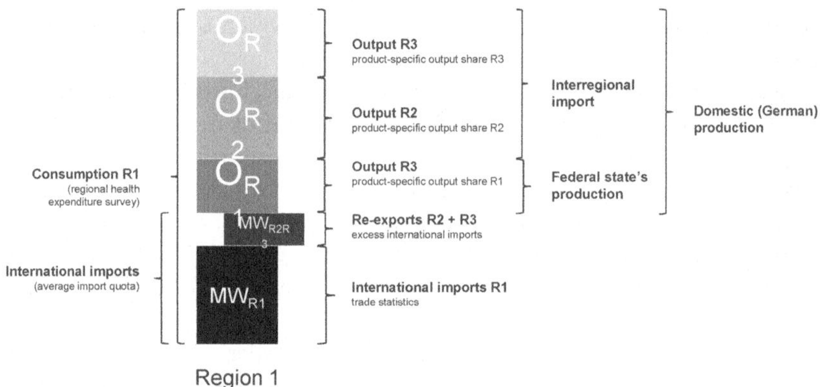

Source: Own illustration.

In a first step, we assume that each federal state obtains the same share of health expenditures from imports of the product in consideration (i.e. medication or medical products). Hence, we use federal-state-specific health expenditures on the product in consideration to distribute the corresponding national value of imports across federal states. We refer to this amount with 'International imports (average import quota)' in Figure 14. This amount is fixed over all iterations of the algorithm. As illustrated in Figure 14, this value does not necessarily need to equal the specific amount of imports obtained from the trade statistic. We refer to the latter with 'International imports R1 (trade statistics)' in Figure 14. This means we have excess or shortage of imports within each federal state. In the case illustrated in Figure 14, when a federal state shows a shortage of international imports from trade statistics opposed by the just calculated amount of health expenditures from imports, the corresponding missing amount is recorded as re-export from another federal state. We refer to this value with 'Re-exports R2 + R3 (excess international imports)' in Figure 14. The other federal state in turn is of import excess given its amount of imports from trade statistics opposed by health expenditures multiplied with the average import quota. This interrelationship between federal states can be obtained from Figure 15.

Figure 15: Assumptions on the origins of health products in region 1, region 2 and region 3

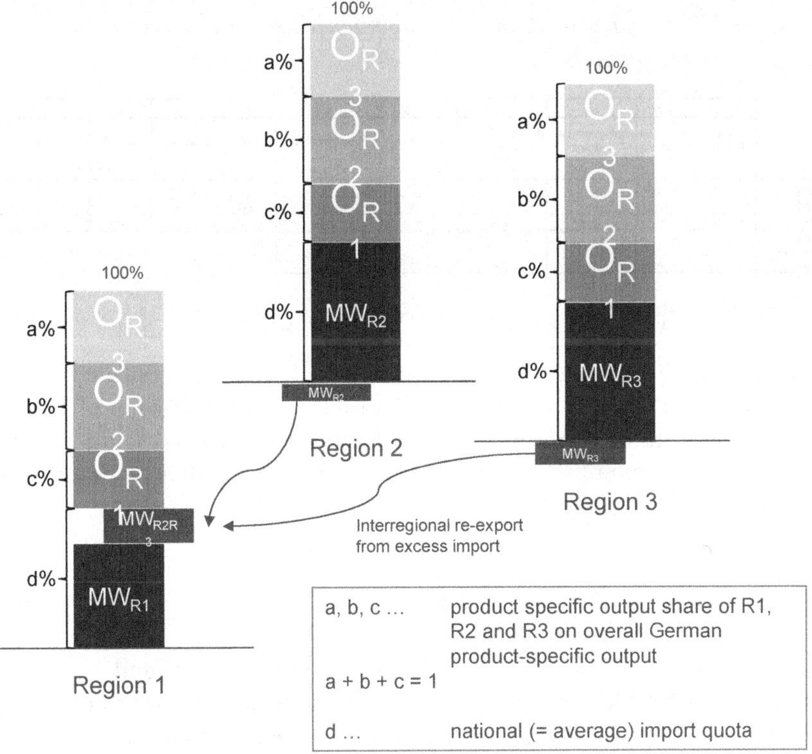

Source: Own illustration.

Due to the assumption of perfectly heterogeneous goods, each federal state obtains a mixture of medication and medical products from all federal states with respect to the amount of the product-sided output manufactured within each of the federal states. For example, federal state 1 supplies 30 percent of overall German output of medicine. Therefore, each federal state obtains 30 percent of its domestic demand from federal state 1. As the algorithm used to obtain the MRHA is of an iterative kind, product-specific output shares change within each stage of calculation.

This situation of interregional dependency in the case of manufactured health products is shown in Figure 15. Health products obtained within each region comprise of the exact equal share of interregional imports and moreover the exact equal share of involvement of each federal state.

Table 4: Numerical example on the assumption of origins of manufactured health products.

	C1	C2	C3	C4	C5	C6	C7	C8	C9	C10
	Overall Health Expenditure	**Import quota**	**International imports**	**domestic health expenditures**	**Output**	**Output share**	**Supply R1**	**Supply R2**	**Supply R3**	**Sum**
			*(C1 * C2)*	*(C1-C3)*	*iteratively changing*	*iteratively changing*	*(C4 * C6[R1])*	*(C4 * C6 [R2])*	*(C4 * C6[R3])*	*(C7 + C8 + C9) = C4*
R1	35	0,3	10,5	24,5	70	35%	8,575	3,675	12,25	24,5
R2	10	0,3	3	7	30	15%	2,45	1,05	3,5	7
R3	55	0,3	16,5	38,5	100	50%	13,475	5,775	19,25	38,5
Germany (given data)	**100**	**0,3**	**30**	**70**	**200**	**100%**				

Source: Own illustration.

At the end of this procedure we obtain fixed values for the consumption of manufactured health products, which all refer to the categories of private and public consumption in use tables. However, these fixed values change with each iteration of the algorithm. Table 4 shows a numerical example of the just described procedure.

3.4.2. Alignment of the initial matrix

In subsection 3.4.1 we describe the preparation of primary and secondary data for the MRHA. In this subsection we focus on the alignment of the initial matrix, in advance to applying the iterative algorithm on the overall concept elaborated within the preceding and this subsection. In order to compile the initial matrix a few additional assumptions and manipulations have to be conducted. Those consist of the general arrangement of matrices for the multiregional framework and the handling of given data, such as the ones derived within the previous subsection.

In a first step, we establish the multiregional framework according to Figure 8 and Figure 9, but for the 16 federal states of Germany, therefore replacing three by 16 regions. At the beginning, all matrices involved in the multiregional table are consistent with national tables, therefore picturing the German overall economy each. In accordance to sub-subsection 3.4.1.5, however, the supply tables are adjusted with respect to additional information in order to take into account the imbalance between industry information and the number of product categories referring to it. Use tables are adjusted accordingly in order to keep tables balanced with regard to supply and use.

Tables also need to fulfill the requirement that the sum of the initial matrix equals the overall amount of the final matrix. Hence, the 16 supply or 16x16 use tables are downgraded so they correspond to the amount of the overall German economy.

The next step concentrates on the setting of use tables. Imagine, we assign the same use matrix to each of the off-block-diagonal elements and the block-diagonal elements, the first referring to interregional trade, the latter to own domestic use of the federal state of concern. This setting would suggest that there are no transportation costs within the German economy nor there are other restrictions such as preferences for regional goods. From a methodological perspective, the algorithm registers only equal values among use tables and hence captures no preferences among interregional trade or domestic use. Unequal values indicate there is a preference among interregional trade and domestic use, i.e. reducing the amount traded due to transportation costs.

The way initial matrices for interregional trade are weighted thus impacts on the degree of openness of federal states. As we have fixed values for the interregional trade balance of federal states it causes changes in the amount of cross-hauling, i.e. the simultaneous export and import of goods and therefore the assumed heterogeneity of goods. Hence, we have to find a reasonable initial matrix, which takes into account a realistic 'openness of the federal state' towards interregional trade.

In order to proceed accordingly we define the openness of each federal state by the ratio of overall public and private consumption to GVA. Both of the two indicators used relate to the federal state in consideration. The first refers to overall regional demand for consumption expenditures to be satisfied, while the latter refers to the regional value added caused by the supply of products. This way we can approach differences of federal states in their capability of supplying regional demand as we calculate the deviation from the average value of this indicator for each federal state. We apply these 16 values to the diagonal elements of a 16x16 weighting matrix, each cell referring to exactly one federal state or the respective interregional trade.

In a next step, we concentrate on the direction of openness in terms of interregional export, hence the off-diagonal elements of the 16x16 weighting matrix. We only have to define one side - interregional exports or interregional imports - as the distribution of one of the directions of trade leads to the other.

One possible solution to this is to apply spatial interaction models. Többen and Kronenberg (2015) discuss and summarize different approaches. Over here, we assume that the exporting federal state distributes its products among the other regions with respect to the purchasing power of recipients. Hence, we calculate the share on overall GVA of each federal state in 16 variations, each time omitting the federal state which is represented in the diagonal element. This way, we can approach a first guess on the distribution of destinations for interregional exports for each federal state. We insert these values into the off-diagonal elements of the 16x16 weighting matrix. Within a final step, we rescale this matrix to one so that the national domestic use table, available 16x16 in the initial framework, multiplied by the weighting matrix, equals to the overall amount of the national domestic use table.

Figure 16: Weights for the initial matrix on domestic (German) use.

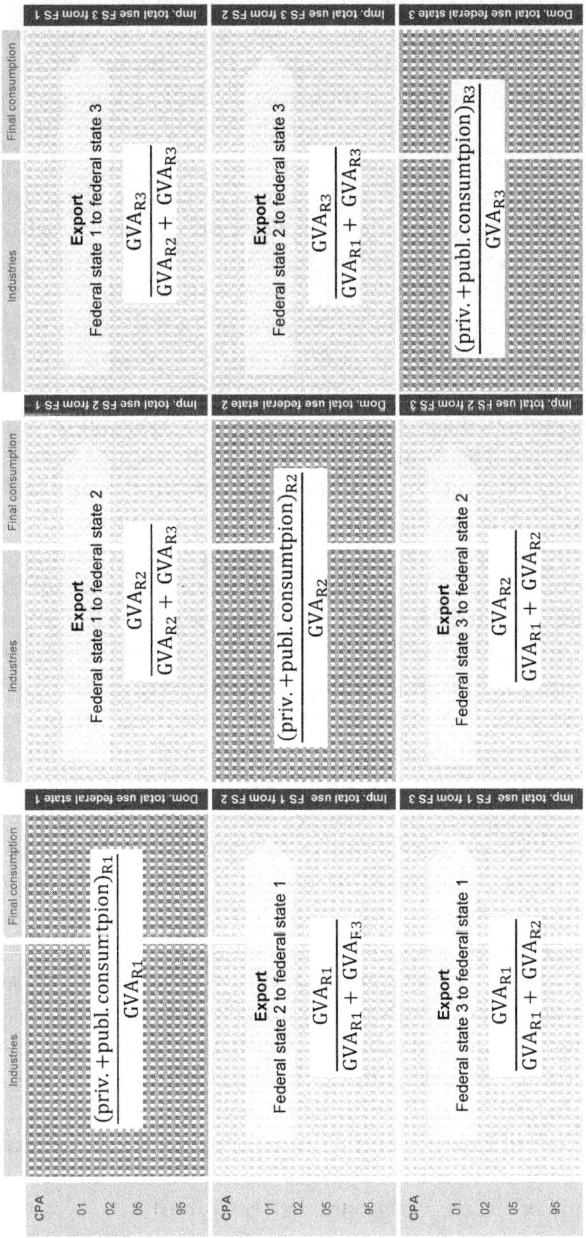

Source: Own illustration.

We multiply supply tables accordingly by assigning row sums of the weighting matrix, as the concept of interregional trade does not apply to the supply tables. The only reason for the weighting of supply tables is that supply and use tables are balanced again. It has no further impact on the supply tables since output of industries, which is going to be assigned within the iterative algorithm, adjusts the overall amount of supply tables immediately.

As there is a possibility of interregional re-exports of international imports, we have to apply a similar procedure on the initial matrix of the national import use table. We do not have any information or approaches to calculate the individual openness for re-exports of federal states, hence we apply the national share of non-re-exports on overall imports to the diagonal elements of the import weighting matrix. Consequently, each federal state has the same – national – propensity for re-exports. The direction of re-exports is evaluated again in consideration of GVA ratios of the destination federal states. The final weighting matrix is aligned to one in the end and applied on the 16x16 framework of national import use tables.

At this point it is essential to note that preceding steps, which involve the alignment of the initial matrix according to the openness for interregional trade of federal states, do not imply any fixed values of the final matrices. The initial matrix is only a general setting, which is adjusted within the algorithm afterwards. There are no binding restrictions, so that the amounts of interregional trade still adjust iteratively.

In a next step we eliminate entries within matrices where we have fixed values such as international exports or private and public consumption on health care goods and services. Experience has also shown that it is essential to make restrictions upon changes in inventories too, as they consist of positive and negative entries and make up substantial amounts of some product groups at the detailed level we are working with. Consequently, we restrict changes in inventories to the place of production. Moreover, we distribute the national value among federal states in accordance to the ratio of exports to changes of inventories at the national level. This only applies in cases the latter has significant importance on the overall value of the product group in consideration. In cases changes in inventories only have a low impact on the product output, the distribution of changes in inventories among federal states is adjusted with each iteration in accordance to the distribution of product output among federal states. Consequently, we now also have fixed values for changes in inventories and set respective values within the initial multiregional matrix to zero.

Furthermore, we restrict interregional trade on some services, involving administration, education, health services, social work activities, services concerning sports, entertainment and recovery, other personal services and private households with employed persons. We proceed accordingly due to the domestic concept those services apply to. This means we ignore the existence of online training in the context of tertiary education or telemedicine in the case of health care due to their very rare occurrence to the current point of time.

3.4.3. Basic concept of the SUT-RAS algorithm

The SUT-RAS algorithm (Temurshoev and Timmer 2011) intends to project supply and use tables in an iterative and mutually dependent matter with respect to information on the industry side and sums of final consumption categories. Hence, there is no urgent need for product-specific information in order to project tables. This circumstance constitutes a major difference to related iterative algorithms such as RAS.

At the national level, we use the SUT-RAS algorithm exactly with its initial intention, which is to project available national tables on supply and use. We proceed accordingly, so we are able to quantify the economic impact of the health economy also apart from the years the generic national supply and use tables refer to. This is important, as tables are only available for a number of years at the current statistical standard of NACE 2008 and ESA 2010. We describe the underlying data base and the algorithm applied for the national case in detail in Schwärzler and Kronenberg (2016).

Since this chapter focusses on the further development of the SUT-RAS algorithm into the MR-SUT-RAS algorithm, we present the main underlying formulas over here as well. The intention is to provide a broad picture and facilitate a better understanding regarding developing the MRHA.

At this point we want to emphasize that there are several ways to apply the SUT-RAS algorithm in general. The choice of procedure depends on the available data set of supply and use tables. It is possible to project tables at purchasers or at basic prices, applying the algorithm on domestic and import use tables separately or on the overall sum of the two tables. Moreover, it offers the possibility to include additional specific information on either the supply or the use side.

Within the next few paragraphs we present the formulas of the SUT-RAS, which correspond to the setting of basic prices and separated use tables. This reflects the requirements that are met by the special evaluation on supply and use tables from national accounts. Moreover, we expand this setting due to available information on product-specific export and import data. Hence, the provided formulas do not refer to Temurshoev and Timmer (2011) exactly, as no section focusses precisely on the setting available in this case. In fact, it is a combination of different situations evaluated in Temurshoev and Timmer (2011).

As already mentioned, information on industries and final use categories are prerequisites for the projection of supply and use tables in accordance to the SUT-RAS algorithm. Moreover, the minimum of information we need in our case in addition is the overall sum of imports and taxes less subsidies. Those critical areas of data supply refer to the red colored areas in Figure 17. In formula notation, industry output refers to vector $\bar{x}$, while vector $\bar{u}$ indicates total use and therefore the individual sums of intermediate and final use.

Additional information on i.e. exports and imports can be implemented to increase the validity of projected tables. Those areas show a red frame in Figure 17. Product information on imports are denoted by $\overline{mt}$, with respective information on re-exports already subtracted. Product information on exports from domestic production refer to certain cells of the use table, while their appearance among industries in the supply table is not known. Hence, additional information we have on the use side are denoted by vector $(-f)$. Referring cells in the use table are set to zero. Vector $(-f)$ consequently indicates the resulting difference in sums over products of the supply and the domestic use table. Consequently, final supply and use tables are balanced the moment we insert the information on exports into the target cells of final tables, due to having considered the difference along the iterative algorithm.

Note at this point, that the respective information has to be subtracted from the vector $\bar{u}$ as well, as it contains information on the final value of overall exports as well. In the case the overall amount of exports comes from secondary data and is hence manually set, not only the overall respective vectors in both use tables have to be set to zero, but also to be completely removed, as a vector of purely zeroes cannot be applied within the algorithm.

Figure 17: Data requirements for the SUT-RAS algorithm

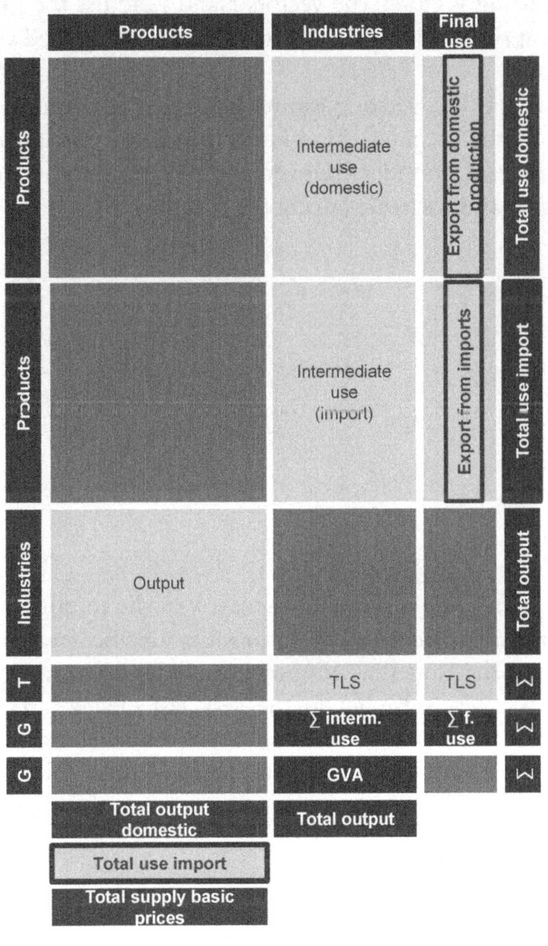

Source: Own illustration.

N_0^v and P_0^v denote the initial and hence the to be projected supply table, which is separated into a negative and positive matrix, both showing the corresponding entries in absolute positive values. The same procedure is applied on the domestic use table, indicated by N_0^d and P_0^d, and on the use tables of imported products with the corresponding notation N_0^m and P_0^m. Vector m_0 indicates overall product-specific imports of the initial import use table.

The SUT-RAS algorithm is applied iteratively, focusing on four interdependent adjusting vectors. The vectors r_d and r_m adjust the initial matrices of use tables at the product side. Vectors s_u and r_v are applied at the industry side.

To be more specific, vector r_d assures balancing conditions of the supply table and domestic use table. In order to include given information on i.e. domestic exports, r_d considers the vector $(-f)$ as an authorized difference between supply and use table during the compilation.

$$r_d = 0.5 * \hat{p}_d^{-1} \left(f + \sqrt{f \circ f + 4 * p_d \circ n_d} \right) \tag{21}$$

where

$$p_d = P_0^d s_u + N_0^{v'} \hat{r}_v^{-1} i \tag{22}$$

$$n_d = N_0^d \hat{s}_u^{-1} i + P_0^{v'} r_v . \tag{23}$$

The vector r_m is applied on the initial matrix of the import use table in order to obtain consistency with given product-specific data on imports, denoted by vector $\overline{mt}$. Note that this vector includes information on the overall sum of taxes less subsidies in the very last element. This one corresponds to the final row of the initial import use table, reflecting information on taxes less subsidies among industries and final consumption categories.

$$r_m = \sqrt{\widehat{P_0^m s_u}^{-1} \left(N_0^m \hat{s}_u^{-1} i + \hat{r} m_0 \right)} \tag{24}$$

where

$$r = \overline{mt} / \left(m'_0 \hat{r}_m^{-1} i \right). \tag{25}$$

On the industry side, s_u is applied on the initial matrices of domestic and import use tables in order to reflect given industry-specific data on intermediary and final use, denoted by vector $\overline{u}$.

$$s_u = 0.5 * \hat{p}_s^{-1}\left(\bar{u} + \sqrt{\bar{u} \circ \bar{u} + 4 * p_s \circ n_s}\right) \tag{26}$$

where

$$p_s = P_0^{d\prime} r_d + P_0^{m\prime} r_m \tag{27}$$

$$n_s = N_0^{d\prime} \hat{r}_d^{-1} i + N_0^{m\prime} \hat{r}_m^{-1} i. \tag{28}$$

Vector r_v adjusts the supply table to given output of industries, denoted by $\bar{x}$.

$$r_v = 0.5 * \widehat{P_0^v \hat{r}_d^{-1} i}^{-1}\left(\bar{x} + \sqrt{\bar{x} \circ \bar{x} + 4 * \left(P_0^v \hat{r}_d^{-1} i\right) \circ \left(N_0^v r_d\right)}\right) \tag{29}$$

The iterative algorithm stops as soon as changes in r_d and r_m correspond to a specific chosen level of tolerance. The four major adjustment vectors obtain projected supply and use tables by performing the following procedure on initial matrices:

$$\bar{V} = \hat{r}_v P_0^v \hat{r}_d^{-1} - \hat{r}_v^{-1} N_0^v \hat{r}_d \tag{30}$$

$$\bar{U}_d = \hat{r}_d P_0^d \hat{s}_u - \hat{r}_d^{-1} N_0^d \hat{s}_u^{-1} \tag{31}$$

$$\bar{U}_m = \hat{r}_m P_0^m \hat{s}_u - \hat{r}_m^{-1} N_0^m \hat{s}_u^{-1} \tag{32}$$

In a very last step, product-specific fixed data, i.e. domestic exports and re-exports, are assigned to the projected tables. Final tables correspond to given data on industry output and intermediate use, are balanced between supply and domestic use, include fixed values on i.e. exports and match given data on product-specific import.

The result of this procedure is projected national tables. Hence, the described formulas correspond to the generic intention of the SUT-RAS algorithm according to a specific case of Temurshoev and Timmer (2011), which is basic prices, separation of domestic and import use tables and given information on product-specific exports and imports. We derive from this point in order to further develop the just described procedure into a multiregional framework.

3.4.4. The MR-SUT-RAS

In this section, we depict the adjustments we made to the SUT-RAS algorithm in order to apply it for the multiregional context. We hence take knowledge upon the generic formulas from subsection 3.4.3 as given.

One of the major advantages of the SUT-RAS algorithm is that no information on the product-side is necessary in order to adjust an initial matrix to new information on industries and final use. However, in a multiregional context we do not just update an initial matrix to unknown product-specific information. Yet, we know that the sum of each specific product, available once in each of the 16 federal states, has to equal the national value.

Consequently, this is the most essential additional restriction of the MR-SUT-RAS, since it assures the multiregional table to correspond to product-specific national values in addition to industry-specific national values. The latter restriction is easily implemented and not further discussed, since industry-specific information is directly assigned to the algorithm, in accordance to the original SUT-RAS algorithm.

The second important adjustment refers to iteratively changing fixed values concerning health product consumption (see sub-sub-section 3.4.1.6 for more details) and changes in inventories (see end of subsection 3.4.2 for more details).

Over here we want to mention that some adjustments to the original formulas lead to a number of further adaptations and restrictions. This becomes important especially in the case of fixed values concerning changes in inventories. The special evaluation on supply and use tables at hand plays a decisive role in this matter. Sometimes, detailed data lack accuracy. In our case, doubtful data refers to high ratios of changes in inventories on remaining categories of demand for relatively unspecific data (i.e. 'other products of ...'). This encourages the assumption that these categories meet compensatory requirements of tables. Product output equaling to zero, due to changes in inventories and the remaining categories of use leveling each other out, are another example of critical data. Hence, the more information we implement on product-specific data, the more we have to cope with probably unreliable data. This is why we will add some extensions on 'further restrictions' to our adjustments below. Those take care of certain circumstances, which might appear during the computation due to special cases in the characteristic of some product groups.

After we gave a first introduction on additional adjustments and challenges concerning the MR-SUT-RAS we proceed with the concrete steps of compilation. In order to do so, we refer to the formulas in subsection 3.4.3 and add our adjustments to the formula in consideration including a reference in lowercase letters.

In order to apply the MR-SUT-RAS we start with 3.4.3) and 3.4.3). Before we calculate the vector r_d,according to 3.4.3, which balances supply and use in consideration of fixed values represented by $(-f)$, we compute the latter first.

Figure 18: Calculation of iteratively changing fixed values.

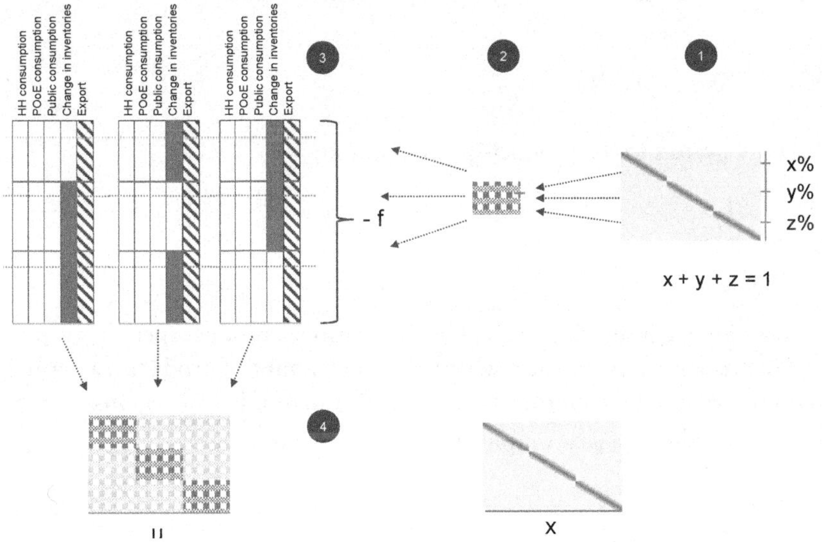

Source: Own illustration.

In sub-subsection 3.4.1.6 we explain the reasons for calculating iteratively changing fixed values for health care products, which are part of (– f), next to changes in inventories and international exports. Summarized, we have information on regional health products consumption. However, we do not know the federal state of origin of the consumed products and respective interregional trade. Hence, we assume perfect heterogeneity of medication and medical products. In practice, this means people and health facilities spare no expenses on the appropriate health product in terms of transportation costs. Moreover, they show no preference for regional products. Therefore, we distribute the origins of consumed products with respect to output share of federal states. Consequently, each federal state obtains the same mixture of health products in terms of their origins. Due to the iterative calculations, the product-specific output and hence its distribution among federal states adapts with each round. This is why we do not obtain constant fixed values for the interregional trade of health care products. Figure 18 represents an overview of the necessary steps to calculate an iteratively changing value for (– f). We will refer to the compilation steps indicated in Figure 18 in the following.

We obtain the distribution of product-specific output from the current supply table. Therefore, we calculate the supply table corresponding to the current iteration by applying the following formula, which is equal to 3.4.3 except for the subscript k referring to its iterative character.

$$\bar{V}_k = \hat{r}_v P_0^v \hat{r}_d^{-1} - \hat{r}_v^{-1} N_0^v \hat{r}_d \tag{23a}$$

Vector $\bar{v}_{ki}$ refers to the product-specific output:

$$\bar{v}_{ki} = \sum_{j=1}^{j=b*64} \bar{v}_{kij} \tag{23b}$$

Hence, for $\bar{v}_{Ni}$ indicating the replicated national product-specific output, defined as a b x n X 1 vector, where n is the amount of products categories within the overall economy and b refers to the number of regions, we obtain the product-specific output share $\tilde{\bar{v}}_{ki}$ of federal states by

$$\tilde{\bar{v}}_{ki} = \frac{\bar{v}_{ki}}{\bar{v}_{Ni}} \tag{23c}$$

We picture the compilation of the federal- and product-specific output share on the national values from the current multiregional supply table by step one and two in Figure 18.

We now distribute the health expenditures on products of federal states among regions in order to model interregional trade. Overall health expenditures are denoted by matrix E in the dimension of n X b x 3, the number 'three' indicating the categories of final consumption essential in this matter – households, non-profit organizations serving households and governments. Product categories refer to n in dimension, but all elements not corresponding to health products of concern being set to zero. In order to apply output shares on the expenditure of federal states, we expand E to $\tilde{E}$, the b-fold health expenditure matrix with the dimension n x b X b x 3:

$$\widetilde{E} = \begin{matrix} E \\ \dots \\ E \end{matrix} \tag{23d}$$

We now obtain adjusted health expenditure of federal states, which is distributed in origins according to the product-specific output share by:

$$\dddot{E} = \widetilde{E} * \widetilde{\overline{v}_{ki}} \tag{23e}$$

This procedure corresponds to step three in Figure 18. This way, the overall amount of consumption expenditure of federal states does not change. However, the origins of products adapt, modelling interregional trade in accordance to the respective amount of output of federal states.

The same applies for changes in inventories, which can also be observed from Figure 18. According to the last few paragraphs of subsection 3.4.2, we assume that changes in inventories only occur at the place of production. Consequently, we exclude the possibility of interregional trade from changes in inventories, which makes our final matrix look like a block-diagonal matrix with the dimensions of n x b X b x 1, changes in inventories corresponding to only one column of each use table.

$$\dddot{C} = \begin{matrix} c_1 & \dots & 0 \\ \dots & \dots & \dots \\ 0 & \dots & c_b \end{matrix} \tag{23f}$$

Moreover, we assume that the product-specific amount of changes in inventories depends on the amount produced. Accordingly, we distribute the national values of changes in inventories in accordance to the product-specific output share. Matrix C_N contains the national vector of changes in inventories c_N with length n and replicated b-fold at the block-diagonal elements, such as

$$C_N = \begin{matrix} c_N & \dots & 0 \\ \dots & \dots & \dots \\ 0 & \dots & c_N \end{matrix} \tag{23g}$$

With the product-specific output share already derived in (23d) we obtain our final matrix $\dddot{C}$, representing national values on changes in inventories distributed among federal state in accordance to their product-specific output share:

$$\dddot{C} = C_N * \dddot{\bar{v}}_{ki} \tag{23h}$$

This causes the matrix of changes in inventories to adapt within each iteration as well.

However, since there are single product groups, which show a high amount of changes in inventories and therefore have a high impact on the corresponding output share, there is a special case for which we add a further restriction. This exclusively refers to cases when the absolute value of changes in inventories of a product group makes up more than half of domestic use in the generic national table excluding exports. The latter applies since exports refer to fixed data as well. We exclude these product groups from adjustment according to output share, since the iteratively changing value on changes in inventories has too much impact on output. In these cases we apply the ratio of exports to changes in inventories of generic tables on the fixed values of exports to obtain product-specific values on changes in inventories of federal states.

At the end of this procedure – including special cases - we obtain a new matrix of *changing* fixed values. Within a next step we combine the calculated matrices with information on *constant* fixed values, such as domestic exports or health services. We calculate row sums of the overall matrix in order to obtain $(-\mathrm{f})$.

At this point, we emphasize that we performed this procedure on two different indicators with a different intention each: Adjustments regarding the interregional trade of health product consumption do not have any impact on the overall sum of consumption of each federal state. Hence, no further adjustments are necessary. However, in the case of changes in inventories, we just calculated an adjusted overall sum of this category for each federal state. This is due to our assumption that changes in inventories only occur at the federal state of production. According to the procedure described above, the amount of changes in inventories of a product increases with a higher product-specific output share. This in turn influences the overall amount of changes in inventories of each federal state. Hence, we need to adjust the respective values of the vector $\bar{\mathrm{u}}$, which corresponds to intermediate use of industries and final consumption categories, the sum of changes in inventories among them. This is shown by step four in Figure 18. At the end of this step, we obtain an adjusted vector $(-\mathrm{f})$and a slightly changed vector $\bar{\mathrm{u}}$with respect to the entries referring to the overall sum of changes in inventories of the federal state. We then proceed with the calculation of rd, applying equation 3.4.3.

Over here, we also add a further restriction for cases in which all information on use comes from (– f). This situation implies that the use matrix consists of only zeroes and balancing between supply and use happens between the supply table and (– f). However, equation 3.4.3 cannot be applied in this case. Hence, we use a modified version for this case:

$$r_d = \frac{\hat{r}_v P_0^v i}{-f} \tag{33a}$$

and go on with equations 3.4.3 to 3.4.3.

At the end of this first iteration we calculate the current tables for supply and domestic use by applying equation 3.4.3 and 3.4.3. This procedure deviates from the original version. Usually, the main decision criterion upon the convergence of the algorithm are the changes of rdand rmto the respective values from the iteration before. In the case these values are below a certain range of tolerance the algorithm is said to have converged. However, in the multiregional case, we have another criterion to be met. We want the sum of each single product over all federal states to meet the national value.

In order to implement this restriction we remove the block diagonal shape of the current multiregional supply table. This way, the number of industries stays equal, representing 64 industries in each of the b regions. However, this matrix only refers to n product categories anymore, opposed to n x b from before. We call this procedure 'to de-diagonalize' the multiregional supply table. $\bar{V}'_k$ refers to the multiregional supply table, while $\hat{\bar{V}}'_k$ represents its 'de-diagonalized' version.

$$\bar{V}'_k = \begin{matrix} \bar{v}'_{k1} & \dots & 0 \\ \dots & \dots & \dots \\ 0 & \dots & \bar{v}'_{kb} \end{matrix} \tag{30a}$$

$$\hat{\bar{V}}'_k = \bar{v}'_{k1} \dots \bar{v}'_{kb} \tag{30b}$$

We know x, the column sums of $\hat{\bar{V}}'_k$, referring to the industry-specific output of federal states, and the wanted row sums of $\hat{\bar{V}}'_k$, the national product-specific value. Thus, we apply the GRAS algorithm over $\hat{\bar{V}}'_k$ until the latter corresponds to national product output. At the end of this procedure we restore the 'block-diagonal' shape again in order to separate federal states from each other again. This yields in $\bar{V}'_{kGRAS}$. This supply table corresponds to national values in both industries and products.

However, we have a special case over here as well, since we know some entries of $\bar{V}'_{kGRAS}$ by definition if all information on use is exclusively included in $-f$, i.e. only consists of exports and changes in inventories and possibly private and public consumption on health. Hence, we include this given information in these cases:

$$\bar{V}'_{kGRAS} = -f \tag{30c}$$

In order to implement information on $\bar{V}'_{kGRAS}$ into our algorithm we compare product-specific information on $\bar{V}'_k$ with product-specific information on $\bar{V}'_{kGRAS}$ and calculate a product-specific rescaling vector.

$$resk_V = \frac{\sum_{j=1}^{j=b*64} \bar{V}_{kGRASij}}{\sum_{j=1}^{j=b*64} \bar{V}_{kij}} \tag{30d}$$

We apply the same procedure to the domestic use table as well. However, we have to define a vector, which incorporates the information on $(-f)$. The denominator refers to the vector of product-specific information from the current domestic use table.

$$resk_{U_d} = \frac{\sum_{j=1}^{j=b*64} \bar{V}_{kGRASij} - (-f)}{\sum_{i=1}^{i=b*64} \bar{u}_{d\,kji}} \tag{31a}$$

We apply rescaling vectors $resk_V$ and $resk_{U_d}$ on the matrices Pv and Pd. After that, we restore column sums of Pd and rerun the iterative algorithm.

Again, we have some special cases over here. First of all, $resk_V = 1$ if all information on use is exclusively included in $(-f)$. Second, if $resk_{U_d} < 0$, we rescale the product-specific distribution of concern of Pd to 0.1, since the use table cannot exhibit negative values due to the fact that we determine fixed values on export and changes in inventories.

Third, it appears that values of $resk_{U_d}$ remain far below zero over several iterations. This causes the algorithm failing to convergence if we leave it that way. Taking a closer look at these occasions reveals that this circumstance is attributable to fixed product-specific values being of a higher amount opposed to industry-specific output. This mainly occurs in the Hanseatic cities Bremen and Hamburg when exports are higher than output. This needs us to introduce the possibility of re-exports between federal states, which we have excluded so far. In order to do so, we proceed the following:

The first time, the absolute difference of the multiregional supply table and multiregional domestic use table is smaller than five million, we look at values of $resk_{U_d} < -100{,}000$.[7] We reduce the amount of corresponding exports so it matches product-specific output of the current multiregional supply table and assign subtracted values to re-exports from other federal states. We perform this procedure only once in order to introduce constant fixed values on re-exports. In order to provide the algorithm the correct information on external information, such as the amount of re-exports, from the very beginning, we restart the algorithm with the now adjusted information on exports.

We rerun this iterative algorithm with all its special cases until $\max|r_d - r_{d-1}| < 0.00001$ and $\max|r_m - r_{m-1}| < 0.00001$. The moment this applies, we calculate final multiregional supply and use tables according to (30), (31) and (32).

3.4.5. First evaluation of the derived multiregional supply and use tables

In this section, we provide a short first evaluation of the derived multiregional tables. A thorough validation regarding the reliability of the developed tables is subject of chapter 4 and chapter 5. Over here, however, we intent to establish an initial assessment of the impact the elaborated algorithm has on the initial tables in order to obtain the final tables.

Golan and Vogel (2000) present their approach to derive the degree of similarity of two matrices in the context of a cross-entropy approach, which is similar to the procedure applied in the RAS family. Their main objective is the same, however, which is to conclude upon the similarity of the initial and the estimated final matrix. Hence, we pursue the same approach, which relies on the log-likelihood, or entropy-ratio statistic *W*. The null hypothesis claims that *W* converges in distribution to $\chi^2_{(i-1)*(j-1)}$.

7 In our setting, this is the case at around 50 iterations.

Hence, we can test our results under the null hypothesis that A and A_0, which is the final and the initial matrix in our context, are stochastically dependent in accordance to

$$\chi^2_{(i-1)*(j-1)} = \sum_i \sum_j \frac{1}{a^0_{ij}} \left(a_{ij} - a^0_{ij} \right)^2 \tag{34}$$

We obtain a $\chi^2 = 210{,}000$ on 225 degrees of freedom. The resulting p-value $<< 0.01$ indicates that we have to reject the null hypothesis for the domestic use table. Hence, A and A_0 are stochastically independent when we apply this procedure on totaled up federal state matrices as shown in Figure 19 and Figure 20.

This result favors our approach, since we did not put much effort on the compilation of the initial matrix in order to hand this task over to the elaborated algorithm. A high deviation between the initial matrix and the final matrix hence implies that we obtained a great amount of additional information from applying the algorithm.

Furthermore, we find a high degree of differences between the initial and the final supply table when we focus on one exemplary field of the economy – the pharmaceutical industry – in a next step. These findings support the high impact of our approach, since the final supply table exhibits strongly adjusted production structures of industries. Those altered in the course of the calculation and now reveal certain characteristics in auxiliary production, such as R&D or wholesale among others. Reliability of these emphases in production of federal states have to be tested in a further step, however. This is the goal of the subsequent chapter, chapter 4.

Figure 19: Aggregated initial domestic use matrix

	BW	BY	BE	BB	HB	HH	HE	MV	NI	NW	RP	SL	SN	ST	SH	TH
BW	578,177	38,844	11,576	3,082	3,230	9,172	23,083	4,823	24,278	47,076	13,685	4,282	12,450	7,744	9,552	7,054
BY	38,068	705,112	13,695	3,559	3,820	10,849	27,315	5,705	28,717	55,697	16,189	5,065	14,726	9,159	11,299	8,343
BE	8,694	10,414	103,636	2,158	862	2,450	6,261	1,287	6,493	12,661	3,678	1,143	3,325	2,070	2,557	1,883
BB	4,679	5,558	1,670	57,174	458	1,304	3,383	684	3,458	6,781	1,969	608	1,770	1,102	1,364	1,002
HB	2,189	2,655	787	550	35,170	624	1,570	328	1,652	3,210	931	291	847	527	650	480
HH	7,565	9,213	2,718	1,899	759	133,664	5,422	1,134	5,738	11,072	3,215	1,006	2,927	1,820	2,246	1,658
HE	18,645	22,494	6,710	4,682	1,871	5,313	287,427	2,794	14,063	27,273	7,931	2,481	7,212	4,486	5,534	4,086
MV	2,963	3,506	1,056	723	289	822	2,147	33,035	2,180	4,285	1,244	383	1,115	695	860	631
NI	19,032	22,688	6,806	4,694	1,874	5,331	13,741	2,799	317,844	27,640	8,029	2,485	7,235	4,505	5,570	4,096
NW	46,880	56,351	16,834	11,703	4,676	13,285	33,711	6,982	35,181	874,505	19,886	6,200	18,032	11,220	13,851	10,214
RP	9,547	11,435	3,418	2,367	945	2,688	6,873	1,412	7,122	13,901	133,108	1,254	3,648	2,270	2,805	2,066
SL	2,563	3,070	919	636	254	723	1,847	380	1,914	3,733	1,085	37,347	981	610	754	555
SN	8,062	9,547	2,876	1,972	787	2,240	5,841	1,175	5,942	11,665	3,390	1,044	107,679	1,894	2,344	1,720
ST	4,301	5,090	1,534	1,051	419	1,194	3,117	626	3,167	6,220	1,307	556	1,620	56,555	1,249	917
SH	6,186	7,438	2,207	1,524	608	1,731	4,455	909	4,594	9,020	2,306	807	2,352	1,463	76,985	1,330
TH	4,114	4,881	1,468	1,008	402	1,145	2,977	601	3,037	5,958	1,731	534	1,554	968	1,198	50,027

Source: Own illustration.

Figure 20: Aggregated final domestic use matrix

	BW	BY	BE	BB	HB	HH	HE	MV	NI	NW	RP	SL	SN	ST	SH	TH
BW	532.759	53.219	10.126	6.121	2.537	9.780	25.676	2.921	25.451	70.600	10.947	3.196	9.717	5.803	7.196	5.130
BY	51.946	636.125	12.659	7.737	3.161	12.181	32.131	3.703	31.933	87.839	13.884	3.955	12.337	7.361	9.074	6.499
BE	8.348	10.735	111.673	1.249	529	2.138	5.453	616	5.029	13.848	2.226	620	1.927	1.150	1.510	1.002
BB	6.035	7.893	1.609	69.417	392	1.576	3.951	476	3.851	10.621	1.715	474	1.504	908	1.147	788
HB	1.962	2.446	443	272	39.486	433	1.176	128	1.202	3.122	483	146	429	254	319	228
HH	4.995	6.296	1.324	748	339	127.051	3.244	358	2.976	8.205	1.325	374	1.164	688	887	592
HE	18.512	23.948	4.909	2.898	1.237	4.874	269.312	1.386	11.445	32.016	5.142	1.425	4.486	2.674	3.405	2.315
MV	4.040	5.285	1.047	660	260	1.032	2.626	45.209	2.592	6.919	1.137	310	1.005	609	773	532
NI	25.045	32.103	6.149	3.789	1.549	5.997	15.767	1.808	313.645	41.971	6.731	1.895	5.871	3.533	4.450	3.121
NW	60.917	79.010	15.915	9.504	3.965	15.642	39.472	4.544	37.776	763.080	16.906	4.798	14.782	8.814	11.235	7.669
RP	12.477	16.307	3.257	1.980	796	3.183	8.116	949	7.848	22.100	150.371	971	3.062	1.849	2.312	1.611
SL	2.879	3.671	709	435	179	688	1.811	203	1.785	5.099	768	44.863	683	405	509	360
SN	12.079	15.543	3.017	1.826	737	2.923	7.621	875	7.439	20.688	3.276	931	125.719	1.704	2.155	1.501
ST	5.778	7.639	1.514	948	371	1.514	3.856	444	3.702	10.503	1.704	456	1.426	69.304	1.107	758
SH	7.954	10.322	2.043	1.265	515	2.051	5.116	608	4.975	13.574	2.193	606	1.926	1.166	91.643	1.010
TH	5.938	7.754	1.516	931	370	1.474	3.845	445	3.733	10.514	1.676	465	1.435	869	1.098	62.949

Source: Own illustration.

3.4.6. Calculation of the satellite account from multiregional accounts

At this point of calculation we managed to compute a multiregional account of the overall economy corresponding to the same level of detail of the national special evaluation on supply and use tables. Hence, we obtain one multiregional supply table in the dimension of n x b X 64 x b, n representing the number of products consistent with the national special evaluation, 64 indicating the amount of industries and b referring to the number of regions. Moreover, we calculated multiregional use tables for domestic production and imports in the size of n x b X (64 + 7) x b, including information on both, industries and categories of final use. The use table for imports shows one row in addition, representing information on taxes less subsidies. All tables refer to basic prices.

Summarizing, we established a b X b multiregional framework of national accounts. In the case of compiling the NHA, data on national accounts were provided by the Federal Statistical Office, represented by single supply and use tables. This in turn means, that we have now established the same data base for the multiregional case as was already available for the NHA.

Consequently, the remaining steps of calculating the MRHA refer identically to the procedure described in chapter 2 of this contribution. This is due to the fact that we aim to apply the very same methodology for the multiregional case as was developed for the national case. Since there are no supply and use tables for the German federal states available, it was necessary to establish this primary data base first. Hence, we can proceed to compile the satellite account next.

In order not to replicate the descriptions from chapter 2, we just summarize the calculation steps necessary in the following:

In order to quantify the core area of the health economy, we match data on regional health expenditure with private and government final consumption from multiregional accounts. Next, we apply additional secondary data base in order to quantify the extended area of the health economy. Within further steps we form feasible groups of the health economy in products and industries. As an interim step, we reconcile intermediate consumption patterns in order to honor the health-related characteristics of involved products. After we established the multiregional satellite account comprising supply and use tables, we calculate the multiregional health input-output table (MR-HIOT) from obtained tables. In doing so, we apply commodity technology assumption like in the national case. This approach also refers to the procedure of the Federal Statistical Office concerning the calculation of input-output tables. We adjust the MR-HIOT by manual manipulation in order to handle negative entries evolving from applying the commodity technology assumption.

At the end of this procedure we succeed to compile the MRHA, which consists of one multiregional supply table, two multiregional use tables and one multiregional input-output table. From the derived model we can obtain information on i.e. direct GVA, employment and trade of the health economy in the German federal states. The health economy refers to a product-specific definition and bears information on regional health expenditure in order to obtain a valid quantification. The MR-HIOT does not only allow to conduct input-output analysis in order to evaluate the overall impact of the health economy, but describes interregional dependencies with special emphases on the health economy.

3.5. Concluding remarks

The MRHA is a further development of the NHA, an already established reporting tool for the national health economy of Germany. It refers to a satellite account of the national accounting framework emphasizing on the product-sided defined health economy. It implements secondary data on health expenditure in order to assure a valid quantification of this cross-industrial sector. For the compilation of the MRHA we aim to use the same methodology, which was developed for the national case in order to assure consistency and comparability of results. Unlike the national case, no supply and use tables are available for the German federal states. Hence, it is indispensable to compile multiregional supply and use tables first. This procedure is in the focus of the present chapter.

In order to calculate multiregional supply and use tables for the overall economy, we developed and implemented a new way to multiregionalize national tables. This procedure uses the main principles of the known SUT-RAS Algorithm (Temurshoev and Timmer 2011) and develops it further for the multiregional case. This MR-SUT-RAS is an iterative algorithm, which is applied on an initial multiregional table in order to update it to given regional data. This provided regional data refers to output and intermediate use of industries and use of final consumption categories. Moreover, the approach takes into account given information on fixed values, i.e. on exports or any other values we can specify precisely. A special feature of the SUT-RAS and consequently the MR-SUT-RAS is that it includes given information and simultaneously applies it in the supply and use tables.

Hence, no further adjustment is necessary after performing the algorithm since all information available is considered within the procedure. Moreover, the algorithm considers the process of balancing supply and use tables. The resulting multiregional tables correspond to the national tables in the sum of industries and products.

We are well aware of the fact that this procedure, like most other approaches concerning the (multi-)regionalization of national accounts, cannot keep up with survey-based tables. Hence, we aim at a holistic approach of our model. This means, we do not pursue accuracy in each cell of the tables, but an accurate picture of economic flows. We specifically make use of a closed mathematical model in order to rely on a rather mechanical approach. It makes use of the interdependencies of the economic cycles of supply and use.

The developed approach involves a more pronounced mathematical background than the FLQ or CHARM approach, and challenges some of their essential drawbacks. However, its first implementation takes more effort as well. The circumstance that misspecifications often lead to a non-converging algorithm, is both a blessing and a curse of this approach. However, everyone, who is capable of algorithm programming and with sufficient knowledge of national accounts can apply this algorithm. There are no specific requirements concerning hardware and software to be met. For the implementation we used the free statistical software R at a standard computer with extended working storage capacity of 16 GB RAM. Moreover, the procedure can easily be applied to multiregionalize national accounts from other countries as long as sufficient data is available.

Certainly, there is a potential for improvements of the current MR-SUT-RAS algorithm. Most of it refer to additional data. However, data has to fit the framework of national and regional accounts, otherwise additional assumptions have to be taken, which might have a reverse effect on overall data quality in the end. In the case of regional accounts, in turn, more data is actually available opposed to what we were able to access, suggesting implementing a revised data base in future.

Another critical factor is the compilation of the initial matrix and the resulting amount of cross-hauling. However, we do not want to put too much emphases on this matter in order to keep the focus on the algorithm and its power first. Moreover, we applied the same idea of regional openness among all federal states in the same way, never putting any emphases on special regions. This was necessary in order to observe the power of the algorithm in depicting specific characteristics of federal states. This way, each federal state was treated identically. Hence, we think that this leads to a general bias of a direction unknown, which, however, makes it possible to compare results among regions.

The developed model at hand exhibits some specifics, which favor a thorough validation of results within a next step. First, the model builds up on a special evaluation of national supply and use tables and hence offers a high degree of detail on the product side. Moreover, we calculated a satellite account in a final step. This one allows to evaluate the product-sided defined health economy. This enhances a variety of analyses, i.e. on the regional production structure of health products, such as regional specialization in production processes, in retail or in research and development. Putting emphasis on the field of the health economy makes it easier to develop a proper assessment on the quality of results. The field of health economy has for long now been our field of expertise, not only from a theoretical, but also from a practical approach. Hence, we see a great advantage in the further development into a satellite account.

Further contributions will focus on the results of the MRHA in order to evaluate the quality of the developed approach. We will look at direct effects in chapter 4 and spill-over effects in chapter 5 and will even question time series results of direct effects in chapter 4. Moreover, we will apply the model to a certain economic policy issue – lagging investments in German hospitals in chapter 6.

4. Validation of Direct Effects of the Health Economy[8]

The Multiregional Health Account is a satellite account focusing on the economic impact of the health economy in German federal states. It was developed as an enhancement of the existing National Health Account for Germany. In contrast to the subject of matter over here, the calculations of the National Health Account are based on available national supply and use tables. Since there are no according tables available for the German federal states, we developed a methodology, which allows to calculate supply and use tables at the subnational multiregional level. The present chapter focusses on the results of the MRHA for the reason of a thorough validation procedure of the developed approach. We evaluate regional direct effects of the health economy by comparing derived characteristics with company data and evaluate the performance of the algorithm in a time series. We find that the elaborated approach shows reasonable results in both dimensions evaluated.

4.1. Introduction

Both the National (NHA) and the Multiregional Health Account of Germany (MRHA) refer to satellite accounts of the health economy and aim to quantify the economic contribution of this cross-sectoral industry in terms of gross value added (GVA), employment and trade. Unlike the MRHA, the concept of the NHA already exists for several years, promoted and initiated by activities of the Federal Ministry for Economic Affairs and Energy (Henke et al. 2010; Ostwald et al. 2014; Schneider et al. 2016; Bundesministerium für Wirtschaft und Energie (BMWi) 2015 & 2016 & 2017). The MRHA was published in 2017 and extends the existent calculations by a regional component (Ostwald et al. 2017).

In order to assure consistency of national and multiregional results, we pursued the intention to apply the same methodology of satellite account compilation in both cases. This approach is based on the elaborated methodology, which was devised over several years in the context of the NHA and described in chapter 2 of this contribution. This intention, how-

8 This chapter is based on Schwärzler and Kronenberg (2017b).

ever, leads to a great challenge. The NHA is based on official supply and use tables of national accounts. Since there are no such tables available for the federal states of Germany, multiregional supply and use tables had to be compiled first.

Hence, we developed the MR-SUT-RAS algorithm to calculate multiregional supply and use tables. This approach derives from the SUT-RAS algorithm of Temurshoev and Timmer (2011) and was further developed for the multiregional case in the context of compiling the MRHA, which is described in chapter 3 of this contribution. The elaborated procedure is an iterative algorithm, which incorporates all given information simultaneously, balances supply and use table mutually and is restricted by meeting national values in industries and products. The concept of the MR-SUT-RAS relies on the economic conditions and therefore the fact that all supplied output is used at some place. Regional diversification and specialization hence leads to interregional interaction and interdependencies.

After presenting the motivation for this chapter in section 4.2, we show the basic results of the MRHA, including direct effects of the overall health economy, its subcategories and fields of specialization of federal states in section 4.3. Moreover, we apply the elaborated approach for several different years in order to analyze the development of the health economy in German federal states over time in section 4.4. We close this chapter with concluding remarks in section 4.5. Since calculations were conducted on behalf of the Federal Ministry for Economic Affairs and Energy, the description of results in section 4.3.1 and 4.4.1 mostly refers to the corresponding report (Ostwald et al. 2017).

4.2. Motivation

In this chapter, we focus on the results of the MRHA in order to challenge the elaborated algorithm, MR-SUT-RAS. Hence, it is our intention to critically scrutinize the reliability of the approach before applying it to answer specific economic policy issues. This proceeding is especially challenging since no official supply and use tables are available for German federal states. Therefore, it is reasonable to question the reliability of the approach in the context of a satellite account, which allows to focus on a specific field of the economy. This way, we are able to oppose and compare results with qualitative information or related but not in the calculation integrated data. Since we carry out calculations in the context of the health economy on a wider basis already for several years, we can fall back on knowledge, which favors the focus on the health economy in this context.

Focusing on industry information of multiregional supply and use tables does not lead to new findings, since corresponding values refer to data directly applied to the model. However, compiling a satellite account in accordance to the methodology developed in the context of the NHA allows us to concentrate on the product-specific defined health economy, which accordingly refers to modelled information. Hence, we can reasonably question the reliability of the elaborated model from this perspective.

Our main database for the MRHA, the national supply and use tables, refer to the years 2010 and 2011. They correspond to the statistical standards of NACE 2008 and ESA 2010. In Schwärzler and Kronenberg (2016) we depict on how to project these available tables for the years before and after the referring point of time. This procedure is necessary in order to quantify the contribution of the national health economy for the corresponding years, since generic tables on supply and use tables consistent with the latest statistical standards are available for the years 2010, 2011 and 2012 only at the time of writing.[9] We present results of the MRHA for 2011 in section 4.3, since our latest official national supply and use tables refer to this very same year. Accordingly, we present direct effects for the years 2006 to 2015 in section 4.4 to show that the elaborated approach manages to depict the macroeconomic development of the health economy despite the lack of generic national supply and use tables for all these years.

As aforementioned, we aim to challenge the developed approach of the MR-SUT-RAS in this chapter. In a subsequent step, we evaluate indirect effects of the health economy in order to challenge a further dimension of the elaborated model in chapter 5. The overall goal of the MRHA is to focus on interregional spillover effects from patient treatment and resulting implications on the lagging investments in German hospitals, which is discussed in chapter 6.

4.3. Direct effects of the health economy in 2011

In this section, we focus on the direct effects of the health economy in German federal states for the year 2011. This includes the main economic indicators GVA, employment, export and import of the overall health econo-

9 Tables for 2012 are not available due to high costs involved.

my in subsection 4.3.1. This way, we are able to present the big picture of heterogeneity German federal states exhibit in the case of the health economy. We show this in order to reach out for the reader's attention towards the need for the MRHA. In subsection 4.3.2, we look at a specific field of the health economy in order to challenge obtained results with secondary data. In this context, we make use of the fact that federal states exhibit a great heterogeneity in their specialization regarding the supply of medication in terms of manufacturing, R&D and wholesale. We challenge results with company data in order to see whether the algorithm is capable of elaborating the same characteristics of federal states observed in reality.

4.3.1. The overall health economy in the German federal states in 2011

The German health economy contributes 11.2 percent to overall GVA in the year 2011. Figure 21 exhibits this indicator for the federal states, ranging between 14.7 in Schleswig-Holstein and 9.1 percent in Hamburg. We can depict an East-West divide to some extent. All new German Laender including Berlin show an above average share of the health economy. In Western German states, the sector exhibits outstanding significance for the overall economy only in Schleswig-Holstein, Rhineland-Palatinate, Hesse and Saarland. The health economy shows low significance for the overall economy of the city states Hamburg and Bremen and the economy of Bavaria. The latter is characterized by several well performing industries contributing to a high GDP per capita of this federal state. This causes the health economy to be of minor significance for the overall economy. Hence, we see the necessity to consider a further indicator, which is unrelated with the overall economic structure of the respective federal state.

Figure 21: GVA share of the health economy, 2011

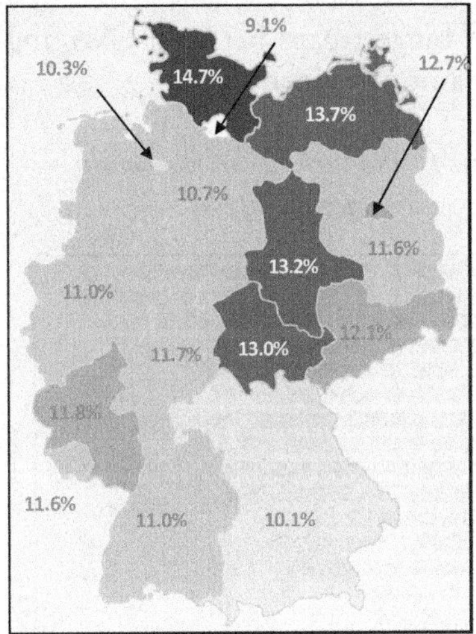

Source: own illustration b.o. Ostwald et al. (2017).

Figure 22: GVA of the health economy per inhabitant, 2011

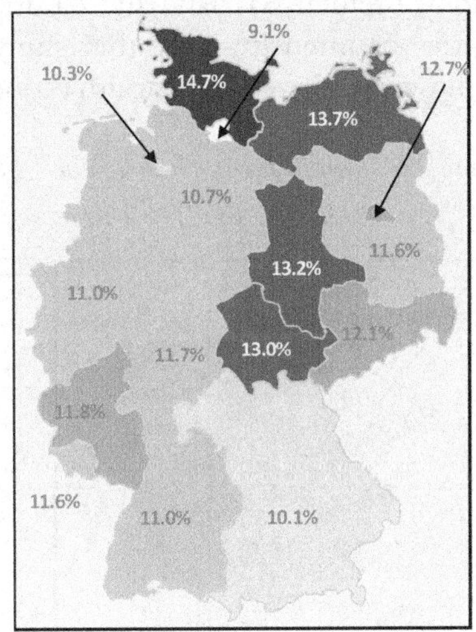

Source: own illustration b.o. Ostwald et al. (2017).

GVA per capita generated by the health economy reveals the performance of the industry opposed to its significance for the overall economy as previously described. As exemplified by Hamburg, we observe the difference of these two indicators. Hamburg obtains a well performing overall economy, resulting in a high GDP per capita. Accordingly, the influence of the health economy – and hence its significance for the overall economy – is low. This is due to the fact that the health economy is a considerably stable part of the economy with a relatively low range of possible outcomes compared to other industries. Hence, the indicator of the industry's performance offers an additional perspective, placing Hamburg at the top of the ranking.

In the following, we present figures on the significance of the health economy for employment in accordance to the previously shown GVA share of the health economy. The overall German health economy contributes 15.3 percent to employment in 2011. Again, this indicator shows a great variation among federal states, which is 13.5 percent in Hamburg and 18.2 percent in Schleswig-Holstein. In general, a high share of employees working in the health economy points towards a labor-intensive service orientation of the respective health economy. This is especially the case when we observe great disparities between GVA and employment shares. We hence conclude that the health economy in the federal states Lower Saxony, Bremen, Saarland and Bavaria are above average characterized by a high labor intensity, since they show the biggest gaps between GVA and employment share of the health economy among federal states.

Figure 23: Employment share of the health economy, 2011

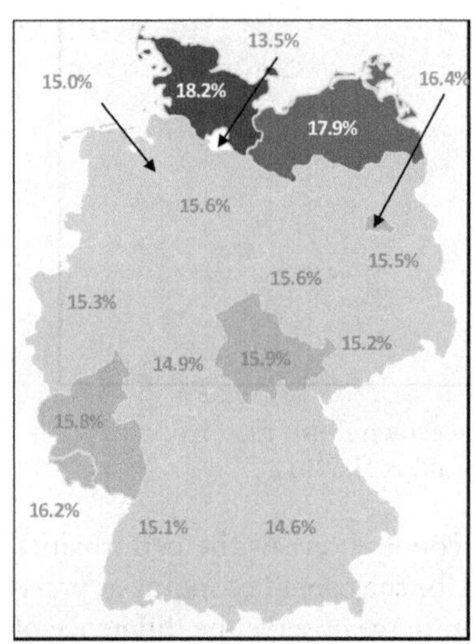

Source: own illustration b.o. Ostwald et al. (2017).

Figure 24: Productivity of the health economy, 2011

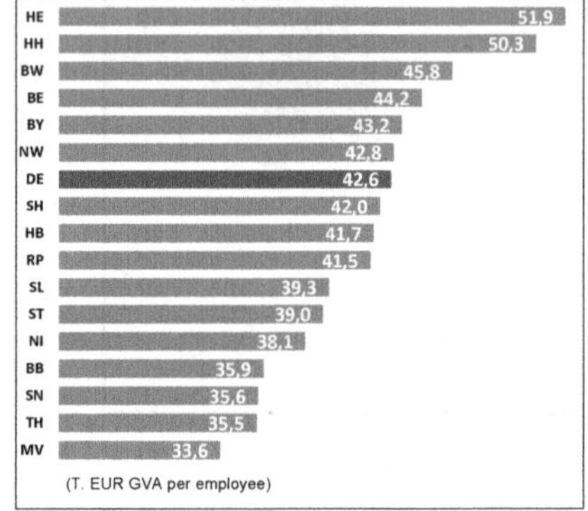

Source: own illustration based on Ostwald et al. (2017).

Productivity is in some way related to the conclusions just described, since it provides an additional perspective on the matter of specialization the health economies of federal states exhibit. We define productivity as the ratio of GVA per employee. The overall German health economy is characterized by a relatively low productivity compared to the overall economy. While the latter shows a productivity level of 58,400 € of GVA per employee, the health economy is characterized by a productivity level of 42,600 € GVA per employee in the year 2011. Reasons for this difference are the high labor intensity of the health economy accompanied by a relatively low degree of automatization of processes compared to manufacturing industries. The cross federal state comparison exhibits the highest level of productivity for Hesse with 51,900 € GVA per employee. This corresponds to a more than 20 percent gap between the average German level and

Hesse. Moreover, among all Western German federal states, this one shows the lowest gap between the productivity of the health economy compared to the overall economy.

Figure 25: Relationship between labor productivity of the health economy and share of industrial segment, 2011

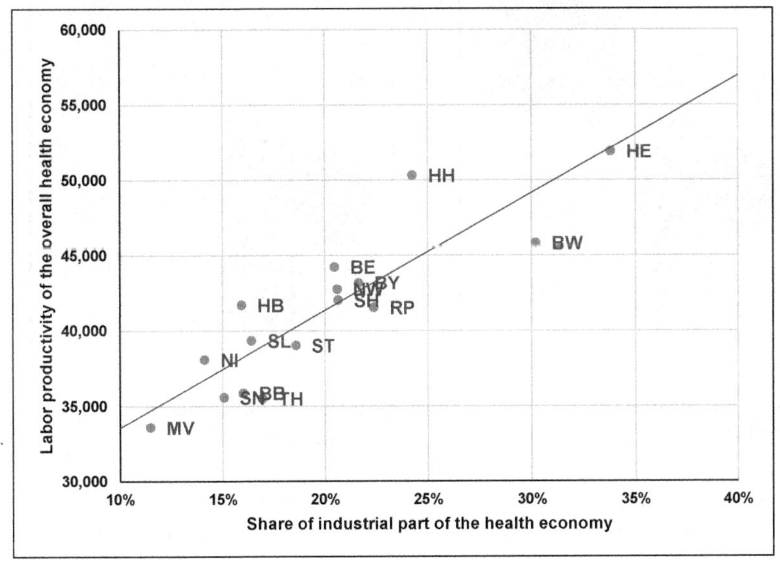

Source: own illustration based on Ostwald et al. (2017).

Key driver of this circumstance is the high amount of medication manufacturing taking place in Hesse. Operating companies are for example Sanofi-Aventis Deutschland GmbH and Merck KGaA. In general, we observe a relationship between the significance of the industrial segment of the health economy on the one hand and the level of productivity of the health economy on the other hand, as shown in Figure 26.[10] Since labor productivity of the overall economy is below-average for all Eastern German federal states in 2011 (Statistische Ämter des Bundes und der Länder 2017), it is essential to be aware of the general discrepancy of productivity levels among Eastern and Western German federal states in this case.

10 The definition of industrially characterized categories can be retrieved from Ostwald et al. (2017).

Figure 26: International export share of the health economy, 2011

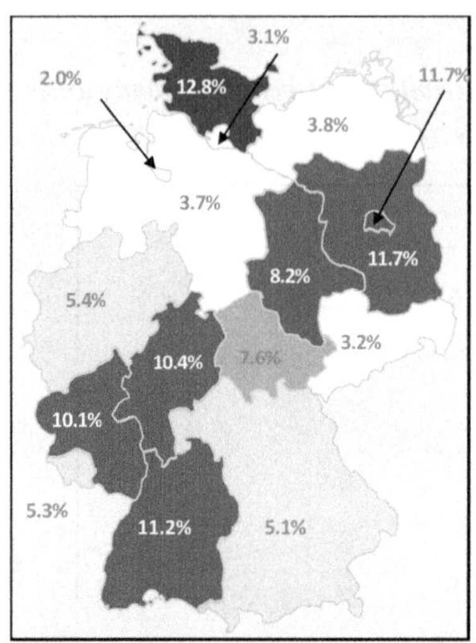

Source: own illustration b.o. Ostwald et al. (2017).

Figure 27: Import share of the health economy, 2011

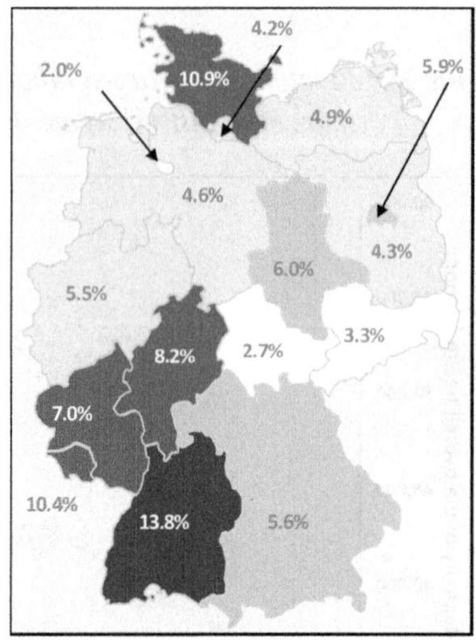

Source: own illustration b.o. Ostwald et al. (2017).

The German health economy contributes 7.0 percent to international exports in 2011. There is only minor significance of exports in the Hanseatic Cities Bremen and Hamburg with 2.0 and 3.1 percent. In contrary, the health economy has relatively large impact on overall international exports in Schleswig-Holstein, Berlin, Brandenburg, Baden-Württemberg, Hesse and Rhineland-Palatinate with shares all above 10 percent. Baden-Württemberg is the driving force of international exports, not in terms of relative but absolute importance, with an amount of 24.9 Bn. € in 2011. This corresponds to a 30 percent share of overall exports of the German health economy. North Rhine-Westphalia and Bavaria follow with 13.1 and 11.1 Bn. €. Adding Hesse with corresponding 9.4 Bn. € in fourth place, the overall export amount of named federal states corresponds to around 70 percent of overall German exports of the health economy.

Figure 28: International trade balance of the health economy, 2011

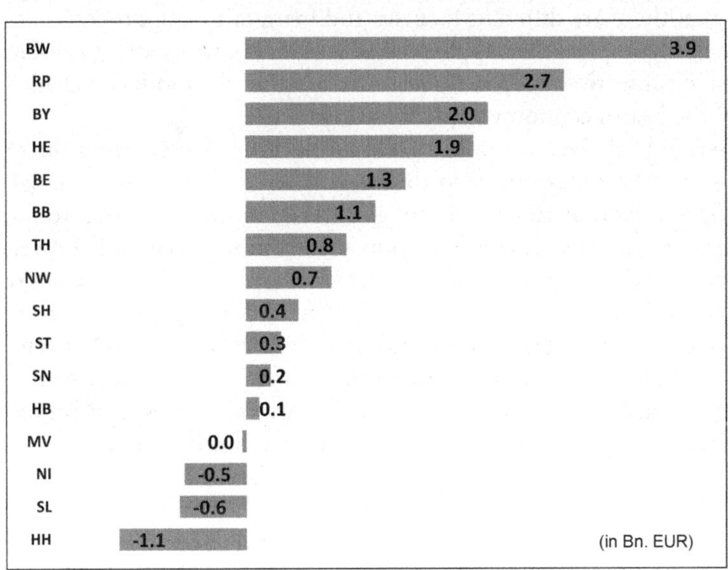

Source: own illustration based on Ostwald et al. (2017).

A high amount of exports often entails a similar characteristic regarding imports in the sense of mutual transfer of knowledge. International collaboration and cross-national manufacturing processes are essential characteristics of the health economy. Depicting the import share of the health economy therefore shows a similar scheme as the previous figure. Compared to the overall German health economy import share of 6.9 percent in 2011, the federal states Baden-Württemberg, Schleswig-Holstein, Saarland, Hesse and Rhineland-Palatinate show an above average relevance of this cross-sectoral industry for overall import activities. Named federal states are responsible for more than half of overall imports of the German health economy. On average, medication makes up about 50 percent of imports of the health economy. Baden-Württemberg, however, is characterized by a 70 percent share of imports reflected by medication. Influence of medication products on the national health economy is high in this context. About 45 percent of overall medication imports corresponds to Baden-Württemberg. Its export share is only slightly lower. This circumstance reflects the special role of Baden-Württemberg as an important supplier and international trading partner for medication. However, it is interesting to see in this matter that the importance of Baden-Württemberg is outperformed by Hesse when we look at medication output. We hence can conclude that there are different focusses and manufacturing processes applying when it comes to the supply of medication. We will look at this circumstance in subsection 4.3.2 in order to see whether the modelled characteristics of the health economy apply in reality.

The external trade balance of the German health economy amounts to 13.2 Bn. € in 2011. Opposing it to the overall German external trade balance results in a ratio of 10 percent, the health economy contributes to the overall characteristic. With the exception of Hamburg, Saarland, Lower-Saxony and Mecklenburg Western Pomerania, all other federal states show a positive trade balance from international activities in the context of the health economy. The highest contribution goes back to Baden-Württemberg with 3.9 bn. € external trade balance, followed by Rhineland-Palatinate, Bavaria and Hesse, which all show a similarly high degree of importance regarding output of industrially manufactured health products.

4.3.2. Characteristics of medication supply in German federal states in 2011

In the previous subsection, we looked at the results of the overall health economy in German federal states for 2011 in order to establish a big picture regarding intention and use of the model. This subsection concentrates on figures in the context of medication supply exclusively in order to conclude upon the reasonability of results.

One advantage of this focus is we can challenge the MRHA results with information on operating companies. Moreover, manufacturing industries show a much more diverse structure in auxiliary production compared to service-oriented industries. This means that obtained product-specific information differs from given industry-specific information to a larger amount compared to i.e. the industry of health services, which exhibits hardly any auxiliary production. Hence, we expect to obtain the best impression regarding the reliability of the model if we look at product-specific output related to industrial production, which is accordingly supposed to differ from given industry-specific information to a higher extent.

The product-specific approach we pursue in the context of the satellite account implies we look at medication for human use only, regardless of the question by which industry it is produced. Moreover, we do not consider any other output of the involved industries, which is not directly related to human health, e.g. chemical or veterinary products. Hence, we refer to this as 'medication.' The product-specific approach also implies that we are able to define certain additional categories in the satellite account, including the differentiation between manufacturing, R&D and wholesale in the context of medication. Therefore, we are able to analyze the defined different categories of the health economy in terms of output, GVA, export and import. Table 1 of chapter 2 provides an overview of all categories of the health economy.

Since we have now discussed the object of further investigation, we look at the different characteristics of medication supply in the context of the MRHA. We distinguish between manufacturing, wholesale and R&D. In order to get a sense of the reliability of the elaborated approach, we look at the respective characteristics of federal states to see whether we can find any explanations in additional secondary data, which were not included in the compilation of the model.

In order to proceed accordingly, we focus on some federal states, which show specific characteristics and for which secondary information is available. Hence, we hypothesize that in reality and hence according to the results of the MRHA shown in Figure 29 and

Figure 29: Output of medication in German federal states by characteristic, absolute values, 2011

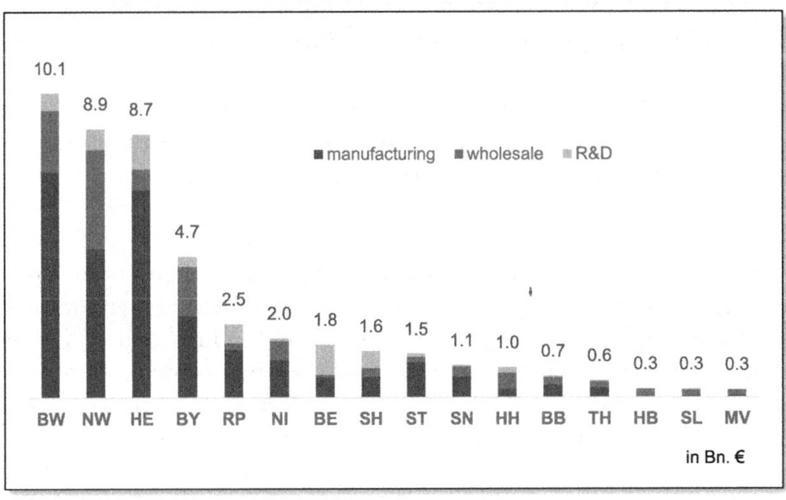

Source: own illustration based on Ostwald et al. (2017). 4.3.2

Figure 30, Hesse, Saxony-Anhalt and Baden-Württemberg exhibit high amounts of manufacturing activities, North Rhine-Westphalia and Bavaria are characterized by larger shares of distribution and Berlin, Rhineland-Palatinate and Schleswig-Holstein represent important locations for R&D activities.

Figure 30: Output of medication in German federal states by characteristic, relative shares, 2011

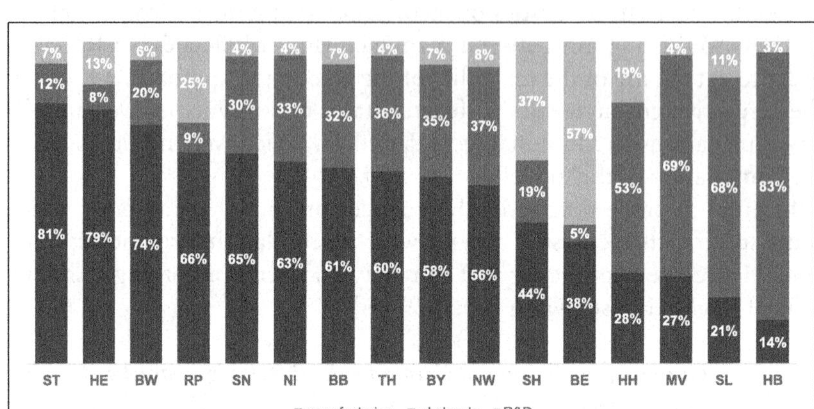

Source: own illustration based on Ostwald et al. (2017).

Figure 60 in the appendix contains information on the name and focus of active companies in German federal states. However, we want to point out that this information does not provide a complete picture of operating companies, since the map focusses on companies conducting R&D. Hence, companies performing e.g. wholesale or manufacturing exclusively are not represented in this figure. In order to make the amount of included information manageable, we compiled a summary of represented information, putting emphases on selected pharmaceutical industries only, in Figure 31. We decided upon their relevance by referring to the top ten companies, which generate the highest revenue in Germany on the one hand (IMS Health 2015) and on known German brands on the other hand.

Large crosses indicate a high relevance of the operating company in the federal state in terms of employees, whereas small crosses indicate a lower relevance. We do not provide exact numbers, since the quality of referring data base and the period in consideration differ among companies. Moreover, we are not able to distinguish between the subsidiaries of companies in terms of employees. Hence, the table aims at providing an overview and an initial assessment of operating countries only.

Figure 31: Sites and subsidiaries of selected pharmaceutical companies

	(Research)/ preclinical development	Clinical development	Distribution & shipping	API production	Production of finished pharmaceuticals
BW	✖✖	✖✖	✖✖	✖✖✖	✖✖✖✖✖✖
BY	✖✖	✖✖		✖	
BE	✖	✖✖✖✖	✖		✖✖
HE	✖✖✖	✖✖✖✖✖	✖✖	✖✖✖✖	✖✖✖✖
NW	✖✖	✖✖		✖✖	✖
RP	✖	✖✖	✖✖	✖	✖✖
SH	✖	✖✖	✖✖✖	✖	✖
OT					✖

AbbVie	Allergopharma	Astra Zeneca	Bayer	Berlin-Chemie	Boehringer Ingelheim	GlaxoSmithKline	Lilly Pharma	Merck	Novartis	Pfizer	Roche	Sanofi
✖	✖	✖	✖	✖	✖	✖	✖	✖	✖	✖	✖	✖

Source: own illustration based on Verband Forschender Arzneimittelhersteller (vfa) (2015).

First, we take a closer look at federal states with above-average activities in manufacturing, which is Hesse, Saxony-Anhalt and Baden-Württemberg, according to our results.

In Hesse, Sanofi-Aventis Deutschland GmbH and Merck KGaA mostly shape this characteristic since both have manufacturing sites located here. Sanofi-Aventis Deutschland GmbH employs about 7,300 people in Hesse, performing manufacturing, R&D and administration over there. Distribution is carried out by about 1,100 employees in Berlin (Sanofi-Aventis Deutschland GmbH 2017b). Moreover, the Sanofi-Aventis Deutschland GmbH site in Hesse is one of the most important locations for manufacturing of the overall and worldwide operating Sanofi-Group (Sanofi-Aventis Deutschland GmbH 2017a). Merck KGaA in Hesse does not reveal specific numbers. They employ about 10,900 people in overall Germany in all sections, including business in pharmaceuticals, chemicals, life science and material science. Hence, the number of employed people applying to the considered case is probably reasonable lower, since about 40 percent of worldwide sales originate from the chemical division in 2011 (Merck

KGaA 2012a). Nevertheless, Merck KGaA carries out production next to distribution, R&D and administration in Hesse. Moreover, we know that Merck KGaA increased their tablet production from four billion to eleven billion tablets during the period 2003 to 2011 (Merck KGaA 2012b).

Baden-Württemberg also shows a strong focus on manufacturing, similarly to Hesse. The most influencing company over here is Boehringer Ingelheim GmbH with about 5,500 employees (Boehringer Ingelheim GmbH 2015). This company owns one of the largest manufacturing plants worldwide and puts emphasis on R&D at this site. Pfizer Deutschland GmbH contributes about 1,000 employees exclusively to manufacturing and 100 employees to distribution (Pfizer Deutschland GmbH 2017b; Steibadler 2012), while Roche Pharma AG focusses merely on marketing, sales and R&D with 1,200 employees in Baden-Württemberg (Roche Pharma AG 2017).

Saxony-Anhalt shows the greatest share of manufacturing among all federal states. Over there, Bayer HealthCare AG produces Aspirin® in one of the biggest sites worldwide in this context, employing about 350 people (Bayer AG 2017b). Moreover, additional data sources reveal activities of Novartis with about 1,500 employees working on manufacturing and distribution in Saxony-Anhalt (Pavel et al. 2015; Salutas Pharma GmbH 2015).

We hence can conclude that the relatively large share of manufacturing in Hesse, Baden-Württemberg and Saxony-Anhalt resulting from the MRHA is reasonable due to the existence of large production sites in each of the federal states, without showing any contradictory information on different emphases.

In the following, we take a closer look at federal states particularly characterized by distribution activities of medication, North Rhine-Westphalia and Bavaria amongst them. The first is dominated by the activities of the company Bayer HealthCare AG employing about 13,000 people. Novartis is the main contributor to activities in Bavaria with having about 4,000 people employed in the context of medication. However, neither of these companies exhibit distribution and shipping activities according to Verband Forschender Arzneimittelhersteller (vfa) (2015), which contradicts our results. Unfortunately, this is caused by the focus on companies dedicated to R&D on the map.

However, according to Pavel et al. (2015), two reasonably large sites of Novartis AG conduct distribution of medication next to development, manufacturing, marketing and R&D of medication. Each of the sites employs about 2,000 people. However, the main production facility of Novartis AG is located in Baden-Württemberg. In the case of North Rhine-Westphalia we discover the high relevance of Bayer Vital GmbH, which is the distribution company of Bayer HealthCare AG, employing 1,700 people (Bund-Verlag 2011). Moreover, additional distribution activities are conducted by relatively smaller companies such as Janssen-Cilag GmbH and Grünenthal GmbH in North Rhine-Westphalia, employing an overall amount of about 800 and 1,800 people in this federal state (Janssen-Cilag GmbH 2017; Grünenthal GmbH 2017). In conclusion, a higher focus on distribution compared to the federal states aforementioned is reasonable, since both main contributing companies in these federal states, Novartis AG and Bayer HealthCare AG, conduct a reasonable amount of wholesale activities over there.

In the case of R&D, we find above-average shares for Berlin, Schleswig-Holstein and Rhineland-Palatinate. Since overall output of medication is reasonable lower in these federal states compared to the ones already described, the amount of available information is accordingly less, especially in the case of Rhineland-Palatinate and Schleswig-Holstein.

We suggest that the strong impact of Boehringer Ingelheim GmbH with an above-average R&D intensity of 13.4 percent (Boehringer Ingelheim GmbH 2015) compared to overall German pharmaceutical industries has a high impact on this characteristic for Rhineland-Palatinate.

AstraZeneca GmbH operates in Schleswig-Holstein, conducting R&D in addition to manufacturing and marketing with about 800 employed people (AstraZeneca GmbH, 2015). The company is known for its high investments in R&D, resulting in an overall R&D intensity of around 16.5 percent, which is reasonable well above the German average (AstraZeneca GmbH 2012). Another company operating and participating in R&D in Schleswig-Holstein is Allergopharma GmbH & Co. KG, a subsidiary of Merck KGaA with about 480 employees of which 12.5 percent are dedicated in R&D (Allergopharma GmbH & Co. KG 2014).

Last, but not least, Berlin shows the highest share of R&D activities among all German federal states. Manufacturing is only conducted by the companies Bayer HealthCare AG and Berlin-Chemie AG. The first employs about 4,900 people in Berlin but conducts manufacturing activities to a considerably low amount only. This is due to the fact that this location is one out of four main sites for R&D of Bayer HealthCare AG worldwide. Therefore, the Berlin site focusses on R&D in particular (Bayer AG 2012; Bayer AG 2017a). Berlin-Chemie AG employs about 1,800 people in Berlin, about 400 among them focusing on research and development (Berlin-Chemie AG 2017). Moreover, Pfizer Deutschland GmbH and

Sanofi-Aventis Deutschland GmbH have sites in Berlin as well, employing about 650 and 1,100 people. Pfizer Deutschland GmbH focusses on R&D, administration and marketing (Pfizer Deutschland GmbH 2017a), while Sanofi-Aventis Deutschland GmbH conducts marketing and distribution over there (Sanofi-Aventis Deutschland GmbH 2017b). Putting together all this information, we can indeed obtain a focus on R&D in the three federal states Berlin, Schleswig-Holstein and Rhineland-Palatinate, supporting our MRHA results.

Summarizing, we managed to find reasonable qualitative information that support our findings of the MRHA regarding direct effects of manufacturing, wholesale and R&D activities in the context of medication supply. In the following, we look at overall time series results of the MRHA in a first step and see whether we can find reasonable explanations for obtained developments in a second step.

4.4. Direct effects of the health economy during the period 2006 to 2015

While we focused on MRHA results for the year 2011 in section 4.3, we look at the development of key figures during the period of 2006 to 2015 in this section. In general, the elaborated MR-SUT-RAS can be applied to calculate multiregional supply and use tables for several different years. However, we are well aware of the fact that we move along a small ridge between methodological appropriateness and technical feasibility in this case. This is the reason we do not focus on the application of the algorithm in a time series in general. We want to demonstrate its performance in this matter nevertheless, since it provides a good opportunity to look at the reliability of the approach from a different perspective.

Therefore, we describe the results on the overall health economy in German federal states during the period 2006 to 2015 in order to enable a basic understanding of use and aim of this application in subsection 4.4.1. In subsection 4.4.2 we continue with a special focus on the supply of medication similarly to subsection 4.3.2. Instead of focusing on just one year we look at the modelled dynamics over time again. We challenge obtained results with industry specific information and company data in order to question their consistency with reality. Again, the overall goal is to develop an assessment concerning the validity of the elaborated approach.

4.4.1. The overall health economy in the German federal states during 2006 to 2015

The GVA average annual growth rate of the German health economy amounts to 3.8 percent in nominal terms during the period 2006 to 2015. If we compare this indicator to the overall economic development we find a higher growth rate for the health economy to the extent of 0.8 percentage points. In German federal states, growth rates of the health economy range between 4.7 percent in Brandenburg and 2.9 percent in Bremen. At this point, it is worth noting that the health economy grew faster than the overall economy in all federal states (Statistische Ämter des Bundes und der Länder 2017), even in those with the lowest GVA growth rates of the health economy. Moreover, the federal states Hamburg, Rhineland-Palatinate and Saarland show the greatest positive gap between the growth rates of the health economy and the overall economy. In those regions, the dynamic of the health economy tops the overall economic development by about 2.0 percentage points. In Hamburg, this development is driven by the largest increase in health expenditures among all federal states in the same period of time. This way, the sector outperforms the city state's overall economic development. Brandenburg, the federal state with the highest GVA growth rate, exhibits about 60 percent of overall increase from inpatient and outpatient treatment. Moreover, supply of medication increased in Brandenburg in terms of manufacturing, wholesale and R&D activities from nearly non-existent to about 0.6 Bn. € in 2015.

The heterogeneous composition of the health economy is responsible for the different picture employment growth rates of this cross-sectoral industry show in contrast to GVA growth rates. Hamburg, Berlin, Bavaria and Rhineland-Palatine exhibit the highest growth rates for the period 2006 to 2015 among all federal states. A high increase of employees in the context of inpatient and outpatient treatment causes this development in Hamburg and Bavaria. The very same indicator, however, shows only below-average values for Berlin and Rhineland-Palatine. In Berlin, R&D activities of the health economy are driving forces of increasing employment, due to both high significance and above-average growth rates of this area. In Rhineland-Palatine, employment growth in the context of both, health tourism and supply of organic food, stimulate the development of the overall health economy. Hence, we observe a great variety in determining factors of economic dynamic in the case of the health economy. This example points out the advantage of the MRHA very clearly, since it provides additional information on the development of the health economy in contrary to the NHA, which lacks regional diversification.

Figure 32: GVA growth rates of the health economy, 2006-2015

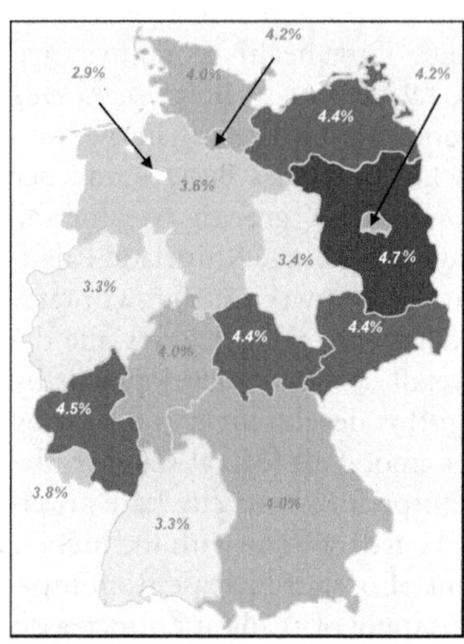

Source: Ostwald et al. (2017).

Figure 33: Employment growth rates of the health economy, 2006-2015

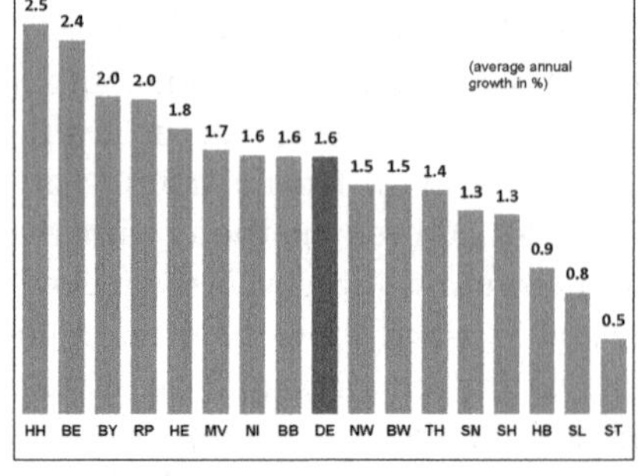

Source: Ostwald et al. (2017).

Export of products and services of the German health economy increased by on average 7.1 percent per annum between 2006 and 2015. Hence, the health economy shows a substantial above average growth of exports, which is 2.9 percentage points higher than the export growth rate of the overall German economy. This indicator differs vastly among federal states. The highest growth rate is observed in Saxony-Anhalt, where exports of the health economy increased by on average 13.7 percent per annum since 2006. This corresponds to a rise from 700 m. € in 2006 to 2.3 bn. € in 2015. About three-quarters of this increase result from export activities in the context of medication. The most significant growth in absolute values is recorded in Baden-Württemberg. Exports went up by 16.6 bn. € between the years 2006 and 2015. This in turn implies that the health economy of this federal state is responsible for about one third of German increase of exports in the field of the health economy.

Figure 34: Export growth rates of the health economy, 2006-2015

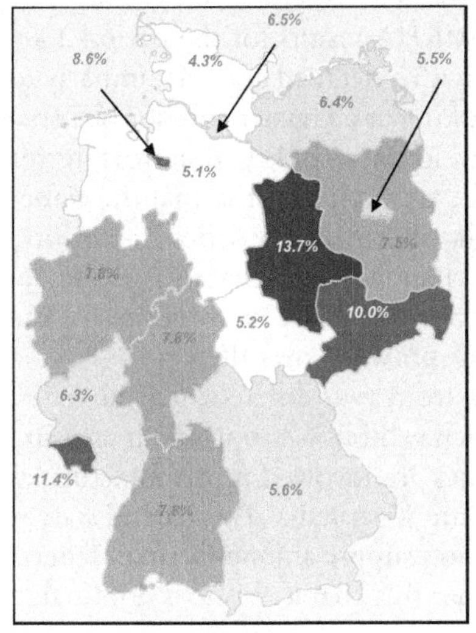

Source: Ostwald et al. (2017).

Figure 35: Import growth rates of the health economy, 2006-2015

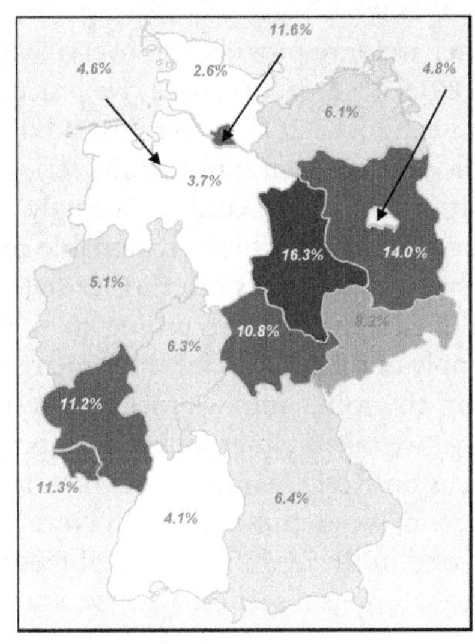

Source: Ostwald et al. (2017).

Imports of the German health economy increased by on average 6.0 percent per annum in the period 2006 to 2015. They hence show a lower dynamic compared to exports in this field. This caused the German external trading balance of products and services of the health economy to increase in that period of time. Similar to exports of the health economy, imports rose to a higher extent compared to overall German imports, resulting in a positive gap of 2.3 percentage points. Again, we recognize similarities between imports and exports in regional characteristics. Saxony-Anhalt shows the highest increase in imports of the health economy to the amount of on average 16.3 percent per annum. This corresponds to an absolute increase of imports of 1.4 Bn. € since 2006. Although international trade of the health economy in Saxony-Anhalt generates a positive external trade balance, this could change in the future, if imports remain to show higher growth rates than exports.

4.4.2. Characteristics of medication supply in German federal states 2006 - 2015

After we have provided an overview of MRHA results for the period 2006 to 2015 in subsection 4.4.1, we proceed with a detailed analysis similarly to subsection 4.3.2. However, instead of looking at characteristics for one specific year, we focus on the time series development of key indicators in this subsection. We proceed accordingly, since we want to verify that the elaborated approach exhibits reasonable results also in a time series framework. Hence, this analysis is a further step to challenge the reliability of the developed approach. According to subsection 4.3.2, we concentrate on the supply of medication for the same reasons provided over there.

In the following, we focus on results from two different federal states. First, we take a closer look at Berlin, which exhibits a strong and increasing focus on R&D, while only two companies are involved in manufacturing. Second, we examine results in North Rhine-Westphalia. This federal state is second in the overall amount of medication supply among German federal states. From subsection 4.3.2 we know that this characteristic is dominated by one main company. This circumstance favors a detailed analysis since we expect to find a direct link between company data and obtained results. Therefore, the two federal states show certain characteristics we pursue to identify in the following, both in results and secondary data.

In order to proceed accordingly, it is not conducive to make use of official statistics regarding the pharmaceutical industry. Official statistics do not account all companies, a common industry representative would assign to the statistical entity of a pharmaceutical industry, as such. For example, the companies Pfizer Deutschland GmbH and Sanofi-Aventis Deutschland GmbH, each of them employing more than 1,000 people in Berlin are accounted as trading companies in official statistics, since they do not manufacture any pharmaceutical products in this federal state. Consequently, neither their employees nor their sales are represented by the indicators of the pharmaceutical industry from official statistics. The same applies to Teva GmbH, Takeda Pharma Vertrieb GmbH & Co. KG and Parexel International GmbH next to some other service companies (Pharmahauptstadt Berlin 2017).

This is the reason why our satellite account does not focus on industry-related but on product-specific data. Hence, we include and separate from each other manufacturing, wholesale and R&D of medication, independently from the fact which industry it produced.

Figure 36 exhibits the results from our model for Berlin, focusing on output of medication in terms of the three named categories for the period 2006 to 2015. As already depicted in subsection 4.3.2, there is a clear focus on R&D, which is in addition growing in relative and absolute importance. Moreover, manufacturing activities declined and show their lowest amount in the years 2011 and 2012.

Figure 36: Output of medication in Berlin by characteristic, absolute values, 2006-2015

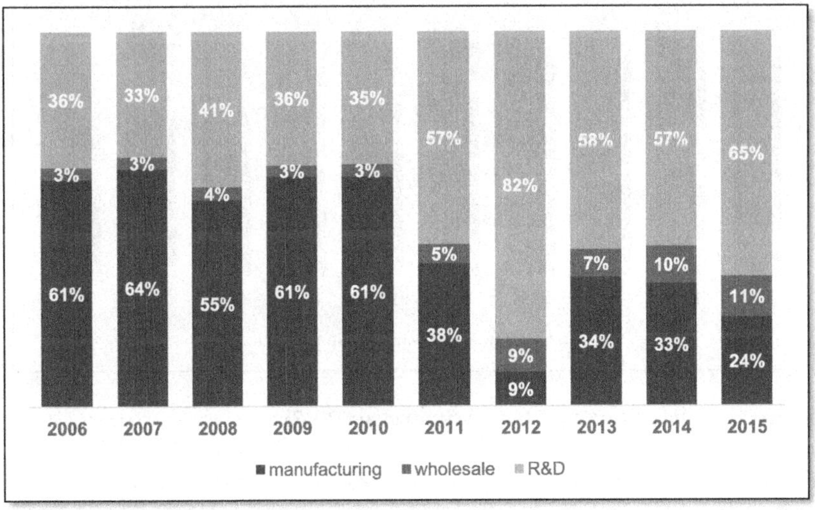

Source: own illustration based on Ostwald et al. (2017).

The existent and growing importance of R&D can be confirmed by secondary data. In general, there is an overall increase in R&D of German pharmaceutical companies (Verband Forschender Arzneimittelhersteller (vfa) and Stifterverband für die Deutsche Wissenschaft e. V. 2016). Moreover, Pfizer Deutschland GmbH has settled in Berlin in the year 2008. This site focuses on R&D next to HR, finance, market access, communication and marketing. Manufacturing and wholesale are both carried out in Baden-Württemberg (Pfizer Deutschland GmbH 2017b). Hence, some of the increases in R&D are certainly attributable to the company Pfizer Deutschland GmbH. Moreover, Bayer HealthCare AG as the biggest company in Berlin with about 4,900 employees, raised its overall expenditures on R&D by on average about 8 percent per annum since 2006 (Bayer AG 2016; Bayer AG 2007). We argue that this has impact on R&D output in

Berlin, since one of Bayer HealthCare AG's worldwide four sites on R&D is located in this federal state (Bayer AG 2016).

Figure 37: Output of medication in Berlin by characteristic, relative values, 2006-2015

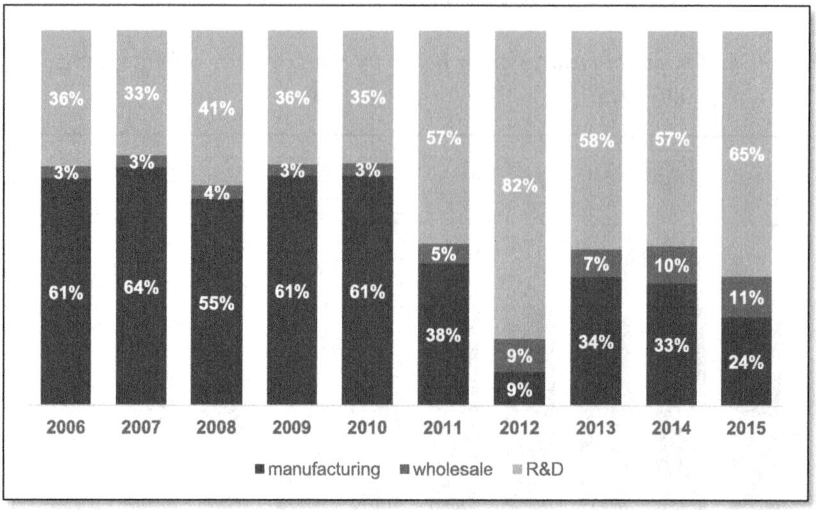

	2006	2007	2008	2009	2010	2011	2012	2013	2014	2015
R&D	36%	33%	41%	36%	35%	57%	82%	58%	57%	65%
wholesale	3%	3%	4%	3%	3%	5%	9%	7%	10%	11%
manufacturing	61%	64%	55%	61%	61%	38%	9%	34%	33%	24%

Source: own illustration based on Ostwald et al. (2017).

The second circumstance Figure 36 exhibits, is a decrease in manufacturing in the years 2011 and 2012, followed by an increase in the years afterwards. Nonetheless, output did not catch up with amounts of output from 2010. Moreover, we can see an absolute and relative increase in wholesale from 2013 on. In the following, we will try to explain this development with information from secondary data.

In Berlin, there are only two main companies involved in manufacturing of medication – Bayer HealthCare AG and Berlin-Chemie AG. Since the first shows about the fourfold of employees compared to the latter, we will focus on the development of the first in order to explain the dynamics from reality.

According to qualitative data sources, the year 2010 was challenging for the pharmaceutical industry, due to cost reductions of health systems all over the world and increased competition from generic drugs. Moreover, demand of the contraceptive pill group YAZ™, Yasmin™ and Yasminelle™, which brought Bayer HealthCare AG revenues to the amount of 1.2 Bn. € in 2009, weakened in a double-digit range (Salz 2010; Mielke

2011). This impacted on the Berlin site, since packaging of these products is one main focus of manufacturing at this location. While these activities were carried out by several extra shifts of employees in Berlin in the years before, decreased demand resulted in a reduction of shifts and output by a quarter (Peters 2009). At the same time, Bayer HealthCare AG announced to reduce employees in Germany by 700 people. All this happened in the course of reorganization aiming at investing more in R&D and reducing costs in administration. It was seen to be very likely that the site of Berlin was highly affected by the reduction in employment, since the decrease in demand of the names contraceptive pills had high impacts on the production site (Salz 2010). Reorganization was said to incur costs at the amount of 1 Bn. €, but supposed to save 800 m. € on a yearly basis from 2013 on (Mielke 2011).

In a retrospective review, the years 2009 until 2011 were characterized by strict cost management (Szent-Ivanyi 2014). From 2012 on, Bayer HealthCare AG was back on the path to growth and experienced a record year in 2013. Simultaneously, Bayer HealthCare AG increased expenditures on R&D favoring the site of Berlin, according to a manager of Bayer HealthCare AG in 2014. The upward trend is also supported by a contract between Bayer HealthCare AG and the labor union IG BCE, which prohibits Bayer HealthCare AG from compulsory redundancies until 2020. The contract is aiming at strengthening the location and ensuring R&D activities in Germany (Mortsiefer 2016).

According to what has just been described, we conclude that the reduction in manufacturing in Berlin shown in Figure 36 is reasonable due to the decrease in demand of Bayer Health Care AG's contraceptive pills, an overall reduction in costs and a reorganization of the company. The depicted increase in R&D can also be explained.

In a next step, we take a closer look at dynamics of medication supply in North Rhine-Westphalia. The right box at the bottom of Figure 38 depicts corresponding GVA according to the MRHA. We observe a dynamic development, which is caused by a high amount of GVA from manufacturing in 2008, decreasing to a lower level with sudden drops in the years 2009 and 2012, which is again followed by an increase in GVA from 2013 on. In the following, we look for secondary data supporting these results.

Figure 38: Comparison of MRHA results with related secondary data in the field of medication.

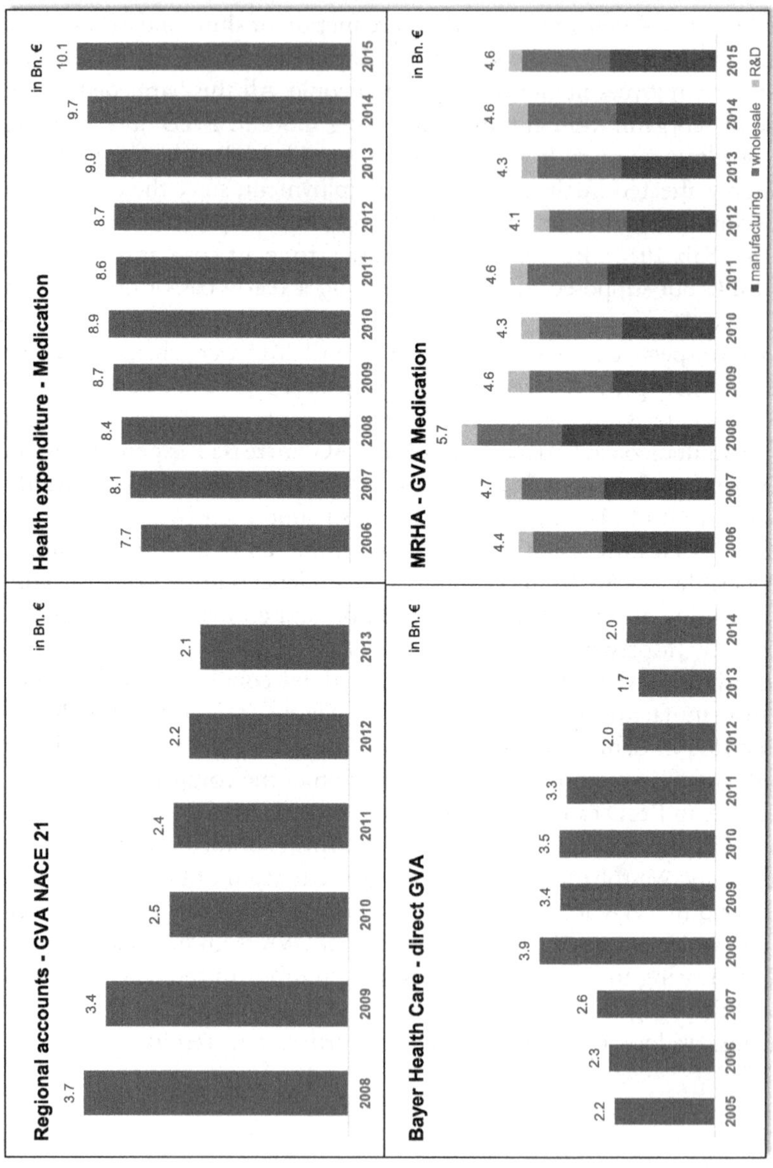

Source: Statistische Ämter des Bundes und der Länder (2016); Ostwald, Zubrzycki and Legler (2015); own illustration based on Ostwald et al. (2017).

Medication supply in North Rhine-Westphalia is mainly dominated by the company Bayer HealthCare AG. Hence, we do not necessarily have to look at a large number of different companies in order to observe a first guess regarding the reliability of the MRHA. Moreover, since we have just looked at Bayer HealthCare AG's site in Berlin, it should be clear so far that not all of the company's dynamics are reflected in medication output of North Rhine-Westphalia. However, the largest share of activities indeed goes back to this federal state since about two thirds of Bayer HealthCare AG's employed people in Germany work at the several sites in North Rhine-Westphalia.

We observe the great opportunity to have data on direct GVA of Bayer HealthCare AG available from a completely unrelated earlier project (Ostwald, Zubrzycki and Legler 2015). This data, shown in the left bottom box of Figure 38, was not incorporated into the MRHA in any way. Therefore, we matched results from the MRHA and GVA of Bayer HealthCare AG for the cause of validation. The level of GVA is a different one due to inaccuracies in the context of the regional differentiation of operating companies involved. This applies to the case of Bayer HealthCare AG itself, as described above, but also to other – reasonably smaller - companies active in North Rhine-Westphalia, such as Janssen-Cilag GmbH, Grünenthal GmbH or Baxter Deutschland GmbH. In addition, results obviously derive from different approaches. The one relies on regional data from national accounts, while the other calculates results from primary company data.

Ignoring the different levels of GVA, we recognize a similar dynamic when we compare results from the MRHA with Bayer HealthCare AG GVA. Both show peaks in 2008 followed by a decrease in GVA to a reasonable lower level in the period 2009 to 2011 and a further significant drop in 2012. Increase in GVA starts in 2013 according to MRHA results opposed by an increase of Bayer HealthCare AG GVA in 2014. However, both data show a general upward trend in the recent years. We hence conclude that the dynamic of medication supply resulting from the MRHA is reasonable.

In a next step, we look at secondary data we implemented in order to the compile the MRHA. First, we focus on GVA of NACE 21 from official regional accounts (Statistische Ämter des Bundes und der Länder 2016), referring to the pharmaceutical industry Bayer HealthCare AG also belongs to. This data exhibits a clear decrease of GVA for the overall available period of 2008 to 2013 including an instant drop in 2010. Official response to this matter revealed a re-classification of one important player from NACE 21 to NACE 20 in 2010, the latter referring to the chemical industry. Since industry-specific GVA clearly represents essential information applied to the MR-SUT-RAS, we find it convincing regarding the reliability of the approach that we do not observe any similar development from MRHA results. Even more, it is a good indicator of quality that similarities of MRHA results are closer to GVA of Bayer HealthCare AG than to regional accounts.

In a further step, we look at data from regional health expenditure (Ostwald et al. 2017)[11], which is another secondary data source we implemented into the model. With the exemption of 2011 and 2012, expenditures on medication continuously increase. Hence, we do not recognize any implausible direct influence of this closely related and implemented data on the results of the MRHA again.

From subsection 4.4.2 we conclude that the MR-SUT-RAS leads to reasonable results even if we apply it to several years. This applies to Berlin as well as to North Rhine-Westphalia, while the latter offers the great opportunity to match results with available company data.

4.5. Concluding remarks

This chapter aims to challenge results from the MRHA with secondary data in order to conclude on the reliability of the elaborated approach. We find that the compiled figures deliver reasonable results in both evaluated dimensions.

First, we discover that provided economic key figures on the health economy for 2011 reproduce specific characteristics of federal states obtained from independent secondary information. We performed this analysis in the context of medication, since industries involved in production are characterized by a reasonable amount of auxiliary production. Hence, we expect significant differences between given industry-specific and modelled product-specific information. We find that the multiregional supply table obtained from the developed approach exhibits essential characteristics, which allow a federal state specific differentiation between manufacturing, wholesale and R&D in the context of medication. Qualitative secondary data indicate the reliability of derived characteristics.

Second, we applied the model in a time series to examine the performance of the MR-SUT-RAS and its application in the context of health, the

11 The calculation on regional health expenditure was conducted by our project partner BASYS in the course of BMWi (2017b).

MRHA, for different data sets. We perform this application for ten years based on the only two tables of national accounts available for 2010 and 2011. Obtained results show that the model is capable of approximately reproducing specific company data. This comparison is possible due to the fact that the company of concern is responsible for the clear majority of activities in the evaluated federal state. This finding is a convincing argument for the reliability of the developed approach particularly in regard of the fact that generic national tables were not available for all of the considered years.

Hence, despite the absence of official supply and use tables for the German federal states, we managed to challenge product-specific satellite account information of the health economy with secondary data. We find that the elaborated approach to compile the MRHA manages to reproduce certain characteristics of federal states in the context of the health economy not only for one specific year but also in a time series. We hence close this chapter on validation of direct effects in order to look at indirect effects in the next chapter. However, this procedure was essential to conduct in advance, since a valid data base in the context of product-specific output is essential for further input-output analysis.

5. Validation of Indirect Effects of the Health Economy[12]

The Multiregional Health Account is a methodological enhancement of the National Health Account and adds a subnational regional dimension to the latter. Both satellite accounts aim to quantify the contribution of the German health economy in terms of gross value added, employment and trade. Moreover, since they are based on supply and use tables and thus input-output tables of the national accounting system, both models allow input-output analysis for a more thorough evaluation of the national and multiregional health economy. The challenge addressed in this chapter consists in questioning the reliability of the results from multiregional input-output analysis based on the Multiregional Health Account. This is necessary due to the circumstance that no official multiregional input-output tables are available for German federal states and we elaborated a new methodology to derive multiregional tables on our own. Hence, we conduct input-output analysis to evaluate the performance of the multiregional input-output table in modelling intra- and interregional interdependencies. We find that the model succeeds in reproducing certain regional characteristics.

5.1. Introduction

The main database for the subsequent described input-output analysis is the Multiregional Health Account (MRHA), which is a methodological enhancement of the National Health Account (NHA). The latter was developed over years commissioned by the Federal Ministry for Economic Affairs and Energy (e.g. Henke et al. 2010; Ostwald, Henke, et al. 2014; Schneider et al. 2016). The high heterogeneity of categories of the health economy observed during these research activities and from first attempts for an equivalent database on the subnational level (Ostwald, Legler, Schwärzler, Plaul, et al. 2015; Ostwald, Legler, Schwärzler and Tetzner 2015a; Ostwald, Legler, et al. 2014; Ostwald and Schwärzler 2015; Ranscht 2009; AG GGRdL 2016; Schneider 2013; Schneider et al. 2003; Schneider et al. 2000a; Schneider et al. 2000b; Schneider et al. 1998; Schneider et al.

12 This chapter is based on Schwärzler and Kronenberg (2017c).

2002; BASYS and GÖZ 2012) led to this research in the field of the multiregional health economy.

Hence, we pursued to apply the same methodology to compile this satellite account on health, which has been elaborated at the national level, also for the multiregional level for the sake of consistency in methodological terms and results. The main challenge, however, consists in the circumstance that the main database for the compilation, official supply and use tables of the national accounting system, are not available for German federal states. Hence, we developed a new methodology to compile multiregional supply and use tables for this purpose in chapter 3.

Subsequent processing into a satellite account favors analyses regarding the reliability of the approach, since it enables focusing on specific characteristics. We want to point out here that the methodology of the NHA and therefore the MRHA refers to a product-specific approach. The ratio behind this is that we want to quantify the economic contribution of all health care products and services irrespective of questions regarding responsibility in financial terms and the producing industry. Consequently, the direct effects of the health economy in terms of i.e. GVA already refer to modelled information, since only industry-specific information but no product-specific information is available for German federal states in this context. This is the rationale behind the already conducted assessment of direct effects of the MRHA in chapter 4 in order to challenge result calculated (Ostwald et al. 2017).

Hence, this chapter on the assessment of indirect effects of the multiregional health economy is already the second step of the validation procedure, since the assessment on direct effects found that the model succeeds in reproducing certain characteristics of the health economy not only for one year but also in a time series in the preceding chapter 4. Indirect effects are derived from conducting input-output analysis. It captures the complex interdependencies of the economy. Therefore, it is challenging to conduct a reliable validation without having a survey-based multiregional input-output table at hand. This is the rationale for focusing on the main beneficiaries of effects among federal states and industries in this chapter in order to assess the reliability of the approach in the context of intra- and interregional dependencies. The results refer to 2011, since the latest and for the compilation necessary generic supply and use tables at the national level available to us correspond to that year.

The remainder of this chapter is structured as follows. Section 5.2 starts with initiating the results with a general assessment of interregional interdependencies. Subsequently, we focus on indirect output effects of five specific categories of the health economy, which is medication manufacturing, medical products manufacturing, in- and outpatient treatment, organic food supply and health tourism. Section 5.3 summarizes and concludes.

5.2. Indirect output effects of selected categories of the health economy

In this section, we evaluate indirect output effects of the health economy by conducting input-output analysis based on the standard static open model. In order to facilitate an assessment regarding the reasonability of the results, we aim to identify specific characteristics of intra- and interregional contributors in contrast to just name most important beneficiaries of indirect effects in the following subsections.

Indirect effects highly depend on the amount of interregional trade. A high proportion of interregional imports implies lower indirect effects in the federal state of concern, while it results in higher indirect effects for the interregional exporting federal states. The same applies vice versa. For this reason we refer to the following tables, which focus on overall interdependencies of German federal states. They depict modelled direct intra- and interregional dependencies in absolute and relative terms according to the domestic use table.

Table 5: Direct overall interdependencies of German federal states in M. €, 2011

	BW	BY	BE	BB	HB	HH	HE	MV	NI	NW	RP	SL	SN	ST	SH	TH
BW	532.759	53.219	10.126	6.121	2.537	9.780	25.676	2.921	25.451	70.600	10.947	3.196	9.717	5.803	7.196	5.130
BY	51.946	636.125	12.659	7.737	3.161	12.181	32.131	3.703	31.933	87.839	13.884	3.955	12.337	7.361	9.074	6.499
BE	8.348	10.735	111.673	1.249	529	2.138	5.453	616	5.029	13.848	2.226	620	1.927	1.150	1.510	1.002
BB	6.035	7.893	1.609	69.417	392	1.576	3.951	476	3.851	10.621	1.715	474	1.504	908	1.147	788
HB	1.962	2.446	443	272	39.486	433	1.176	128	1.202	3.122	483	146	429	254	319	228
HH	4.995	6.296	1.324	748	339	127.051	3.244	358	2.976	8.205	1.325	374	1.164	688	887	592
HE	18.512	23.948	4.909	2.898	1.237	4.874	269.312	1.386	11.445	32.016	5.142	1.425	4.486	2.674	3.405	2.315
MV	4.040	5.285	1.047	660	260	1.032	2.626	45.209	2.592	6.919	1.137	310	1.005	609	773	532
NI	25.045	32.103	6.149	3.789	1.549	5.997	15.767	1.808	313.645	41.971	6.731	1.895	5.871	3.533	4.450	3.121
NW	60.917	79.010	15.915	9.504	3.965	15.642	39.472	4.544	37.776	763.080	16.906	4.798	14.782	8.814	11.235	7.669
RP	12.477	16.307	3.257	1.980	796	3.183	8.116	949	7.848	22.100	150.371	971	3.062	1.849	2.312	1.611
SL	2.879	3.671	709	435	179	688	1.811	203	1.785	5.099	768	44.863	683	405	509	360
SN	12.079	15.543	3.017	1.826	737	2.923	7.621	875	7.439	20.688	3.276	931	125.719	1.704	2.155	1.501
ST	5.778	7.639	1.514	948	371	1.514	3.856	444	3.702	10.503	1.704	456	1.426	69.304	1.107	758
SH	7.954	10.322	2.043	1.265	515	2.051	5.116	608	4.975	13.574	2.193	606	1.926	1.166	91.643	1.010
TH	5.938	7.754	1.516	931	370	1.474	3.845	445	3.733	10.514	1.676	465	1.435	869	1.098	62.949

Source: own calculations.

Table 6: Direct overall interdependencies of German federal states in percentage shares, 2011

	BW	BY	BE	BB	HB	HH	HE	MV	NI	NW	RP	SL	SN	ST	SH	TH
BW	0,68	0,07	0,01	0,01	0,00	0,01	0,03	0,00	0,03	0,09	0,01	0,00	0,01	0,01	0,01	0,01
BY	0,06	0,68	0,01	0,01	0,00	0,01	0,03	0,00	0,03	0,09	0,01	0,00	0,01	0,01	0,01	0,01
BE	0,05	0,06	0,66	0,01	0,00	0,01	0,03	0,00	0,03	0,08	0,01	0,00	0,01	0,01	0,01	0,01
BB	0,05	0,07	0,01	0,62	0,00	0,01	0,04	0,00	0,03	0,09	0,02	0,00	0,01	0,01	0,01	0,01
HB	0,04	0,05	0,01	0,01	0,75	0,01	0,02	0,00	0,02	0,06	0,01	0,00	0,01	0,00	0,01	0,00
HH	0,03	0,04	0,01	0,00	0,00	0,79	0,02	0,00	0,02	0,05	0,01	0,00	0,01	0,00	0,01	0,00
HE	0,05	0,06	0,01	0,01	0,00	0,01	0,69	0,00	0,03	0,08	0,01	0,00	0,01	0,01	0,01	0,01
MV	0,05	0,07	0,01	0,01	0,00	0,01	0,04	0,61	0,04	0,09	0,02	0,00	0,01	0,01	0,01	0,01
NI	0,05	0,07	0,01	0,01	0,00	0,01	0,03	0,00	0,66	0,09	0,01	0,00	0,01	0,01	0,01	0,01
NW	0,06	0,07	0,01	0,01	0,00	0,01	0,04	0,00	0,03	0,70	0,02	0,00	0,01	0,01	0,01	0,01
RP	0,05	0,07	0,01	0,01	0,00	0,01	0,03	0,00	0,03	0,09	0,03	0,00	0,01	0,01	0,01	0,01
SL	0,04	0,06	0,01	0,01	0,00	0,01	0,03	0,00	0,03	0,08	0,01	0,69	0,01	0,01	0,01	0,01
SN	0,06	0,07	0,01	0,01	0,00	0,01	0,04	0,00	0,04	0,10	0,02	0,00	0,60	0,01	0,01	0,01
ST	0,05	0,07	0,01	0,01	0,00	0,01	0,03	0,00	0,03	0,09	0,02	0,00	0,01	0,62	0,01	0,01
SH	0,05	0,07	0,01	0,01	0,00	0,01	0,03	0,00	0,03	0,09	0,01	0,00	0,01	0,01	0,62	0,01
TH	0,06	0,07	0,01	0,01	0,00	0,01	0,04	0,00	0,04	0,10	0,02	0,00	0,01	0,01	0,01	0,60

Source: own calculations.

The diagonal elements reveal intraregional trade flows, while off-diagonal elements provide information on the interregional export and import of the overall economy. Each row of 5.2

Table 6 sums up to 100 percent since every single cell represents the percentage share of output it obtains from the supplying federal state. We provide this information over here in order to facilitate an initial assessment of interregional dependencies and to challenge these results with different models in the context of multiregional supply and use tables of German federal states.

In order to conduct input-output analysis, we calculated a multiregional input-output table from the compiled satellite account comprising of multiregional supply and use tables. We applied the commodity technology in this case for the sake of consistency with the official input-output table of Germany (Destatis 2010), according to Miller and Blair (2009)

$$Z = U * V'^{-1} * \hat{x} \tag{35}$$

with Z corresponding to the final entries of the input-output table, V and U referring to the supply and use table and $\hat{x}$ representing the diagonal matrix of product-specific total output. We take into account resulting negative values in the input-output table. Schwärzler and Kronenberg (2016) provide a detailed description on the procedure.

The resulting multiregional input-output table exhibits interdependencies of the 16 federal states for non-health and health-related categories. Non-health categories refer to the 63 industries of the official national supply and use tables, of which output and intermediate use of health-related products were subtracted. Categories of health refer to the established definition provided in Table 1 of chapter 2, but can be further differentiated for the sake of enabling certain analyses. This implies that the results provided in the following subsections cannot be directly compared to official ones, since we conduct our calculations based on a health-input-output table with categories deviating from known CPA/NACE categories.

Indirect output effects are calculated according to the Leontief inverse (Miller and Blair 2009):

$$x = (I - A)^{-1} \tag{36}$$

where x corresponds to output and A to the technology matrix, the entries of the latter defined by

$$a_{ij} = \frac{z_{ij}}{x_j} \tag{37}$$

where z_{ij} refers to direct input of product i to industry j.

5.2.1. Indirect effects of medication manufacturing in German federal states in 2011

In this subsection, we evaluate the indirect output effects from medication manufacturing. The national multiplier from the NHA is 1.48, which can be obtained from Figure 40. This category is closest to pharmaceutical products (CPA 21) in terms of its composition of products. Official data shows a multiplier of 1.38 for this category (Destatis 2015).

Figure 39: Indirect output multipliers of medication manufacturing, 2011 (1/2)

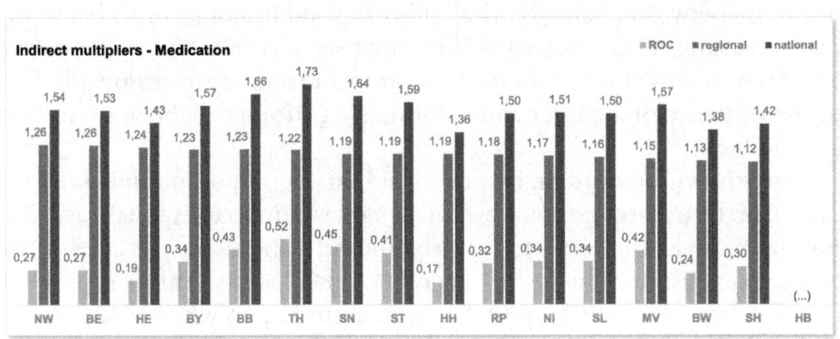

(...) output value too low for reasonable interpretation

Source: own calculations.

As in most cases, North Rhine-Westphalia shows the highest regional multiplier among federal states. This is reasonable since North Rhine-Westphalia is the biggest federal state of Germany in terms of GDP and exhibits a corresponding high diversification of economic activities. In general, industries affected by indirect effects are different regarding the initial impulse. However, some industries show a general high influence, which is energy in the case of North Rhine-Westphalia. This is reasonable, since this federal state supplies one third of overall German energy output (Umweltministerium NRW 2014). In the special case of medication manufacturing, which is the focus of this subsection, an above-average amount of indirect effects also arises from wholesale trade of medication and manufacturing of chemical products. Especially the last fact is not surprising, since the chemical industry of North Rhine-Westphalia generates about one third of overall German sales in this context and looks back at a long and successful history in a close relationship to the coal and steel industry in earlier days (Chemieatlas 2017).

It is quite different in the case of Berlin, which exhibits an indirect regional multiplier of the same amount. This is very special for this city state, since it shows considerably lower multipliers in the context of other categories. Hence, manufacturing of medication is a special case for Berlin. In particular, this is caused by high indirect effects in public administration, consulting services for health facilities and medication manufacturing itself. The first fact is reasonable, since Berlin is the capital city of Germany and consequently shows above-average activities in public administration. Moreover, nine out of the ten leading auditing and tax consultancy companies of Germany (Lünendonk 2016) have branches in Berlin. A close cooperation between pharmaceutical industries and health facilities hence explain resulting effects on related consulting services (Health Capital 2014). Moreover, the high effect on medication manufacturing is reasonable due to the existence of a cluster and accordingly a strong collaboration in this area (idibem).

Hesse shows the third highest regional indirect output multiplier in this case. Due to its strong economy, this is no extraordinary special case. Air transport services contribute to a significantly above-average amount to this characteristic, compared to the other federal states. This is supported by the airport company Fraport AG itself, according to which a vast majority of chemical and pharmaceutical companies could not exist without their closeness to the airport (Fraport AG 2017b). This is mostly due to 7,000 m^2 of space for ground handling operations exclusively for pharmaceutical products (Fraport AG 2017a).

In addition, financial services are a main promoter of indirect effects. This is again reasonable, since the city Frankfurt in Hesse is the most important financial center in Germany due to an agglomeration of important players, the European Central bank, the German Central Bank and the German Stock Exchange among them (Burkert and Garloff 2013). Since manufacturing of medication is of above-average importance for the economy in Hesse, it is plausible that there is an above-average indirect output effect on this category as well. The low rest-of-country (ROC) multiplier of Hesse is remarkable, since it indicates a relatively low dependency on other federal states in the case of medication manufacturing.

From Figure 39 we can also obtain the highest national multiplier for Thuringia, promoted by an accompanying high ROC multiplier. This circumstance mostly derives from an above-average dependency concerning chemical products and wholesale trade of medication manufacturing in this federal state.

Figure 40: Indirect output multipliers of medication manufacturing, 2011 (2/2)

1.48	BW	BY	BE	BB	HB	HH	HE	MV	NI	NW	RP	SL	SN	ST	SH	TH
BW	1.13	0.04	0.01	0.01	0.00	0.01	0.03	0.00	0.02	0.07	0.01	0.00	0.01	0.01	0.01	0.00
BY	0.05	1.23	0.02	0.01	0.00	0.02	0.05	0.00	0.03	0.11	0.02	0.00	0.01	0.01	0.01	0.01
BE	0.03	0.05	1.26	0.01	0.00	0.01	0.04	0.00	0.02	0.07	0.01	0.00	0.01	0.00	0.01	0.00
BB	0.05	0.07	0.02	1.23	0.00	0.02	0.04	0.00	0.04	0.12	0.02	0.00	0.02	0.01	0.01	0.01
HB	...	...	...	...	...	...	...	...	...	...	...	...	...	...	...	...
HH	0.02	0.03	0.01	0.00	0.00	1.19	0.02	0.00	0.01	0.05	0.01	0.00	0.01	0.00	0.00	0.00
HE	0.03	0.04	0.01	0.00	0.00	0.01	1.24	0.00	0.02	0.06	0.01	0.00	0.01	0.00	0.00	0.00
MV	0.05	0.07	0.02	0.01	0.00	0.02	0.05	1.15	0.03	0.11	0.02	0.00	0.01	0.01	0.01	0.01
NI	0.04	0.06	0.02	0.01	0.00	0.02	0.05	0.00	1.17	0.10	0.02	0.00	0.01	0.01	0.01	0.01
NW	0.04	0.06	0.02	0.01	0.00	0.02	0.05	0.00	0.03	1.26	0.02	0.00	0.01	0.01	0.01	0.01
RP	0.04	0.05	0.02	0.01	0.00	0.01	0.04	0.00	0.02	0.09	1.18	0.00	0.01	0.01	0.01	0.01
SL	0.04	0.06	0.01	0.01	0.00	0.01	0.04	0.00	0.03	0.09	0.01	1.16	0.01	0.01	0.01	0.01
SN	0.05	0.07	0.02	0.01	0.00	0.02	0.06	0.00	0.03	0.12	0.02	0.00	1.19	0.01	0.01	0.01
ST	0.05	0.07	0.02	0.01	0.00	0.02	0.05	0.00	0.03	0.11	0.02	0.00	0.01	1.19	0.01	0.01
SH	0.04	0.05	0.01	0.01	0.00	0.01	0.04	0.00	0.02	0.08	0.01	0.00	0.01	0.01	1.12	0.00
TH	0.06	0.08	0.02	0.01	0.00	0.02	0.06	0.00	0.04	0.14	0.03	0.00	0.02	0.01	0.01	1.22

■ national multiplier ■ top 5 regional indirect output multipliers (...) output value too low for reasonable interpretation

Source: own calculations.

We do not want to focus on multipliers exclusively, since it ignores the relative importance of absolute indirect effects for the economy in consideration. Hence, we calculated the share of absolute indirect effects, shown in Figure 41, on the corresponding overall output of the economy in consideration. We highlight calculated above-average values in order to combine information of absolute values and corresponding relevance.

A high relevance of regional indirect effects from own output is indicated by a red frame in Figure 41, pointing towards Baden-Württemberg, Hesse, North Rhine-Westphalia Rhineland-Palatinate and Saxony-Anhalt in this case. This is mostly due to the above-average relevance of medication manufacturing in these federal states. The only exception to this circumstance is North Rhine-Westphalia. However, it is the corresponding high regional multiplier, which results in an above-average relevance of regional indirect effects in North Rhine-Westphalia.

Figure 41: Indirect output effects of medication manufacturing, 2011

	BW	BY	BE	BB	HB	HH	HE	MV	NI	NW	RP	SL	SN	ST	SH	TH
BW	996	334	85	43	21	85	243	18	158	536	89	20	69	40	47	34
BY	128	617	50	21	10	46	141	9	79	294	48	10	36	21	23	17
BE	23	31	173	3	2	8	27	2	13	50	8	2	6	3	4	3
BB	23	33	7	100	2	8	19	2	16	51	9	2	7	4	5	4
HB	...	...	...	...	...	...	...	...	...	...	...	...	...	...	...	...
HH	6	8	3	1	0	53	7	0	4	13	2	0	2	1	1	1
HE	178	243	73	28	14	63	1,670	12	108	396	63	14	49	27	32	23
MV	4	5	1	1	0	1	4	11	2	8	1	0	1	1	1	0
NI	52	73	20	9	4	19	57	4	214	123	20	4	15	9	10	7
NW	214	294	86	35	17	76	242	15	131	1,298	79	17	59	33	39	28
RP	62	86	25	10	5	22	71	4	38	143	293	5	17	10	11	8
SL	2	3	1	0	0	1	2	0	2	5	1	10	1	0	1	0
SN	38	53	16	6	3	14	43	3	23	88	14	3	133	6	7	5
ST	56	78	22	9	4	20	63	4	35	130	21	4	16	219	10	7
SH	24	33	10	4	2	9	28	2	15	54	8	2	7	4	85	3
TH	20	29	7	4	2	7	19	2	13	49	9	2	6	4	4	75

indicating direct relationship; top 5 most affected regions by indirect effects from own output

top 3 most affected regions by indirect effects from federal state in y-axis

(...) output value too low for reasonable interpretation

Source: own calculations.

A high relevance of regional indirect output effects from output of other federal states is indicated by a blue filling in Figure 41. Accordingly, the overall economies of Berlin, Hamburg, Hesse and North Rhine-Westphalia profit the most from medication manufacturing in other federal states. Berlin profits in an extraordinary way from high indirect effects contributed by public administration, while Hamburg benefits in terms of refined petroleum products due to their high importance for this federal state (Statistisches Amt für Hamburg und Schleswig-Holstein 2016) and the fact that respective refineries are at the start of industrial value-added chains (Mineralölwirtschaftsverband e.V. 2015). Large indirect effects arise in medication manufacturing in Hesse, while wholesale trade and manufacturing of chemical products in North Rhine-Westphalia profit in an extraordinary way from medication manufacturing in other federal states.

5.2.2. Indirect effects of medical products manufacturing in German federal states in 2011

The category of medical products refers to products mostly from CPA 26 and CPA 31-32, which is 'Computer, electronic and optical products' and 'Manufacture of furniture; other manufacturing'. The national indirect output multiplier of medical products manufacturing is 1.65. The corresponding multipliers from related CPAs are 1.62 and 1.66 according to official data (Destatis 2015).

In the case of medical products manufacturing, North Rhine-Westphalia again exhibits the highest regional indirect output multiplier among federal states. Next to chemical products, wholesale trade and energy, manufacturing of basic metals and fabricated metal products profit from this activity in North Rhine-Westphalia. This is reasonable, since North Rhine-Westphalia supplies about 38 percent of overall German steel and employs about 56 percent of corresponding employees. (Wirtschaftsministerum NRW, IG Metall and Wirtschaftsvereinigung Stahl 2015).

The previous paragraph already indicates certain differences between medication and medical products. In the following, we will obtain the high diversification of medical products even more when we look at the characteristics of indirect effects. Hence, it is useful to recall the product range of this category involving large medical equipment, wheelchairs, visual aids, human medicine instruments and dental products among other things.

Figure 42: Indirect output multipliers of medical products manufacturing, 2011 (1/2)

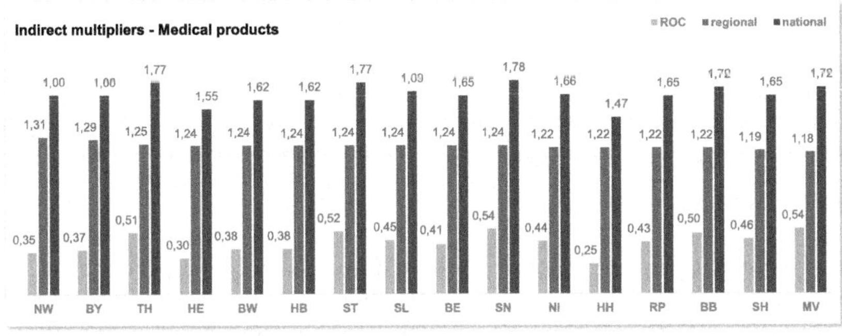

Source: own calculations.

Hence, manufacturing of medical products causes indirect effects on a highly differentiated product range, especially such as computer, electronic and optical products in Bavaria and products of wood, cork, rubber, plastic and fabricated metal in Thuringia. Moreover, it shows a strong reciprocal relationship, since it causes again high indirect effects on medical products in Bavaria, Thuringia and Baden-Württemberg. The latter federal state is especially interesting in this case, since it shows relatively low regional multipliers in general due to a strong international orientation. However, large indirect effects in computer, machinery, electronic and optical products cause this significant high regional multiplier in Baden-Württemberg. Reality supports the depicted high effects on the regional economy, since activities in that field nearly cover the overall product range of medical products and are characterized by close collaborations with practice-oriented research facilities (Baden-Württemberg International 2017).

Figure 43: Indirect output multipliers of medical products manufacturing, 2011 (2/2)

1.65	BW	BY	BE	BB	HB	HH	HE	MV	NI	NW	RP	SL	SN	ST	SH	TH
BW	1.24	0.08	0.01	0.01	0.00	0.02	0.04	0.00	0.03	0.11	0.02	0.00	0.01	0.01	0.01	0.01
BY	0.06	1.29	0.02	0.01	0.00	0.02	0.04	0.00	0.03	0.12	0.02	0.00	0.02	0.01	0.01	0.01
BE	0.06	0.08	1.24	0.01	0.00	0.02	0.04	0.00	0.03	0.11	0.02	0.00	0.01	0.01	0.01	0.01
BB	0.07	0.09	0.02	1.22	0.00	0.02	0.05	0.00	0.04	0.13	0.02	0.01	0.02	0.01	0.01	0.01
HB	0.04	0.06	0.01	0.01	1.20	0.01	0.03	0.00	0.03	0.09	0.01	0.00	0.01	0.01	0.01	0.01
HH	0.04	0.05	0.01	0.00	0.00	1.22	0.03	0.00	0.02	0.07	0.01	0.00	0.01	0.00	0.01	0.00
HE	0.04	0.06	0.01	0.01	0.00	0.01	1.24	0.00	0.03	0.09	0.01	0.00	0.01	0.01	0.01	0.01
MV	0.07	0.10	0.02	0.01	0.00	0.02	0.05	1.18	0.04	0.14	0.02	0.01	0.02	0.01	0.01	0.01
NI	0.06	0.09	0.02	0.01	0.00	0.02	0.05	0.00	1.22	0.12	0.02	0.01	0.02	0.01	0.01	0.01
NW	0.06	0.09	0.02	0.01	0.00	0.02	0.05	0.00	0.04	1.31	0.02	0.01	0.02	0.01	0.01	0.01
RP	0.06	0.08	0.02	0.01	0.00	0.02	0.04	0.00	0.03	0.12	1.22	0.00	0.02	0.01	0.01	0.01
SL	0.06	0.08	0.01	0.01	0.00	0.02	0.04	0.00	0.03	0.12	0.02	1.24	0.02	0.01	0.01	0.01
SN	0.08	0.10	0.02	0.01	0.00	0.02	0.05	0.00	0.04	0.15	0.02	0.01	1.24	0.01	0.01	0.01
ST	0.07	0.10	0.02	0.01	0.00	0.02	0.05	0.00	0.04	0.14	0.02	0.01	0.02	1.24	0.01	0.01
SH	0.06	0.09	0.02	0.01	0.00	0.02	0.05	0.00	0.04	0.12	0.02	0.01	0.02	0.01	1.19	0.01
TH	0.07	0.10	0.02	0.01	0.00	0.02	0.05	0.00	0.04	0.14	0.02	0.01	0.02	0.01	0.01	1.25

■ national multiplier ■ top 5 regional indirect output multipliers (...) output value too low for reasonable interpretation

Source: own calculations.

The highest ROC multipliers from manufacturing medical products occur in Saxony and Mecklenburg-Western Pomerania. The first is highly dependent on metal products and electrical equipment from North Rhine-Westphalia, next to medical products from Bavaria. Mecklenburg-Western Pomerania also exhibits a high dependence on medical products from

Bavaria, next to extraordinary high indirect output effects in rental and leasing services in North Rhine-Westphalia.

The five most affected regions by absolute indirect output effects from own supply are Baden-Württemberg, Bavaria, Hamburg, Schleswig-Holstein and Thuringia. All show above average relevance of medical products for the economies in consideration.

Figure 44: Indirect output effects of medical products manufacturing, 2011

	BW	BY	BE	BB	HB	HH	HE	MV	NI	NW	RP	SL	SN	ST	SH	TH
BW	1,244	414	74	44	21	79	211	20	168	580	87	25	76	45	51	43
BY	435	2,088	108	64	30	116	308	29	246	840	127	36	110	66	75	63
BE	58	80	239	8	4	15	43	4	32	109	16	5	14	8	10	8
BB	29	40	7	93	2	8	21	2	17	58	9	2	8	5	5	4
HB	6	9	2	1	29	2	4	0	4	12	2	1	2	1	1	1
HH	45	03	12	8	3	278	32	3	24	82	12	3	11	6	8	6
HE	106	147	28	16	7	30	579	7	60	204	31	8	27	16	18	15
MV	22	31	6	3	1	6	16	52	12	40	6	2	5	3	4	3
NI	89	122	22	13	6	24	64	6	310	171	26	7	22	13	15	13
NW	279	383	70	42	19	76	201	19	158	1,389	83	23	71	42	48	41
RP	48	67	13	7	3	14	37	3	28	96	179	4	12	7	9	7
SL	14	20	4	2	1	4	10	1	8	28	4	57	4	2	2	2
SN	64	88	16	9	4	17	45	4	35	125	19	5	204	9	11	9
ST	28	39	7	4	2	8	21	2	16	55	9	2	7	97	5	4
SH	70	97	17	10	5	19	50	5	39	134	20	6	17	10	216	10
TH	45	63	11	7	3	12	32	3	26	89	14	4	11	7	8	166

indicating direct relationship; top 5 most affected regions by indirect effects from own output

top 3 most affected regions by indirect effects from federal state in y-axis

Source: own calculations.

The federal states Bavaria, Hesse, North Rhine-Westphalia and Thuringia profit the most from indirect effects caused by medical products manufactured in other federal states. Referring industries are computer, electronic, optical and medical products in Bavaria, financial and airport transport services in Hesse, basic metal in North Rhine-Westphalia and medical, rubber, plastic, fabricated metal and wood products in Thuringia. Especially the last federal state shows specifies in this category, since it does not reveal the same economic diversification as the other named regions. However, medical products are indeed a special field in Thuringia, due to clusters consisting of innovative companies and research facilities (Thüringen innovativ 2006). Moreover, the demonstrated high relevance of Bavaria is not surprising in this context, since activities in this area are perceived as extraordinary important drivers for innovation and economic growth. Moreover, they generate significant effects for supplier industries in this federal state (Forum MedTech Pharma e.V. 2015).

5.2.3. Indirect effects of in- and outpatient treatment in German federal states in 2011

The closest related category of inpatient and outpatient treatment corresponds to 'Human health services' (CPA 86). Official data exhibits an indirect output multiplier of 1.40 for this category (Destatis 2015). The national multiplier of inpatient and outpatient treatment according to the NHA is 1.41, which can be obtained from Figure 46.

The highest regional indirect output multiplier from inpatient and outpatient treatment occurs in North Rhine-Westphalia. Among others, already described general contributing industries, an extraordinary amount of indirect output effects emerge in retail trade with medical products, related collaborating health service facilities and wholesale trade with medical products and medication.

Figure 45: Indirect output multipliers of inpatient and outpatient treatment, 2011 (1/2)

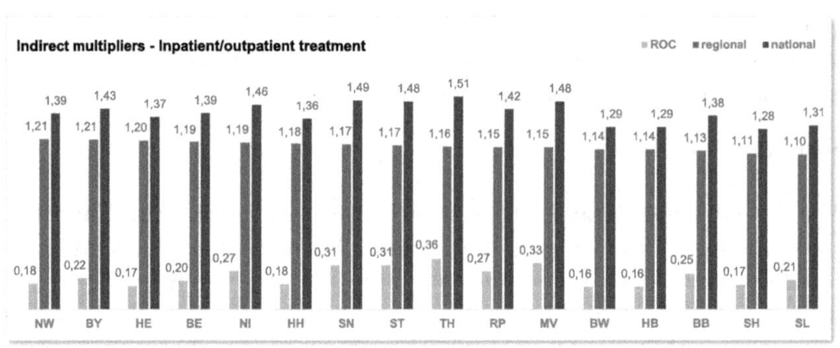

Source: own calculations.

In Bavaria, manufacturing, related health service facilities and trade services of medical products are in an extraordinary way responsible for the high regional indirect output multiplier. Medication manufacturing and health care facilities contribute largely to the high regional multiplier in Hesse.

Figure 46: Indirect output multipliers of inpatient and outpatient treatment, 2011 (2/2)

1.41	BW	BY	BE	BB	HB	HH	HE	MV	NI	NW	RP	SL	SN	ST	SH	TH
BW	1.14	0.03	0.01	0.00	0.00	0.01	0.02	0.00	0.01	0.05	0.01	0.00	0.01	0.00	0.00	0.00
BY	0.03	1.21	0.01	0.01	0.00	0.01	0.03	0.00	0.02	0.07	0.01	0.00	0.01	0.01	0.01	0.00
BE	0.03	0.04	1.19	0.00	0.00	0.01	0.02	0.00	0.02	0.05	0.01	0.00	0.01	0.00	0.01	0.00
BB	0.03	0.04	0.01	1.13	0.00	0.01	0.03	0.00	0.02	0.07	0.01	0.00	0.01	0.00	0.01	0.00
HB	0.02	0.03	0.01	0.00	1.11	0.01	0.02	0.00	0.01	0.05	0.01	0.00	0.01	0.00	0.00	0.00
HH	0.02	0.03	0.01	0.00	0.00	1.18	0.02	0.00	0.01	0.05	0.01	0.00	0.01	0.00	0.00	0.00
HE	0.02	0.03	0.01	0.00	0.00	0.01	1.20	0.00	0.01	0.05	0.01	0.00	0.01	0.00	0.00	0.00
MV	0.04	0.06	0.01	0.01	0.00	0.01	0.04	1.15	0.03	0.08	0.01	0.00	0.01	0.01	0.01	0.01
NI	0.04	0.05	0.01	0.01	0.00	0.01	0.03	0.00	1.19	0.08	0.01	0.00	0.01	0.01	0.01	0.00
NW	0.03	0.04	0.01	0.00	0.00	0.01	0.03	0.00	0.02	1.21	0.01	0.00	0.01	0.00	0.01	0.00
RP	0.04	0.05	0.01	0.01	0.00	0.01	0.03	0.00	0.02	0.07	1.15	0.00	0.01	0.01	0.01	0.00
SL	0.03	0.04	0.01	0.00	0.00	0.01	0.02	0.00	0.02	0.05	0.01	1.10	0.01	0.00	0.01	0.00
SN	0.04	0.06	0.01	0.01	0.00	0.01	0.04	0.00	0.03	0.08	0.01	0.00	1.17	0.01	0.01	0.01
ST	0.04	0.06	0.01	0.01	0.00	0.01	0.04	0.00	0.03	0.08	0.01	0.00	0.01	1.17	0.01	0.00
SH	0.02	0.03	0.01	0.00	0.00	0.01	0.02	0.00	0.01	0.05	0.01	0.00	0.01	0.00	1.11	0.00
TH	0.05	0.06	0.02	0.01	0.00	0.01	0.04	0.00	0.03	0.09	0.01	0.00	0.01	0.01	0.01	1.16

■ national multiplier ■ top 5 regional indirect output multipliers (...) output value too low for reasonable interpretation

Source: own calculations.

Thuringia is most dependent on the rest of the country when it comes to indirect output effects, indicated by the highest ROC multiplier. Unlike manufacturing industries, supply of inpatient and outpatient health care does not require specific intermediate consumption in regard of the federal state in consideration. Hence, the composition of national indirect output effects of inpatient and outpatient service does not vary among federal state to a great amount. The ROC multiplier behaves similarly for the same reason. Therefore, we cannot distinguish any specific characteristic for Thuringia. The most driving forces however, but not exclusively for Thuringia, are supply of energy, food products, imputed rents including owner-occupied dwellings and construction of health care facilities.

The top five most affected regions by indirect effects from own output are Berlin, Mecklenburg-Western Pomerania, North Rhine-Westphalia, Saxony and Thuringia. All these regions show an above-average importance of inpatient and outpatient treatment for their economy.

Figure 47: Indirect output effects of inpatient and outpatient treatment, 2011

	BW	BY	BE	BB	HB	HH	HE	MV	NI	NW	RP	SL	SN	ST	SH	TH
BW	3,765	889	215	97	43	179	555	51	399	1,288	184	49	165	95	126	79
BY	1,182	7,085	392	178	79	327	1,015	93	732	2,358	337	89	302	174	230	145
BE	263	363	1,879	39	17	72	231	20	160	528	74	20	66	38	50	32
BB	166	229	55	639	11	45	144	13	102	333	47	12	42	24	32	20
HB	47	65	16	7	222	13	41	4	29	95	13	4	12	7	9	6
HH	135	186	46	20	9	1,008	117	11	83	269	38	10	34	20	26	16
HE	382	525	128	57	26	107	3,186	30	235	763	109	29	97	56	74	47
MV	171	237	57	26	11	47	148	620	106	342	48	13	44	25	33	21
NI	777	1,074	258	116	51	213	673	61	3,843	1,556	221	58	198	115	152	95
NW	1,557	2,144	519	233	106	432	1,349	122	960	10,500	440	117	396	228	302	189
RP	344	475	115	51	22	94	300	27	212	691	1,477	26	87	50	67	42
SL	72	99	24	11	5	20	62	6	44	144	20	270	18	11	14	9
SN	407	561	134	61	27	110	351	32	251	817	116	31	1,712	60	79	50
ST	223	308	74	33	15	60	193	17	138	448	64	17	57	907	43	27
SH	163	224	54	24	11	45	140	13	101	325	46	12	42	24	756	20
TH	249	345	82	37	16	67	216	19	154	501	71	19	63	37	48	842

indicating direct relationship; top 5 most affected regions by indirect effects from own output

top 3 most affected regions by indirect effects from federal state in y-axis

Source: own calculations.

Economies of Bavaria, Berlin, Hesse and North Rhine-Westphalia are most affected by indirect output effects from inpatient and outpatient treatment in other federal states. This is reasonable, since all these federal states exhibit extraordinary characteristics in certain activities regarding manufacturing and trade services of medical products and medication. In Bavaria this applies to medical products, while it is medication in the case of Berlin and Hesse. In North Rhine-Westphalia, wholesale of both, medication and medical products, profit in an above-average way from inpatient and outpatient treatment of other federal states.

5.2.4. Indirect effects of organic food supply in German federal states in 2011

Organic food supply consists of selected categories of 'Products of agriculture, hunting and related services' (CPA 01) and 'Food products, beverages and tobacco products' (CPA 10-12). Corresponding indirect output multipliers from official data are 1.86 and 1.11 (Destatis 2015). The national multiplier of organic food supply according to the NHA can be obtained from Figure 49, referring to 1.99.

In this subsection, we focus on indirect output effects from organic food supply of German federal states in 2011. We chose this category, since it provides another and quite different area compared to what has been evaluated in this section so far. Moreover, evidence shows that domestic effects from agri-food production are high even for industrialized countries (Semerák et al. 2010). Hence, we find it interesting to take a closer look at this often underestimated part of the economy in the present multiregional context.

Figure 48: Indirect output multipliers of organic food supply, 2011 (1/2)

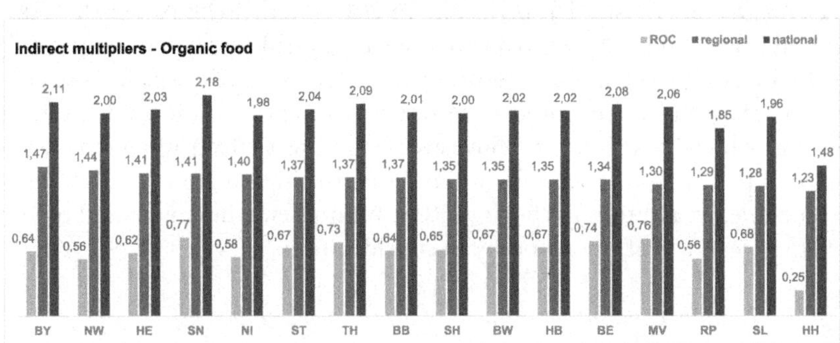

Source: own calculations.

The highest regional indirect output multiplier can be observed in Bavaria, showing specific characteristics regarding high amounts of indirect output in products of agriculture, food and machinery. This is not surprising, since Bavaria exhibits the highest absolute area of both, agricultural land and organic farming (Hemmerling et al. 2013). The growing relevance of machinery in agriculture favors the production of corresponding products. In addition to a general high importance of machinery in Bavaria, important manufacturers of harvesting machines are based in this federal state, Fendt® (AGCO GmbH 2017) and CLAAS KGaA mbH (CLAAS KGaA mbH 2017) among them.

North Rhine-Westphalia, second in the ranking of regional indirect output multipliers, shows no characteristics exclusively specific to organic food supply. In fact, the general high contribution of energy and wholesale trade are the usual industries, which show above-average relevance compared to other federal states.

In the case of Hesse, rental and leasing services next to advertising and market research activities show extraordinary high contributions in this special case. The latter fact may seem surprising at first but becomes reasonable when considering the rising attention and efforts to market especially organic food (Zühlsdorf and Spiller 2012).

Saxony exhibits the highest ROC multiplier. This circumstance is very interesting, since this federal state also shows a reasonable high regional multiplier. Supply of organic food is above-average characterized by high indirect effects on agriculture over there. This circumstance is supported by Semerák et al. (2010), who find a high importance of indirect effect from agri-food production especially for remote regions. This explanation is supported by the fact of Saxony being among the five German federal states with the lowest GDP per capita in 2011 (Statistische Ämter des Bundes und der Länder 2016). However, Saxony is still by far the biggest federal state among these five in terms of GDP. Moreover, organic food supply is characterized by food processing rather than agricultural production in Saxony, which in turn favors above-average indirect effects in regional agricultural production. Therefore, we find that the high regional multiplier is reasonable, in addition to the high ROC multiplier, which is caused by the relative weakness of the economy in consideration.

Figure 49: Indirect output multipliers of organic food supply, 2011 (2/2)

1.99	BW	BY	BE	BB	HB	HH	HE	MV	NI	NW	RP	SL	SN	ST	SH	TH
BW	1.35	0.14	0.02	0.02	0.01	0.03	0.07	0.01	0.08	0.18	0.03	0.01	0.03	0.02	0.03	0.02
BY	0.09	1.47	0.02	0.02	0.01	0.03	0.07	0.01	0.08	0.18	0.03	0.01	0.03	0.02	0.03	0.02
BE	0.09	0.14	1.34	0.02	0.01	0.03	0.06	0.01	0.08	0.17	0.03	0.01	0.03	0.02	0.03	0.02
BB	0.08	0.12	0.02	1.37	0.01	0.03	0.06	0.01	0.07	0.16	0.03	0.01	0.02	0.01	0.02	0.01
HB	0.04	0.06	0.01	0.01	1.21	0.01	0.03	0.00	0.03	0.07	0.01	0.00	0.01	0.01	0.01	0.01
HH	0.03	0.05	0.01	0.01	0.00	1.23	0.02	0.00	0.03	0.06	0.01	0.00	0.01	0.01	0.01	0.01
HE	0.08	0.12	0.02	0.02	0.01	0.03	1.41	0.01	0.07	0.16	0.03	0.01	0.03	0.02	0.02	0.01
MV	0.09	0.14	0.02	0.02	0.01	0.03	0.07	1.30	0.08	0.18	0.03	0.01	0.03	0.02	0.03	0.02
NI	0.08	0.11	0.02	0.02	0.01	0.03	0.06	0.01	1.40	0.16	0.03	0.01	0.02	0.01	0.02	0.01
NW	0.09	0.13	0.02	0.02	0.01	0.03	0.06	0.01	0.08	1.44	0.03	0.01	0.03	0.02	0.02	0.01
RP	0.07	0.10	0.02	0.02	0.01	0.02	0.05	0.01	0.06	0.14	1.29	0.01	0.02	0.01	0.02	0.01
SL	0.08	0.12	0.02	0.02	0.01	0.03	0.06	0.01	0.07	0.16	0.03	1.28	0.03	0.02	0.02	0.01
SN	0.09	0.14	0.02	0.02	0.01	0.03	0.07	0.01	0.09	0.19	0.03	0.01	1.41	0.02	0.03	0.02
ST	0.08	0.12	0.02	0.02	0.01	0.03	0.06	0.01	0.07	0.16	0.03	0.01	0.03	1.37	0.02	0.01
SH	0.08	0.12	0.02	0.02	0.01	0.03	0.06	0.01	0.06	0.16	0.03	0.01	0.02	0.01	1.35	0.01
TH	0.09	0.13	0.02	0.02	0.01	0.03	0.06	0.01	0.08	0.18	0.03	0.01	0.03	0.02	0.02	1.37

■ national multiplier ■ top 5 regional indirect output multipliers (...) output value too low for reasonable interpretation

Source: own calculations.

Indirect effects from own output are of highest importance for the economies of Bavaria, Brandenburg, Mecklenburg-Western Pomerania, Lower-Saxony and Schleswig-Holstein, which all show reasonable above-average relevance of organic food supply.

Figure 50: Indirect output effects of organic food supply, 2011

	BW	BY	BE	BB	HB	HH	HE	MV	NI	NW	RP	SL	SN	ST	SH	TH
BW	799	316	52	51	17	66	150	18	186	412	70	16	68	41	58	36
BY	239	1,230	61	57	19	77	174	21	211	479	82	19	77	47	66	40
BE	14	22	53	4	1	4	10	1	13	27	4	1	5	3	4	3
BB	30	44	8	140	2	10	22	3	25	60	10	2	9	6	8	5
HB	4	6	1	1	20	1	3	0	3	7	1	0	1	1	1	1
HH	7	12	2	2	1	57	5	1	7	15	2	1	3	1	2	1
HE	56	85	14	13	5	18	287	5	50	111	19	4	18	11	15	10
MV	54	82	14	13	4	17	39	176	48	107	18	4	18	11	15	9
NI	142	207	36	31	11	47	105	12	727	287	50	11	43	27	37	22
NW	156	236	40	37	13	50	114	14	138	794	53	12	50	30	43	26
RP	57	85	15	13	5	18	42	5	49	114	238	4	18	11	15	9
SL	7	11	2	2	1	2	5	1	6	14	2	24	2	1	2	1
SN	36	55	9	9	3	11	26	3	32	72	12	3	154	7	10	6
ST	18	27	5	4	1	6	13	2	16	36	6	1	6	83	5	3
SH	53	75	14	11	4	18	39	4	42	107	19	4	15	10	228	8
TH	17	25	4	4	1	5	12	1	15	34	6	1	5	3	5	71

indicating direct relationship · top 5 most affected regions by indirect effects from own output

top 3 most affected regions by indirect effects from federal state in y-axis

Source: own calculations.

Impacts of output from other federal states are of above average relevance for the economies of Brandenburg, Lower-Saxony and Schleswig-Holstein. Products from agriculture prove to be a major characteristic, since they show a reasonable above-average share of indirect effects in all three federal states. Moreover, refined petroleum products and energy exhibit high shares of indirect effects in Brandenburg, initiated by organic food production in other federal states. This is reasonable, since a significant proportion of electricity generated in Brandenburg is determined for export into other federal states (Amt für Statistik Berlin-Brandenburg 2017) and petroleum products is the second main source of energy supply in Brandenburg (Wirtschaftsministerium Brandenburg 2012). In Lower-Saxony, an extraordinary high share of indirect effects emerge in the area of food products manufacturing. The latter federal state becomes less important in the case of organic food production in Schleswig-Holstein. In this case, the nearby Hanseatic City Hamburg exhibits a higher relevance of indirect effects with above-average shares from refined petroleum products and warehousing, induced by organic food supply in Schleswig-Holstein.

5.2.5. Indirect effects of health tourism in German federal states in 2011

The satellite account category of health tourism is strongly related to 'Accommodation and food services' (CPA 55-56). Official data exhibits an indirect output multiplier of 1.77 for this category (Destatis 2015). The NHA multiplier of health tourism, shown in Figure 52, is 1.87.

North Rhine-Westphalia, Bavaria and Hesse exhibit the highest regional indirect output multipliers from health tourism. In the case of the first, health services and travel agencies are above-average contributors to regional indirect effects, next to the known federal-specific industries of energy supply and wholesale.

Figure 51: Indirect output multipliers of health tourism, 2011 (1/2)

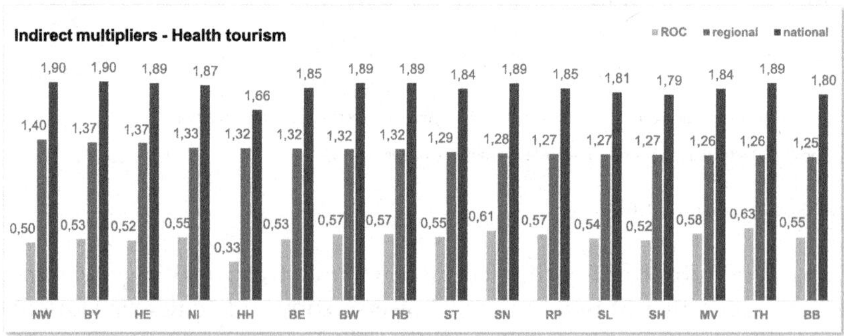

Source: own calculations.

Characteristics of health tourism become even more obvious when taking a closer look at Bavaria, with having real estate service including imputed rents of owner-occupied dwellings and health services as above-average contributors to regional indirect output effects from health tourism. Hesse exhibits extraordinary effects in areas such as travel agencies and air transport services, next to wholesale and financial services.

The general influence of travel agencies, health services and air transport services seem obvious in this case, since those categories exhibit a direct relevance for health tourism. North Rhine-Westphalia and Hesse show an above-average density of travel agencies (DRV Deutscher ReiseVerband e.V.

2017), while again, North Rhine-Westphalia and Bavaria are two among the three federal states profiting the most from tourism in the context of treatment (Juszczak 2016). The relevance of air transport services in Hesse is obviously reasonable due to the largest airport of Germany in terms of passenger volume is based in Frankfurt (Destatis 2016e). A relative high contribution of real estate service including imputed rents of owner-occupied dwellings in Bavaria is argued with the highest price per square meter for land ready for construction in this federal state in 2011, city states excluded (Destatis 2017j).

Figure 52: Indirect output multipliers of health tourism, 2011 (2/2)

1.87	BW	BY	BE	BB	HB	HH	HE	MV	NI	NW	RP	SL	SN	ST	SH	TH
BW	1.32	0.12	0.02	0.01	0.01	0.03	0.06	0.01	0.06	0.16	0.03	0.01	0.02	0.01	0.02	0.01
BY	0.08	1.37	0.02	0.01	0.01	0.03	0.06	0.01	0.06	0.15	0.02	0.01	0.02	0.01	0.02	0.01
BE	0.07	0.10	1.32	0.01	0.01	0.02	0.05	0.01	0.05	0.13	0.02	0.01	0.02	0.01	0.02	0.01
BB	0.07	0.10	0.02	1.25	0.01	0.02	0.05	0.01	0.05	0.13	0.02	0.01	0.02	0.01	0.02	0.01
HB	0.05	0.08	0.02	0.01	1.30	0.02	0.05	0.00	0.04	0.11	0.02	0.00	0.02	0.01	0.01	0.01
HH	0.04	0.06	0.01	0.01	0.00	1.32	0.04	0.00	0.03	0.08	0.01	0.00	0.01	0.01	0.01	0.01
HE	0.07	0.10	0.02	0.01	0.01	0.03	1.37	0.01	0.05	0.14	0.02	0.01	0.02	0.01	0.02	0.01
MV	0.07	0.10	0.02	0.01	0.01	0.02	0.05	1.26	0.06	0.14	0.02	0.01	0.02	0.01	0.02	0.01
NI	0.07	0.11	0.02	0.01	0.01	0.03	0.06	0.01	1.33	0.14	0.02	0.01	0.02	0.01	0.02	0.01
NW	0.08	0.12	0.03	0.01	0.01	0.03	0.06	0.01	0.06	1.40	0.03	0.01	0.02	0.01	0.02	0.01
RP	0.07	0.11	0.02	0.01	0.01	0.03	0.06	0.01	0.05	0.14	1.27	0.01	0.02	0.01	0.02	0.01
SL	0.07	0.10	0.02	0.01	0.01	0.02	0.05	0.01	0.05	0.13	0.02	1.27	0.02	0.01	0.01	0.01
SN	0.08	0.11	0.02	0.01	0.01	0.03	0.06	0.01	0.06	0.15	0.02	0.01	1.28	0.01	0.02	0.01
ST	0.07	0.10	0.02	0.01	0.01	0.02	0.05	0.01	0.05	0.14	0.02	0.01	0.02	1.29	0.02	0.01
SH	0.07	0.09	0.02	0.01	0.01	0.02	0.05	0.01	0.05	0.13	0.02	0.01	0.02	0.01	1.27	0.01
TH	0.08	0.11	0.02	0.01	0.01	0.03	0.06	0.01	0.06	0.15	0.02	0.01	0.02	0.01	0.02	1.26

■ national multiplier ■ top 5 regional indirect output multipliers (...) output value too low for reasonable interpretation

Source: own calculations.

Again, Thuringia shows the highest ROC multiplier in the case of health tourism. This is caused by general interregional interdependencies of travel agencies, real estate services including imputed rents for owner-occupied dwellings and food products, without revealing any characteristics exclusively applying in the case of Thuringia.

Figure 53: Indirect output effects of health tourism, 2011

	BW	BY	BE	BB	HB	HH	HE	MV	NI	NW	RP	SL	SN	ST	SH	TH
BW	366	132	29	16	8	32	72	9	69	180	29	8	27	16	21	13
BY	153	727	47	26	14	53	119	15	115	300	48	13	44	27	35	22
BE	17	24	79	3	1	6	13	2	12	32	5	1	5	3	4	2
BB	8	11	2	28	1	3	6	1	6	15	2	1	2	1	2	1
HB	1	2	0	0	8	1	1	0	1	3	0	0	0	0	0	0
HH	6	9	2	1	1	48	5	1	5	13	2	1	2	1	1	1
HE	61	88	19	10	6	22	321	6	46	120	19	5	18	10	14	8
MV	41	58	12	7	3	14	31	150	31	79	13	3	12	7	10	6
NI	82	118	26	14	8	29	65	8	364	161	26	7	24	14	18	11
NW	115	167	37	19	11	41	92	11	86	572	36	9	33	20	25	16
RP	24	35	7	4	2	8	19	2	18	47	90	2	7	4	5	3
SL	2	3	1	0	0	1	2	0	2	4	1	9	1	0	0	0
SN	13	19	4	2	1	5	11	1	10	26	4	1	49	2	3	2
ST	6	9	2	1	1	2	5	1	5	12	2	1	2	26	1	1
SH	59	84	18	10	5	20	45	6	44	114	19	5	17	11	238	8
TH	11	15	3	2	1	4	8	1	8	21	3	1	3	2	2	36

indicating direct relationship | top 5 most affected regions by indirect effects from own output

top 3 most affected regions by indirect effects from federal state in y-axis

Source: own calculations.

Regional indirect output effects from health tourism have the highest impact on the economies of Bavaria, Hesse, Mecklenburg-Western Pomerania, Lower-Saxony and Schleswig-Holstein. All federal state show above-average relevance of health tourism for their economies with outstanding importance in Schleswig-Holstein and Mecklenburg-Western Pomerania.

Output of health tourism leads to indirect effects outside of the supplying federal states. The economies of Berlin, Hamburg, Hesse and North Rhine-Westphalia are above-average affected by these effects. The industries shaping these characteristics in particular are legal, accounting and management consulting services in the context of Berlin, refined petroleum products in Hamburg, financial services in Hesse and wholesale trade in North Rhine-Westphalia. Moreover, all these federal states show an above-average contribution of travel agencies to regional indirect effects. Apart from this characteristic, benefiting areas of the economies in consideration are specific for the federal states in concern rather than health tourism.

5.3. Concluding remarks

In this chapter, we presented selected results from multiregional input-output analysis based on the compiled MRHA. We focused on the reliability of results in order to provide a foundation on a subsequent application of the model to answer a specific question of political relevance.

We proceeded accordingly in order to conclude upon the performance of the algorithm in the context of intra- and interregional dependencies. Unfortunately, no secondary data is available for this case, since generic multiregional supply and use table are not available for German federal states. Consequently, it is challenging to evaluate the accuracy of results, since input-output analysis aims at capturing inter-industry relationships in terms of a finite geometric series. This implies that input-output analysis captures economic correlations, which are normally unconceivable from pure knowledge of reality. Therefore, we decided to focus on various categories of health when we conducted and assayed results from input-output analysis. We are able to derive explanations from reality for obtained results in all considered cases. This does not only apply to the level of multipliers calculated, but also for the industry-specific characteristics of federal states revealed.

From this chapter and the assessment of direct effects of the health economy in the previous chapter we conclude that the developed model shows reasonable results in the context of 'holistic accuracy' (Jensen 1980). This means the model provides results, which manage to picture a macroeconomic overview of the health economy in German federal states.

Next steps involve the application of the model in a political framework, in order to found certain decisions on macroeconomic and interregional relationships in the context of the health economy. To be concrete, we will address the challenge of lagging investments in German hospitals, which is caused by an underfinancing of responsible federal states in the next chapter.

6. A Financial Equalization Scheme to Cope with Lagging Investments in German Hospitals[13]

Lagging investments in German hospitals have become a serious challenge in recent decades. The responsibility for investment financing lies with the German federal states, the "Bundeslaender", due to the dualistic financing framework applying for German hospitals. Yet, hospital investments experience a field of tension between the availability of financial resources and necessary investments. A possible solution could be a financial equalization scheme for the health economy incorporating an earmarked fund for hospital investments. The rationale for such a system is that health economies of federal states do not represent single closed systems, but depend on interregional trade flows to supply patient treatment. The respective calculations in this chapter are based on our recently compiled Multiregional Health Account for Germany. The model represents a satellite account of the health economy based on national accounts and allows us to calculate spillover effects from patient treatment in federal states by conducting input-output analysis. Based on the results, we derive a sketch of a financial equalization scheme in order to ensure needs-based hospital infrastructure in German federal states.

6.1. Introduction

For a long time, health care supply has been perceived as an economic burden (Hilbert et al. 2002). From the mid-1990s on, however, a paradigm shift shaped its perception in Germany (Goldschmidt and Hilbert 2009). Health care supply was no longer seen as a cost factor exclusively, but also as an important contributor to economic growth, employment and international trade. In addition, a definition of the health economy was established, according to which it comprises both health care services and products, 'which serve for prevention as well as for the provision of health and for rehabilitation.' (Kuratorium Gesundheitswirtschaft 2005).

13 This chapter is based on Schwärzler and Kronenberg (2017a).

This perspective was supported by activities of the Federal Ministry for Economic Affairs and Energy from 2010 on (Henke et al. 2010; Ostwald et al. 2014; Schneider et al. 2016; Bundesministerium für Wirtschaft und Energie (BMWi) 2015 & 2016 & 2017; Henke et al. 2011). These activities concentrated on developing and updating the National Health Account (NHA) for Germany, which quantifies the economic contribution of the health economy to the German economy in total. The underlying methodology is based on the macroeconomic framework of national accounts, incorporates official data on health expenditures and follows international standards (Schwärzler and Kronenberg 2016). In addition, recent initiatives of the World Health Organization incorporate this idea to implement a so called Healthcare Economy Reporting for the European region (Werling, Hamelmannn and Henke 2018).

The NHA reveals a high heterogeneity among the many categories of the health economy in terms of their contribution to gross value added (GVA), employment and international trade. In addition, first attempts to establish a similar database on the federal state level stressed different characteristics among regions of Germany (Ostwald, Legler, Schwärzler, Plaul, et al. 2015; Ostwald, Legler, Schwärzler and Tetzner 2015b; Ostwald, Legler, et al. 2014; Ostwald and Schwärzler 2015; Ranscht 2009; AG GGRdL 2016; Schneider 2014; Schneider 2013; BASYS and GÖZ 2012). In order to establish a data base, which incorporates both the heterogeneity of involved categories and of different regions in a consistent manner, we developed and compiled the Multiregional Health Account (MRHA). It corresponds to the NHA in terms of methodology and overall results but adds a further component in terms of regional diversification. The underlying methodology of both the NHA and the MRHA is based on national accounts and hence allows to conduct input-output analysis. The latter is frequently used to study several fields of economic policy action (Eurostat 2008a).

Hence, we apply input-output analysis in this chapter not only to address a current challenge in German health policy but also to demonstrate the relevance of the health economy in the political context. In this framework, we establish an approach to cope with lagging investments in hospitals by making use of multiregional input-output analysis.

This chapter is structured as follows: Section 6.2 describes background and challenges of lagging investments in German hospitals. We discuss existing approaches and address the problem formulation in section 6.3. Section 6.4 describes the data base and the empirical approach used in order to establish the financial equalization scheme that aims to cope with lagging investments in German hospitals. We present and discuss the results in section 6.5, followed by concluding remarks in section 6.6.

6.2. *Background and challenges in the context of investments in German hospitals*

This section aims at describing the general setting of hospital investments. Subsection 6.2.1 focusses on determining factors of existing heterogeneities among federal states and the political framework influencing hospital investments. Subsection 6.2.2 describes the current situation on lagging investments in German hospitals and subsection 6.2.3 addresses future challenges, which may even toughen the existing situation.

6.2.1. Determining factors

In this subsection, we first describe regional heterogeneities between influencing factors of health in order to establish a fundamental understanding for the regional setting of the subsequent analysis. Second, we introduce the legal framework regulating the financing responsibilities of hospital investments. Third, we evaluate existing compensation mechanisms in order to figure out whether sufficient attention is paid to the responsibility of federal states in this matter.

6.2.1.1. Heterogeneities among federal states

The determinants of peoples' health status represent important aspects for health policy. A high heterogeneity of the demographic situation, life expectancy and of the status of health across federal states requires a regionally differentiating health policy. Both health expenditures and demand for inpatient health care services are affected by current and future heterogeneities of federal states.

Figure 54: Expenditures per insured people for publicly insured people (left) and adjusted expenditures for publicly insured people (right), 2009

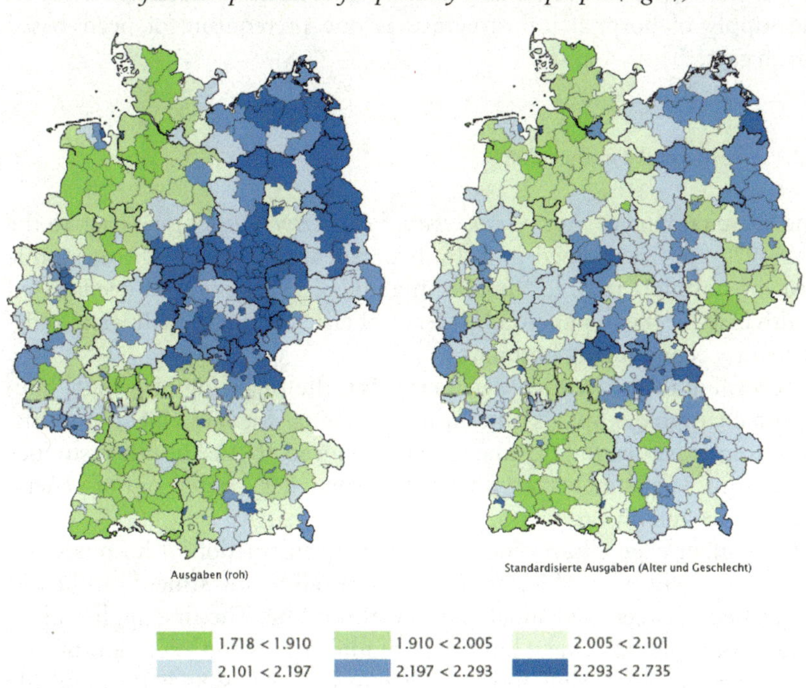

Source: Göpffarth (2011)

On the left side of Figure 54, we observe expenditures per person insured under the statutory health insurance scheme in German districts. The right side of Figure 54 shows the same expenditures, but adjusted by gender, age and morbidity derived from conducting a regression analysis on several defined risk categories of patients' characteristics (Drösler et al. 2011). Hence, we observe the influence of these factors on health expenditures and therefore on the way they are financed.

Needs-based health care is a major criterion for the supply and provision of health care (Sachverständigenrat zur Begutachtung der Entwicklung im Gesundheitswesen (SVR) 2014). It calls for equal treatment in qualitative and quantitative measures in accordance to objective patient needs. This implies that the severity and kind of illness decides upon the treatment irrespective of the patient's financial and family status, income, gender, place of residence, profession, social background or origin.

Hence, supply of needs-based health care has to cope with several factors, which depend on regional characteristics. In this chapter, we focus on the supply of hospital infrastructure as one prerequisite of needs-based health care.

6.2.1.2. Hospital Finance Act

The Hospital Finance Act (*Krankenhausfinanzierungsgesetz*) goes back to the year 1972 and was revised in 2016. It pursues safeguarding the economic basis of hospitals in order to offer high-quality, patient- and needs-based health care for the population by means of efficient, high-quality and independently economizing hospitals.

According to the Hospital Financing Act, the financing of private, public and charitable hospitals is performed in a dualistic way. Operating costs, including expenses for treatments, are financed by the health insurance funds whilst investments are financed by the federal states, out of general revenue, i.e. mainly taxes.

Investment expenditures include costs for construction of hospitals and the replacement of fixed assets. The kind of public investment can be distinguished between individual and global funding. The first applies upon request to expenses of new buildings, modifications and extension of hospitals, next to purchasing and replacement of fixed assets with useful life over three years. Global funding addresses annually expenses for replacements of short-term assets and minor construction measures.

Current challenges regarding financing of investments in hospitals led to adjustments in the Hospital Finance Act in 2016 (*Krankenhausfinanzierungsgesetz*). Accordingly, federal states are currently obliged to provide at least the annual average amount of the years 2012 to 2014 for further investments in hospitals in each year from 2016 to 2018. On top of this, and therefore unrelated to investments, 500 M. € are provided for restructuring of hospitals, such as initiatives regarding scaling down excess capacities or concentration of locations.

Observed heterogeneities among federal states regarding age, gender and morbidity of the population hence influence the financial resources of health insurance funds and federal states. Therefore, we focus on existing compensation mechanisms, which may influence the regionally different characteristics of health care financing in the following.

6.2.1.3. Existing compensation mechanisms in the German health system

Since hospital financing is performed according to a dualistic framework, there are two compensation mechanisms with potential influence on respective financial resources. On the one hand, the morbidity-oriented risk structure compensation (Morbi-RSA) focusses on compensating expenditures among health insurance companies according to age, gender and morbidity of patients. On the other hand, the Federal Financial Equalization System (*Länderfinanzausgleich*) distributes revenues among federal states so the latter are able to fulfill their assigned tasks.

Both compensation mechanisms are relevant in the case of hospital investments. We want to gather arguments for compensation from the Morbi-RSA, which do not only apply to current expenditures, but also to financing of investments. The Federal Financial Equalization System is not related to health, but aims to enable federal states to fulfill their assigned tasks. We describe main characteristics of both in the following.

The Morbi-RSA aims to enable both solidarity and competition in the statutory health insurance market (Bundesversicherungsamt 2008). Solidarity applies since the patient's contribution rate does not depend on health risk but on her or his income. Moreover, statutory health insurance is obliged to contract with providers, irrespective of age, gender or well-being of the patient. Under normal circumstances, competition for young and healthy individuals would arise among insurance companies. The Morbi-RSA, however, aims to adjust influencing factors of insurers' characteristics in order to enable fair competition among health insurance companies based on effective and efficient economizing only. In Figure 54 we can observe the difference between 'original' health expenditures and health expenditures subject to adjustments according to the Morbi-RSA in terms of age, gender and morbidity. Some literature suggests there are additional so far unconsidered exogenous regional factors, which influence supply and demand of health care, such as the level of prices and income (Ulrich and Wille 2014; Göpffarth 2011). Hence, the aforementioned sources propose to implement a regional factor to the Morbi-RSA to increase fairness of competition among health insurance companies in addition.

We suggest that differences in demand for health care regarding age, gender and morbidity among others, apply not only to current costs, but also to investments of hospitals. Federal states and their hospitals need to be able to supply needs-based health care, run their business economically and compete in an environment, which is independent of the financial resources of federal states. The Morbi-RSA has so far no effects on financial resources of federal states. Hence, we turn to the Federal Financial Equalization System in the next step, aiming to figure out whether it copes with regional heterogeneity in health care supply in a similar way the Morbi-RSA does.

Since tax revenues are unequally distributed among German regions due to a diversified economy, certain instruments are necessary to ensure federal states to be able to meet their responsibilities. The existing Federal Financial Equalization System is meant to represent this instrument and aims to establish 'equivalent living conditions throughout the federal territory', based on the German Constitution (Lenk 2008). Figure 55 shows the preliminary calculations of the Federal Financial Equalization System for 2016 in order to enable a general assessment on its impact for the reader.

Figure 55: Preliminary calculations of the German equalization scheme for 2016.

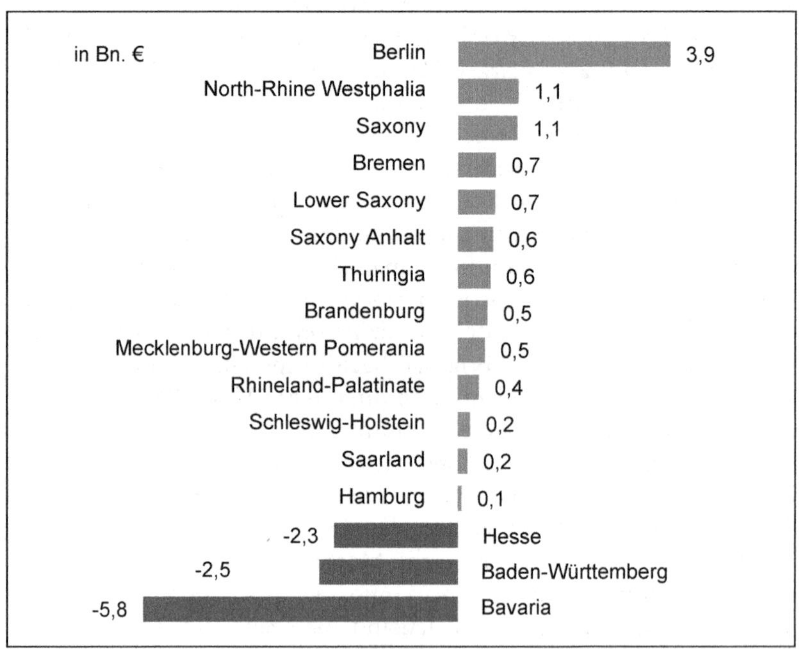

Source: own illustration based on Bundesministerium für Finanzen (2017).

The legal framework of the Federal Financial Equalization System is being revised at the moment. Basic principles, to be applied from 2020 on, have already been settled. Unfortunately, it turns out that the reorganization did not lead to the intended reduction in complexity of the redistribution mechanisms. Hence it lacks improvements, which make it more transparent, systemic and computable in order to fuel financial incentives of federal states (Schäuble 2017).

According to the recent adjustments, the federal government will support federal states with a higher amount of additional 9.5 Bn. € (Bundesministerium für Finanzen 2016) from 2020 on in order to enable them to meet their responsibilities. Associated therewith, the completion of tasks of the federal states will be adjusted and the competencies of the federal government regarding investment decisions will be increased. Special attention is brought to investments in education, federal motorways, the indebted federal states Saarland and Bremen, seaports and Local Community Transport. Apart from this, value-added tax continues to be distributed among federal states in consideration of the number of inhabitants.

So far, we observe no special attention to health care. Therefore, we take a closer look at the applied distribution concept based on the number of inhabitants, which may impact health-related characteristics. Different weights apply for inhabitants in order to include certain characteristics of federal states. This is 1.35 for city states, 1.05 for Mecklenburg-Western Pomerania, 1.03 for Brandenburg and 1.02 for Saxony-Anhalt. This weighting is argued with higher financial needs for city states and sparsely populated regions. The ratio of actual financial capacity and the accordingly weighted target figure reflects the relative position of a federal state. A value below 1 indicates the federal state in consideration is entitled to receive funds and vice versa. Allocation does not lead to a complete equalization of tax revenues, in order to maintain incentives for effective economizing (Lenk 2008).

Hence, we observe a relatively unspecific mechanism to distribute financial resources according to the Federal Financial Equalization System until now. Recent reform proposals suggest to assert fixed amounts to investments for education, science, family policy, environment and nature protection (Lenk 2008). It therefore seems like there is some awareness towards necessary additional actions that need to be taken, however, leaving health ignored in this case. Yet, different literature addresses implementing health-related factors, which enable rural regions to keep up with economic and social developments and prevent a further growing disparity among regions (Kersten, Neu and Vogel 2015). In addition, a demographic factor was discussed in order to consider a decreasing population. However, this is challenging, since the direction of interdependencies of expenditures and demographic constitution depends on the applied field, such as education or health among others (Wissenschaftlicher Beirat beim Bundesministerium der Finanzen 2013). Moreover, the weighting factors applied on the number of inhabitants are criticized by some commentators, who argue that in the case of city states the weighting is too high and too general (Sachverständigenrat zur Begutachtung der gesamtwirtschaftlichen Entwicklung and Statistisches Bundesamt 2014) and does not represent a reliable and verifiable indicator (Bönte and Lucke 2004). In addition, it has been argued that the weighting factors for sparsely populated regions lack a clear scientific foundation (Fuest and Thöne 2012).

So far, we conclude that influencing factors of health are not a subject of the current and future Federal Financial Equalization System. However, since there are adjustments in current expenses regarding gender, age and morbidity in the context of the Morbi-RSA, we can clearly identify need for action regarding the financial resources of the federal states in the context of health.

6.2.2. Current situation on the lagging investments in German hospitals

Federal states increasingly fail to fulfil their obligation to finance investments in hospitals (BDO AG Wirtschaftsprüfungsgesellschaft and Deutsches Krankenhausinstitut e.V. (DKI) 2015; Sachverständigenrat zur Begutachtung der Entwicklung im Gesundheitswesen (SVR) 2014) due to a lack of their financial resources (Clade 2002; Henke 2002; Rehborn and Thomae 2015; Porter and Guth 2012). An analysis conducted by Rösel (2013) confirms this interdependency among other influencing factors such as interest burden and demographic constitution.

Federal states financed about 2.79 Bn. € investments in hospitals in 2015. This is about half of the 6.01 Bn. € projected required investments for 2016. The aforementioned amount of the yearly necessary investment needs of hospitals is derived from investment allocation assessments, which were recently elaborated by the DRG Institute for Hospital Reimbursement (InEK) on behalf of the German Hospital Federation (DKG), the National Association of Statutory Health Insurance Funds (GKV-Spitzenverband) and the Private Health Insurance Association according to the official mandate of § 10 the Hospital Finance Act (KHG). Moreover, the 2.79 Bn. € hospital investments financed by federal states corresponds to a 50 percent real erosion in value since 1991. The investment ratio, calculated as the quota of investments and adjusted costs of hospitals, decreased from 9.7 percent in 1991 to 3.3 percent in 2015. (Deutsche

Krankenhausgesellschaft (DKG) 2017) Nominal development of GDP, adjusted costs of hospitals and public investments in hospitals are depicted in Figure 56.

Figure 56: GDP, adjusted costs of hospitals[14] and public investments in hospitals, 1991-2015

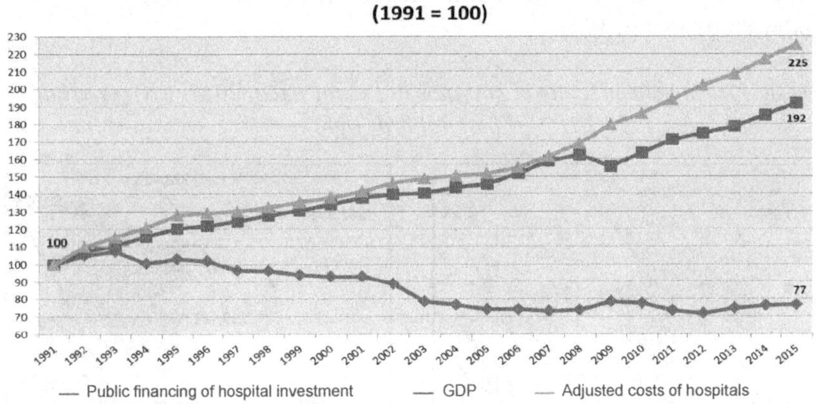

Source: Deutsche Krankenhausgesellschaft (DKG) (2017).

Financing of federal states corresponds to only half of actual hospital investments (BDO AG Wirtschaftsprüfungsgesellschaft and Deutsches Krankenhausinstitut e.V. (DKI) 2015). From an economic perspective necessary additional investments are financed by hospitals themselves, for example from surpluses of current expenses. This circumstance puts several hospitals into financial troubles since surpluses are not meant for financing of investments. Moreover, lacking investments can cause erosion of structural and technical infrastructure, in extreme cases causing limitations in health care supply. In addition, innovative treatments and technical progress are more unlikely to be implemented when hospitals lack investments in structural and medical infrastructure.

Figure 57 shows hospital investments for the German federal states in terms of the investment ratio for 2015 on the left hand side and in terms of the sum of investments taken in the period 1991 to 2015 on the right hand side. The difference between the two figures is mostly due to an invest-

14 Adjusted costs of hospitals refer to gross hospital costs less expenses for outpatient services.

ment program for the Eastern federal states initiated in the course of the Health Care Structure Reform Act of 1992. It aimed to assure equal standards of infrastructure after the unification of Germany by providing around 10 Bn. € for investments in hospitals of Eastern Germany during the period of 1995 to 2014 (Deutsche Krankenhausgesellschaft (DKG) 2017). In the perspective of overall Germany, however, each federal state supplies less financial resources in real terms for investments in hospitals today compared to 1991.

Figure 57: Investment ratio of hospitals in federal states, 2015 (left); investment sum 1991-2015 per hospital bed (right)

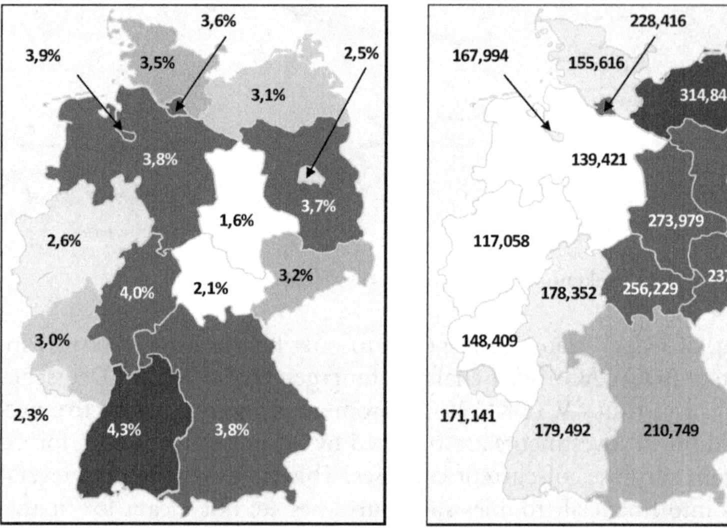

Source: own illustration based on Deutsche Krankenhausgesellschaft (DKG) (2017).

Current discussions focus on a mechanism to calculate the actual need for investments, called investment allocation assessment. Respective calculations have led to the projected need for investments to the amount of 6.01 Bn. € mentioned before (Deutsche Krankenhausgesellschaft (DKG) 2017). The investment allocation assessment aims to provide a basis for federal states' decision making regarding the actual investment need of their hospitals. The mechanism is closely related to Diagnosis Related Groups (DRG) and hence incorporates information on medical and demographic data (Schmid, Stadler and Zipperlen 2016).

For the sake of completeness we want to point out that some literature mentions the so-called ‚investment bottleneck of hospitals', which does not lie in the focus here. We proceed accordingly, since the amount of the investment bottleneck is difficult to measure in an objective way (Sachverständigenrat zur Begutachtung der Entwicklung im Gesundheitswesen 2007).This causes the according calculated amount to differ in a broad range from e.g. 14.6 Bn. € (Augurzky et al. 2014) to 50 Bn. € (Deutsche Krankenhausgesellschaft (DKG) 2009b).

We conclude that the German health policy observes severe challenges resulting from the dualistic framework of health care financing in hospitals. We sympathize with the attempts to improve decision making in the context of investment allocation assessments, since they rely on actual health-related data. However, we find it surprising that this system does not involve a reallocation mechanism between federal states, since financial recourses are to some degree responsible for lagging investments. From what we will see in the next subsection, future challenges may even aggravate the current situation.

6.2.3. Future challenges

We described determining factors and the current situation regarding lacking investments in hospitals in the previous subsections. Now we will look at future developments, which are likely to have reasonable impacts on the existing challenge.

First, the demographic constitution of federal states will influence the further development of hospital infrastructure in different ways. A decreasing population will impact the financial resources of federal states due to the current and future design of the Federal Financial Equalization System (Lenk and Starke 2015). Moreover, the amount of tax revenues generated depend on the number of people in employment, which is again affected by demographic factors. In addition, the latter also impacts the nature and extent of public expenditures, e.g. education for the younger population and retirement homes for elderly people.

The left hand side of Figure 58 exhibits the projected old-age dependency ratio for 2030 in German federal states with highest values for the Eastern federal states. Literature also reveals highest increases compared to 2008 in the same area (Statistisches Bundesamt 2010). Hence, it is likely that Eastern federal states observe greater challenges when it comes to public financing and therefore fulfilling their public duties.

Figure 58: Projected old-age dependency ratio, 2030 (left); change of hospital cases 2008-2030 (right)

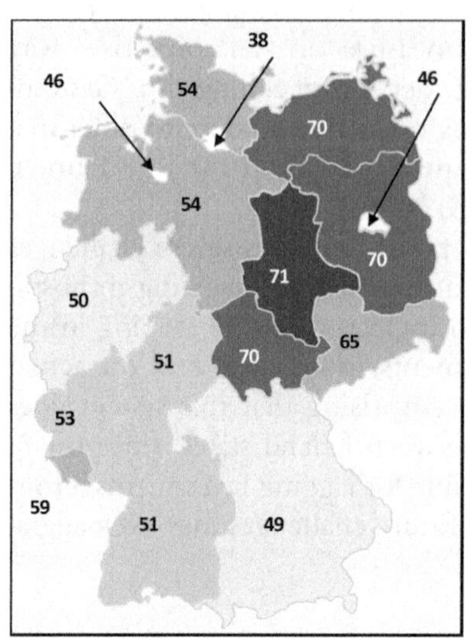

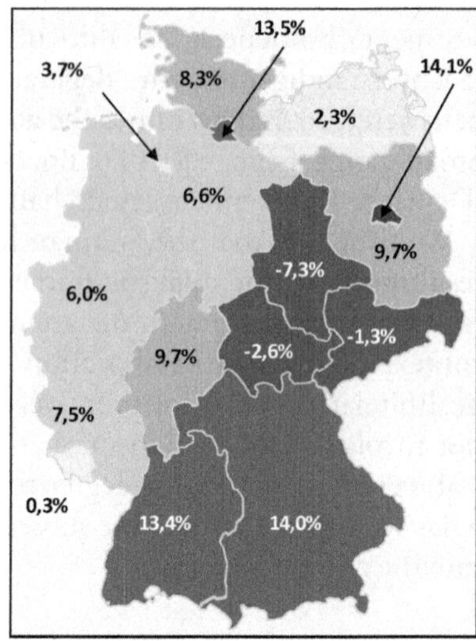

Source: own illustration based on Statistisches Bundesamt (2010); Statistisches Bundesamt (2011).

Projected changes in hospital cases in the period 2008 to 2030 are depicted on the right hand side of Figure 58. The reduction of hospital cases in Saxony-Anhalt is caused by a decrease in population until 2030 while Berlin and Bavaria are expected to cope with the opposite effect due to a slight increase of the corresponding population. Observed changes in hospital cases point towards the necessity for adjustments in the context of health care facilities and medical staff. A lower utilization of health care facilities is especially challenging for larger federal states and regions with low population density and long travel distances in the context of emergency care.[15]

Fortunately, a so-called 'cost explosion' of health care costs is not expected (Nowossadeck 2012; Bowles and Greiner 2012). The slow but long lasting impacts of demographic changes favor planning of a variety of activi-

15 Both projections are based on assumptions, which do not incorporate unexpected demographic developments occurred lately such as the large influx of refugees. At this point there are no revised projections available. Hence, we suggest to interpret this data with respect to a reasonable amount of uncertainty.

ties in medical research, aiming at improved health care provision, prevention, rehabilitation and allocation of resources (Nowossadeck 2012).

Moreover, the impact of financial resources on financing of hospitals is likely to toughen from 2020 on, when the "debt brake" is introduced (Sachverständigenrat zur Begutachtung der Entwicklung im Gesundheitswesen (SVR) 2014). It prohibits federal states from incurring new debt (Deutsche Bundesbank 2011). As already mentioned, the highly indebted federal states Saarland and Bremen receive special attention in the new German equalization scheme (Bundesministerium für Finanzen 2016).

Furthermore, the aforementioned additional resources for hospital investments in Eastern federal states, which were provided from 1995 on, stopped in 2014 (Deutsche Krankenhausgesellschaft (DKG) 2017). This obligates Eastern federal states to provide an even higher amount of financial resources from 2015 on. However, this effect is expected to become visible with delay since hospitals in Eastern Germany currently exhibit a relatively favorable situation due to the expired additional funding (Sachverständigenrat zur Begutachtung der Entwicklung im Gesundheitswesen (SVR) 2014).

Concluding, we observe additional challenges in the future, which may toughen the current situation of lagging hospital investments. In the following, we consider previous approaches, summarize the problem and end with a description on the proposed approach.

6.3. Existing approaches and introduction to the proposed approach

Up to this point, we have introduced the background and challenges in the context of lagging investments in German hospitals. This section focusses on problem solving. Therefore, we summarize existing approaches in subsection 6.3.1, define the problem from our perspective in subsection 6.3.2 and describe our proposed approach in subsection 6.3.3.

6.3.1. Existing approaches

Mentioned adjustments in the Hospital Financing Act from 2016 consist in obligating federal states to finance at least the average annual amount of 2012 to 2014 in each year from 2016 to 2018. There is consensus among several associations about the inadequacy of this regulation (Bundesärztekammer 2015; Leber 2015; Verband der Ersatzkassen (vdek) 2015;

Dachverband Deutsche Hochschulmedizin e.V. 2015). Accordingly, it represents an absolute lower limit of investments but appears to be the only compromise federal states are willing to accept (Verband der Ersatzkassen (vdek) 2015).

The German Advisory Council on the Assessment of Developments in the Healthcare System pursues to introduce monistic hospital financing (Sachverständigenrat zur Begutachtung der Entwicklung im Gesundheitswesen 2007). Health insurance companies would be responsible for financing current expenses and investments in hospitals. The Council suggests to directly link investments to DRG. Consequently, a certain fund is at the free disposal of hospitals. Federal states should nevertheless still be able to oblige hospitals to supply certain services such as emergency care in order to maintain regional and social policy of federal states. The investment fund should still be financed by taxes to avoid additional burden for the statutory health insurance. The opposite would result in a rise of health insurance contribution impacting negatively on the labor market. Federal state contributions to the fund are suggested to be defined according to the number of inhabitants.

This setting considers some challenges of the dualistic financing framework. First, inpatient and outpatient treatment is treated equally, without one of them being partly publicly financed. Second, business decisions in hospitals are made by one player instead of two, which is supposed to improve efficiency and economic profitability. Third, it decreases distorted competition among hospitals, since their equipment is no longer influenced by federal states' decisions (Deutscher Industrie- und Handelskammertag 2010). Fourth, political influence on investments decisions is reduced, which is favorable in respect of the relationship between the short-term budgetary position and lagging investments in hospitals to supply needs-based health care (Sachverständigenrat zur Begutachtung der gesamtwirtschaftlichen Entwicklung and Statistisches Bundesamt 2012).

A more detailed description on the exact procedures of a potential monistic financing framework can be found in Rürup et al. (2008). They pursue to focus on a to-be defined share of value-added tax revenues as part of the current Federal Financial Equalization System. Financial resources are distributed among hospitals in accordance to DRG under the supervision of federal states. Ten percent of the available financial resources should be kept back for financing hospitals in disadvantaged regions.

So far, we observe a general renunciation of the dualistic framework of hospital financing and consensus about relating payments to DRG. However, the source of financing is not quite clear. While the Advisory Council suggests tax payments in accordance to inhabitants, Rürup et al. (2008) suggest to link payments to a specific amount of value-added tax. Both approaches seem relatively unsophisticated considering the heterogeneity among regions and the current inadequacy of federal states' financial contribution. We propose a clear calculation method in this context to favor policy rationale. We think, multiregional input-output analysis is a suitable approach.

6.3.2. Problem formulation

We observe a heterogeneity of German federal states in determinants of health care expenditures, which are considered in financing of current costs by the concepts of the Morbi-RSA. However, no compensation mechanism is available to adjust budgets of federal states enabling them to meet their responsibility of financing hospital investments.

This is crucial since budgetary restrictions play a decisive role in this matter. Neither the current nor the future Federal Financial Equalization System considers determinants of health. However, its future design considers e.g. expenditures for education and hence recognizes financial needs beyond general equalization mechanisms. Therefore, it is surprising that the same mechanism lacks an equivalent adjustment in the context of health especially when we compare its allocation volume of 10.6 Bn. € (Bundesministerium für Finanzen 2017) with annual needs for hospital infrastructure of 6.01 Bn. € in 2016 (Deutsche Krankenhausgesellschaft (DKG) 2017). This dimension clearly indicates the relevance of this topic.

Theoretical approaches suggest to introduce a monistic financing framework, in which health insurance companies come up for current costs and investments. Binding federal states' contributions are supposed to be the source of funding of the latter. We criticize that suggested individual contributions are not linked to any health related characteristics and do not show advantages over the Federal Financial Equalization System regarding the criticized design of the distribution mechanism.

Hence, we aim to establish a macroeconomic model specifying each federal states' contribution to the earmarked fund. This model offers reasonable explanations for due contributions of federal states in the context of the health economy. We propose this direct linkage to the health economy since it potentially promotes understanding and therefore willingness to cooperate of contributing federal states.

6.3.3. Proposed approach

The MRHA is a multiregional satellite account of the health economy based on the macroeconomic framework of national accounts. It reveals intraregional, interregional and interindustry dependencies of the German economy with special emphasis on health care. The model enables input-output analysis in order to examine triggered indirect relationships next to the direct contributions of the health economy to the regional economy. Hence, instead of relying on indicators such as the number of inhabitants to establish an earmarked fund for hospital investments, we make use of modelled interdependencies of federal states with direct link to health care supply.

Indirect effects arise from the interconnectedness of industries and federal states in terms of exchanging products and services for further processing or final consumption. For example, the indirect effects emerge from producing medication and therewith related necessary inputs such as energy. Federal states, which profit to an above average amount from patient treatment in other federal states, since they provide e.g. a high amount of necessary medication or energy, accordingly contribute to the fund to a higher proportion. The allocation of the fund is carried out in accordance to DRG as proposed by previous approaches.

6.4. *Data base and empirical approach*

This section focusses on the data base used and the empirical approach pursued to establish a compensation mechanism for federal states in order to provide needs-based hospital investments.

6.4.1. Data base

The MRHA represents the main data base for further calculations. This satellite account was compiled as a methodological enhancement of the already established NHA and aims at quantifying the economic contribution of the health economy in terms of GVA, employment and trade for the German federal states. While the NHA reveals economic interdependencies of the health economy with the overall economy, the MRHA separates these interdependencies also among federal states in order to evaluate interregional next to interindustry dependencies. The foundation for both models is national accounts. We provide the official definition of national accounts in order to point out its versatility and recognition in the following.

> *National accounts are a coherent, consistent and integrated set of macroeconomic accounts, balance sheets and tables based on a set of internationally agreed concepts, definitions, classifications and accounting rules.*
> *National accounts provide a comprehensive accounting framework within which economic data can be compiled and presented in a format that is designed for purposes of economic analysis, decision-taking and policy-making.*
> *OECD Glossary of Statistical Terms*

Commissioned by the Federal Ministry for Economic Affairs and Energy, we derived the methodology of the current NHA in chapter 2, elaborated the methodology to compile the MRHA in chapter 3 and checked its plausibility and results in chapter 4 and 5 in order to address a current challenge of political matter in this chapter.

For the purpose of this analysis, we use the input-output table of the MRHA, which is derived from the corresponding supply and use tables. Schwärzler and Kronenberg (2016) provide a detailed description on the derivation of the input-output table for the NHA, which applies identically for the multiregional context.

The derived multiregional input-output table with emphasis on the health economy provides information on the production process and the use of goods. Since the economies of federal states do not represent enclosed systems but are related to each other in terms of the supply for and demand of goods and services, this multiregional input-output table allows to calculate interregional dependencies. Emphasis on the health economy make it possible to specifically evaluate categories of the health economy, which cannot be derived from official national tables neither collectively nor separately.

Figure 59: Multiregional input-output table in a 3-region-economy

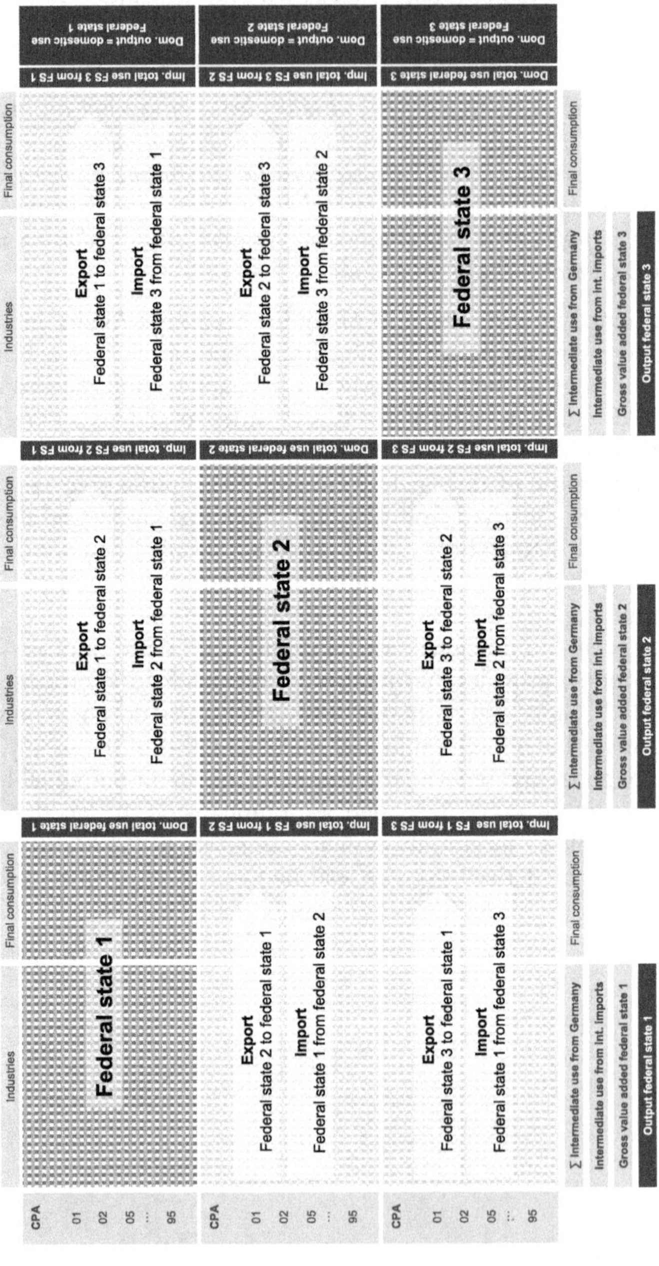

Source: own illustration.

Figure 59 shows the framework of a multiregional input-output table for a three region economy. Included data reveals information on inputs necessary to produce a certain amount of a specific product on the one hand and use of products either for further production or final use on the other hand.

We provide the general notation according to Miller and Blair (2009) over here. Let x_i be the overall produced output of one specific industry i, which only produces one type of good. This output is used as input z_i in n industries or for final consumption f_i, such as private household consumption or exports among others.[16]

$$x_i = z_{i1} + \ldots + z_{ij} + \ldots + z_{in} + f_i = \sum_{j=1}^{n} z_{ij} + f_i \tag{38}$$

Since each industry produces exactly one kind of product, we obtain n industries and hence an *nX(n+1)* matrix, the plus one indicating to final consumption as a single vector. In matrix notation we get

$$x = Zi + f \tag{39}$$

where i denotes a column vector of 1's resulting in a row-wise summation of Z.

6.4.2. Empirical approach

We aim to establish a fund for hospital investments, into which federal states make payments according to their direct and indirect benefits from patient treatment in the rest of the country. Input-output analysis represents the foundation for quantifying indirect effects. In the following we describe the basics of input-output analysis, according to Miller and Blair (2009).

In this context, we rely on the Leontief production function, which is characterized by fixed proportions of inputs. To obtain additional output, all involved inputs need to be increased proportionally. Hence, there is a

16 For the sake of consistency with the notation used in the cited literature, we refer to final consumption as a vector, opposed to its shape in the actual calculation and Figure 59.

direct relationship between necessary inputs and obtained output, defined by the input-output coefficient

$$a_{ij} = \frac{z_{ij}}{x_j} \tag{40}$$

Hence, we can replace z_{ij} by $a_{ij}x_j$ in equation 6.4.1 resulting in

$$x = Ax + f \tag{41}$$

If we want to calculate the amount of output x necessary to supply a specific amount of final demand f, we solve equation 6.4.2 for x and receive the Leontief inverse multiplied by f

$$x = (I - A)^{-1} f = Lf \tag{42}$$

This procedure is special since it calculates round-by-round effects. In the first round, output of one product requires a certain amount of inputs. Those inputs have to be produced themselves, which leads to the second round of effects. Adding all rounds of effects results in a single number from a converging geometric series, caused by economic interdependencies.

Table 7 exhibits exemplary results of direct and indirect effects from patient treatment. Since we only want to focus on effects in the rest of the country, diagonal elements are blanked.[17] The resulting distribution is applied on the given amount of the fund to define each federal state's contribution. The underlying argument is that federal states, which profit from patient treatment in the rest of the country should also be made responsible for investments necessary over there in order to keep up needs-based health care supply.

17 We provide arguments for this approach in subsection 6.5.2.

Table 7: Exemplary results of the allocation mechanism.

	R1	R2	R3	R4	Σ	%
R1	...	3	1	4	8	9%
R2	10	...	23	15	48	52%
R3	13	9	...	3	25	27%
R4	5	2	5	...	12	13%
					93	100%

Source: own illustration.

When we define each federal state's tax contribution to the fund, we will focus on results in terms of GVA. The reason for this approach is a similar challenge in the Federal Financial Equalization System. As mentioned, the latter aims to distribute unequally generated taxes among federal states to ensure the latter are capable to fulfill their duties. Before it gets to the point of re-distributing taxes, however, generated taxes in overall Germany have to be allocated to their 'rightful' owner, which is currently carried out according to the principle of local origin. This becomes tricky when it comes to multiregional companies or employees, who commute over borders of federal states. Special adjustment rules come into action in such situations, which are, however, heavily discussed in the current design of the Federal Financial Equalization System. Consequently, Lenk and Glinka (2015) derive the advantages of allocating taxes according to GVA generated in federal states, due to advancements in transparency and allocation with respect to economic power. Hence, we focus on direct and indirect effects from patient treatment in the rest of the country in terms of GVA in order to define each federal state's contribution to the earmarked fund for hospital investments.

We define 'patient treatment' as public and private expenditures on health according to the health expenditure survey (Statistisches Bundesamt 2011b). In the following analysis, we define three categories:

- Manufacturing of medication including involved retail trade and wholesale trade
- Manufacturing of medical products including involved retail trade and wholesale trade
- Inpatient and outpatient treatment including administration.

Correspondingly, our main foundation for this calculation, the MRHA, incorporates these categories of health, which were obtained from matching compiled multiregional supply and use tables with regional health expenditures. Hence, in technical terms, we calculate direct and indirect input-output effects from current household and government consumption of categories of the health economy based on the standard static open model.

At this point we introduced background and challenges of lagging investments in hospitals, described existing strategies and our proposed approach and explained foundations of the empirical framework. On this basis, we show and discuss results in the next section.

6.5. *Results and discussion*

This section focusses on the results from input-output analysis. Based thereon, we compile the theoretical fund size for hospital investments in a specific federal state according to direct and indirect GVA generated by patient treatment in the rest of Germany. Subsection 6.5.1 describes the results and subsection 6.5.2 discusses further implications.

6.5.1. Results

In our understanding, the economic constitution of the health economy plays a decisive role to secure needs-based health care in hospitals. Yet, the health economy does not operate only within each federal state separately, but depends on products and services from other federal states, i.e. the "rest of the country". Hence, this interdependency implies that certain federal states benefit from patient treatment in the rest of the country. These external effects, however, contradict the concept of dualistic financing of hospitals, according to which investments have to be financed by the responsible federal states exclusively themselves.

Therefore, we pursue the discussion on a compensation mechanism, which is derived from interregional dependencies of the health economy. Direct and indirect GVA generated in federal states due to the treatment of patients in the rest of the country is the main directive to define contributions to the fund. We suggest that federal states, which profit above average from patient treatment in the rest of the country, are obligated to make a greater contribution to the earmarked investment fund.

The overall amount of this fund corresponds to 5.85 Bn. € for 2015, which is derived from investment allocation assessments (Deutsche Krankenhausgesellschaft (DKG) 2017). We refer to 2015, since it represents the most recent data base of federal states' actual investments. We are aware of minor inaccuracies when applying this amount to interregional interdependencies based on data from 2011. However, since our primary objective is to bring the underlying mechanisms into the reader's attention, rather than computing precise numbers, we believe that these inaccuracies are of an acceptable magnitude and ignore them in the following.

Table 8 exhibits the results from input-output analysis, excluding the last column, which represents the share of the overall regional economy in terms of GVA. Summed up over all federal states, we obtain an overall amount of around 48 Bn. € GVA from patient treatment in the rest of the country. We derive individual payments to the fund according to the contribution of each federal state to this amount, indicated by the red frame in Table 8.

This amount includes different categories: medication, medical products and inpatient/outpatient treatment including administration. The latter provides the majority of GVA effects generated, while the first exhibits the highest effects in terms of GVA generated per 100 € spent on this kind of treatment. This is plausible, since health products experience trade between federal states and are therefore responsible for a high degree of interdependencies among federal states for each Euro spent in the rest of the country. Inpatient and outpatient treatment is not part of interregional trade, since this service always takes place at the supplying federal state. This causes GVA generated per 100 € spent on inpatient and outpatient treatment in the rest of the country to be of a lower amount compared to health products. However, inpatient/outpatient treatment and administration represent the biggest contributor to the overall health economy, which makes this part nonetheless powerful in its absolute importance. Its corresponding interregional dependencies come along with necessary inputs like medication and medical products for inpatient and outpatient treatment, but also with energy and food among others.

Table 8: Direct & indirect GVA effects from patient treatment in the rest of country.

	Medication			Medical products			Inpatient/outpatient treatment & administration			Σ patient treatment			Regional economy
	[M. € GVA]	[share]	[€ GVA per 100 € exp.]	[M. € GVA]	[share]	[€ GVA per 100 € exp]	[M. € GVA]	[share]	[€ GVA per 100 € exp]	[M. € GVA]	[share]	[€ GVA per 100 € exp]	[share]
BW	3.012	17,2%	8,40	930	18,0%	7,11	3.394	13,4%	1,73	7.335	15,3%	2,99	15,0%
BY	1.472	8,4%	4,21	1.050	20,3%	8,18	4.180	16,5%	2,21	6.702	14,0%	2,82	17,7%
BE	1.729	9,9%	4,43	149	2,9%	1,04	1.313	5,2%	0,61	3.191	6,7%	1,19	4,0%
BB	363	2,1%	0,92	74	1,4%	0,51	501	2,0%	0,23	937	2,0%	0,34	2,1%
HB	108	0,6%	0,27	57	1,1%	0,38	248	1,0%	0,11	412	0,9%	0,15	1,0%
HH	525	3,0%	1,33	228	4,4%	1,56	1.023	4,0%	0,47	1.777	3,7%	0,65	3,6%
HE	3.989	22,8%	10,55	472	9,1%	3,39	3.100	12,2%	1,49	7.562	15,8%	2,91	8,7%
MV	74	0,4%	0,19	36	0,7%	0,25	275	1,1%	0,12	386	0,8%	0,14	1,3%
NI	661	3,8%	1,82	397	7,7%	2,96	1.959	7,7%	0,96	3.017	6,3%	1,19	8,7%
NW	2.937	16,8%	9,12	1.115	21,5%	9,37	5.612	22,2%	3,23	9.664	20,1%	4,43	21,8%
RP	1.361	7,8%	3,50	155	3,0%	1,08	1.006	4,0%	0,47	2.522	5,3%	0,94	4,4%
SL	124	0,7%	0,31	52	1,0%	0,35	280	1,1%	0,13	456	0,9%	0,16	1,2%
SN	248	1,4%	0,64	120	2,3%	0,84	845	3,3%	0,39	1.213	2,5%	0,45	3,7%
ST	244	1,4%	0,62	63	1,2%	0,43	487	1,9%	0,22	794	1,7%	0,29	1,9%
SH	429	2,5%	1,09	198	3,8%	1,36	693	2,7%	0,32	1.320	2,8%	0,49	2,8%
TH	196	1,1%	0,50	77	1,5%	0,52	406	1,6%	0,19	679	1,4%	0,25	1,9%
Σ	17.471	100%	2,85	5.173	100%	2,29	25.322	100%	0,75	47.967	100%	1,14	100%

Source: own calculations.

By comparing the contribution of each federal state with its share on the overall national economy in terms of GVA shown in the last column of Table 8, we observe an above or below average advantage from patient treatment in the rest of the country. For example, the federal states Baden-Württemberg, Berlin, Hesse and Rhineland-Palatinate profit above average when patients in the rest of the country are treated with medication, since their corresponding GVA share is higher than their share on the national economy. This is legitimate due to large companies operating over there. The companies Sanofi-Aventis Deutschland GmbH and Merck KGaA characterize Hesse as a federal state with strong focus on medication manufacturing as described in chapter 4. Berlin exhibits emphases in R&D in medication especially due to activities of Bayer HealthCare AG, Berlin-Chemie AG and Pfizer Deutschland GmbH. An established cluster in this field and close cooperation between the pharmaceutical industry and health facilities intensify Berlin's activities in corresponding R&D. Boehringer Ingelheim GmbH has high impact on medication supply in Baden-Württemberg and Rhineland-Palatinate. Supply of medication goes in hand with several other indirect effects in these federal states as described in chapter 5.

Bavaria and Baden-Württemberg profit from expenditures on medical products in the rest of Germany, as can be observed from their high shares in the context of medical products from Table 8. Activities in this field have extraordinary importance in these federal states (Forum MedTech Pharma e.V. 2015; Baden-Württemberg International 2017) and exhibit essential interindustry and interregional effects as shown in chapter 5. Both federal states show accompanying regional effects from computer, electronic and optical products next to a strong relationship to machinery in Baden-Württemberg.

As already mentioned, inpatient and outpatient treatment are themselves not subject to interregional trade. However, an essential share of their input does, such as medication, medical products or further services and products related with daily business. This implies high effects for Berlin, Hesse and North Rhine-Westphalia due to their supply of medication. Moreover, high effects arise in administration in Berlin due its characteristic as capital of Germany and in financial activities in Hesse, due to the city of Frankfurt hosting several important players such as the European Central bank, the German Central Bank and the German Stock Exchange among them (Burkert and Garloff 2013). In addition, North Rhine-Westphalia profits from inpatient and outpatient treatment in terms of energy supply, since it provides about a third of overall German energy output.

Hamburg benefits from a wide range in related services, such as trade and warehousing next to insurance, legal, accounting, rental and leasing services.

Summing up all direct and indirect GVA effects from patient treatment in the rest of Germany results in the already mentioned amount of around 48 Bn. €. The more a federal states profits from this effect, the more it should be obligated to contribute to the earmarked fund. When we contrast this share with the regional contribution to the national economy, we obtain above average effects for Baden-Württemberg, Berlin, Hamburg, Hesse and Rhineland-Palatinate, as can be obtained from Table 8. In the following subsection we will apply this allocation to the necessary amount for hospital investments and discuss the results.

6.5.2. Discussion

In the previous subsection, we have derived each federal state's contribution to the earmarked fund for hospital investments. The rationale behind is that federal states should contribute a higher amount to the fund if they profit from patient treatment in the rest of the country in an extraordinary way. This subsection concentrates on further implications of this adjustment scheme. Hence, we conduct another input-output analysis, which focusses on the direct and indirect GVA effects, which arise from current investments in hospitals. We proceed accordingly in order to examine the subsequent step of establishing a fund for investments, which is the effects from actually investing in hospitals.

One essential point is that federal states do not only profit from patient treatment in the rest of the country, but also from investments taken over there. Hence, federal states should indeed be willing to support additional investments in the rest of the country. Even more, as can be depicted from column one and column two of Table 9, returns in terms of GVA generated per 100 € expenditure on investments in the rest of the country exceed those from patient treatment.

Column three depicts the derived relative contributions in the red frame from Table 8 applied to the overall amount of hospital investments necessary in 2015 of 5.85 Bn. € according to Deutsche Krankenhausgesellschaft (DKG) (2017). When we contrast these figures with actual federal states' investments depicted in column four of Table 9, it results in the current implementation rate, shown in column five. The only federal state with accordingly sufficient participation is Mecklenburg-Western Pomerania. Not surprisingly, the five federal states, Baden-Württemberg, Berlin, Hamburg, Hesse and Rhineland-Palatinate, which are supposed to compensate other federal states for their investments in accordance to our calculations, particularly lag behind others in their current participation.

Table 9: Relationship of patient treatment and hospital investments.

	C1	C2	C3	C4	C5	C6	C7
	Effects from patient treatment in ROC	**Effects from investments in ROC**	**Calculated contribution to fund [2015]**	**Current investments [2015]***	**Implementation rate**	**Effects from investments**	**Current gap**
					(C4/C3)		(C4-C6)
	[€ GVA per 100 € expenditure]	*[€ GVA per 100 € investments]*	*[M. € contribution]*	*[M. €]*	%	*[M. € GVA]*	*[M. €]*
BW	2,99	7,00	895	437	49	289	148
BY	2,82	9,64	817	500	61	387	113
BE	1,19	2,11	389	96	25	86	10
BB	0,34	0,98	114	83	72	46	36
HB	0,15	0,44	50	39	77	21	18
HH	0,65	1,17	217	91	42	48	43
HE	2,91	4,88	922	242	26	198	44
MV	0,14	0,67	47	53	112	33	20
NI	1,19	3,97	368	276	75	173	102
NW	4,43	10,39	1.179	515	44	381	134
RP	0,94	2,00	308	120	39	83	37
SL	0,16	0,51	56	29	51	21	8
SN	0,45	2,94	148	131	89	118	13
ST	0,29	1,09	97	39	40	40	-1
SH	0,49	1,12	161	94	59	50	45
TH	0,25	1,58	83	50	60	60	-10
Σ	1,14	2,96	5.850	2.794	48	2.035	759

Source: own calculations, *Deutsche Krankenhausgesellschaft (DKG) (2017), ROC = Rest of Country

At this point, we want to bring the reader's attention back to the positive effects from hospital investments according to the second input-output analysis conducted. Column six of Table 9 depicts the absolute amount of each federal state's current direct and indirect GVA generated by hospital investments in overall Germany. Therefore, we calculate the current gap arising between current expenditures on investments and GVA generated due to investments taken. It follows, that from an overall investment amount of 2,794 M. € in 2015 (Deutsche Krankenhausgesellschaft (DKG) 2017) direct and indirect GVA arises in federal states to the amount of 2,035 M. €. In consideration of this significant amount we suggest to provide more room for a discussion regarding the upsides of investment financing of hospitals in the current political debate.

Next to the additional GVA effects just described, we want to turn to some aspects of more technical nature in the following. There may arise a question on why we refer to GVA effects generated by patient treatment in the rest of the country exclusively in order to calculate individual contributions of federal states, instead of adding effects from treatment in the own federal state.

First, the provided framework is supposed to make involved players aware of the importance and advantages of interregional dependencies for the economy. We believe that if we promote this awareness, it will lead to a higher willingness for any sort of compensation mechanism. Second, we do not intend to interfere with regional policy, which means corresponding decisions regarding general regional health care supply should not impact on the federal state's contribution to the fund. Otherwise, we think, this could affect federal states' incentives to supply needs-based health care in yet unknown directions.

In addition, one may ask whether this compensation mechanism impacts on the federal state's strategic decision regarding their export activities. Federal states would indeed reduce their contribution to the compensation mechanism if they substitute their sales to the rest of the country by international sales. However, companies operate to maximize their profit and therefore look for possibilities all over the world to sell their products. Hence, there is no reason to substitute sales if there is a possibility to increase sales. In addition, federal states probably will not interfere with certain incentives for companies due to additional domestic effects accompanied with interregional trade.

6.6. *Concluding remarks*

This contribution and the underlying model, the MRHA, focus on the economic effects of the health economy in German federal states. Clearly, the perspective on health care as an economic contributor can be criticized. In this perception, the patient is no longer the focus of respective analyses. Related analyses even suggest advantages for the health economy if there is an increased need for patient treatment.

From a scientific view, however, it is beneficial to have additional explanatory factors available for certain analyses. Moreover, supply of health care results in financing responsibilities, hence it is legitimate to pursue the approach of "economizing of health". The macroeconomic framework provides the opportunity to evaluate financing of the health care system in a different picture and puts an alternative light on e.g. investment decisions, with in turn pursue effects on demographic impacts, life expectancy and the degree of pain and suffering of patients.

Both the NHA and the MRHA are macroeconomic models for the German health economy. However, over the years we recognized that the first lacks a certain necessary degree of differentiation. This is the reason we developed the MRHA. It exhibits regional characteristics and reveals intraregional, interregional and interindustry dependencies. Due to its existence we are able to address the current political challenge of lacking investments in German hospitals from a different perspective. This is one example for the close connection between health expenditures and their economic contribution at the same time, since federal states are obligated to finance hospital investments from general revenue, i.e. mainly taxes.

Due to the circumstance that budgets of federal states influence the amount of hospital investments taken, we propose a financial equalization scheme based on modelled interdependencies of federal states caused by patient treatment in the rest of the country. One advantage of this model is a high degree of transparency in the context of the equalization scheme. Another advantage is that the model demonstrates further effects from actual investments. We hence argue that this model has the potential to influence current policy decisions. This is especially important in the context of the inadequacies of two related policy decisions, which is the future design of the Federal Financial Equalization System and the current adjustments in the Hospital Financing Act to cope with lagging investments.

Clear limitations of the approach is the modelled multiregional input-output table, due to its non-availability from statistical offices. Our compilation of the MRHA contributes to existing scientific research in this field, since it incorporates new approaches and exhibits realistic findings in this and two previous chapters. In an overall perspective, we believe it is worth considering to use multiregional tables in the context of financial equalization schemes of federal states in general, since they incorporate actual information on interregional dependencies. However, there is clearly a relatively high effort of such a scientific-based approach associated therewith, since it would require an ongoing monitoring based on a regular updating of the multiregional input-output model.

7. Conclusion

This dissertation deals with the compilation and application of the Multiregional Health Account for Germany, depicted in the form of a satellite account for health based on multiregional supply and use tables from the national accounting framework. It summarizes its foundation - the already established National Health Account for Germany -, describes the steps taken towards developing the Multiregional Health Account for Germany, assesses the general results of the model and applies it in the context of the current challenge of lagging hospital investments in German federal states.

Chapter 2 builds the foundation for the subsequent parts since it describes the historical background, definitions and principles of the already established National Health Account for Germany, which is further developed into a multiregional model in the course of the further chapters of this dissertation. Chapter 3 focusses on the approach to compile the Multiregional Health Account. The contribution of this approach to research in the field of subnational multiregional input-output analyses is in the center of section 7.1 of this chapter. Chapters 4 and 5 of this dissertation evaluate the basic results of the model in terms of the direct and indirect effects of the health economy in the German federal states. General implications of the main findings and their contribution to a more thorough understanding of the German health economy are discussed in section 7.2 of this chapter. Chapter 6 applies the established Multiregional Health Account for Germany to a current challenge in health policy by developing a financial equalization scheme to cope with lagging investments in German hospitals. The contribution of these findings to the discussion about a reorganization of the financing structure of German hospitals on the one hand and the German Federal Financial Equalization System *(Länderfinanzausgleich)* on the other hand are in the center of section 7.3 of this chapter.

7.1. Methodological contribution to subnational multiregional input-output analysis

Chapter 3 of this dissertation presents the established methodology to compile the Multiregional Health Account for Germany. Both the applied approach to compile multiregional supply and use tables and its application in the context of a health satellite account are unprecedented in this research field. Up until the time of writing it has only been possible to compile figures on the health economy for overall Germany, making a distinction between federal states impossible, provided that the established definition of a product-specific health economy is taken into account. Existing approaches have neither been able to quantify the health economy from the product side but relied on an industry-specific approach, nor facilitated multiregional input-output analysis. This is mostly due to the non-existence of officially compiled subnational supply, use and input-output tables for German federal states. It is at the same time the main challenge and contribution of this dissertation that we developed a suitable approach to compile such tables and applied this approach in the course of our research.

We see clear limitations of existing approaches to (multi-)regionalize supply, use and input-output tables for our case, given the data and information we have at hand. However, the existing SUT-RAS approach (Temurshoev and Timmer 2011) shows favorable characteristics we developed further to make it applicable to a multiregional setting. In its origins, the SUT-RAS algorithm aims at projecting supply and use tables of a given year to alternative data points, such as subsequent years. We see its major advantages in its capability to project tables by making use of official data of national accounts, which are available for most years and regions, making it unnecessary for the user to make additional assumptions. However, any additional information available can be implemented into the compilation easily.

We maintain the SUT-RAS algorithm in its original formulation to profit from the described advantages but add further restrictions to make it applicable to the multiregional context. This implies restrictions on the product side to meet the national values summing up across all federal states by providing the algorithm with economic key indicators of the federal states to be considered at the same time. One main advantage over existing approaches following the developed approach comes from the fact that no additional balancing of supply and use is necessary at the end of the overall procedure since balancing conditions are already taken into account during the iterative algorithm.

Another specificity of our approach is the data used. First of all, we have access to a special evaluation on supply and use tables provided by the Federal Statistical Office of Germany, which includes detailed information on the product side for 930 out of 2.643 products making up the overall economy in statistical terms. This detailed level of raw data on the national level, which acts as the foundation for the initial multiregional matrix to be adjusted by the algorithm, is both a curse and blessing at the same time. On the one hand, the detailed level of data favors the validity of results in the context of our satellite account of health and makes it possible for us to implement detailed secondary data as well. On the other hand, the level of detail makes the calculations computational expensive and fragile in the case of occurring poor data quality for some product categories within the special evaluation.

Moreover, we have access to unpublished data on regional gross value added and output, which has positive impact on our results. Additional data on international trade of federal states refers to published information. However, we managed to combine two different trade statistics of unequal detail to gain a maximum of information from available data.

By including several different data bases into our model we also became aware of strongly contradicting information, which was revealed due to a non-convergence of the algorithm. We perceive this as another advantage and at the same time quality label of our approach that its boundaries are so tight that including strongly contradicting information leads to a collapse of the algorithm.

Another important assessment of the quality of the developed model originates from the examination of the final supply and use matrices, which show a significant adjustment compared to the initial ones, on which we apply the algorithm. Production structures and inputs adjust to characteristic specifications of federal states. This adjustment in structures promotes a more thorough understanding of the German health economy, which will be discussed in the next section.

7.2. *Contribution to a thorough understanding of the health economy in German federal states*

Still today, the federal states of Germany are characterized by past events, such as the separation into Eastern and Western Germany until 1990. Moreover, three of the 16 federal states are city states again showing specific characteristics compared to territorial states. In addition, economies of certain federal states are industrially characterized while others exhibit rather agricultural infrastructure. To some point, these characteristics are reflected in the attributes of the health economy in federal states as well, which are described in greater detail in chapters 4 and 5 based on the basic results of the Multiregional Health Account. The two chapters contribute to a thorough understanding of the health economy in German federal states in different ways. While chapter 4 delivers information on the direct effects of the health economy and therefore the direct impact of the health economy on regional GVA, employment and international trade, chapter 5 evaluates the interindustry, intraregional and interregional relationships of the health economies of the German federal states by examining the indirect output multipliers of certain categories of the health economy.

From a scientific perspective, the main contribution of chapter 4 is the unprecedented product-specific evaluation of economic key indicators of the regional health economy. Industry-specific information reporting the economic contribution of companies, which are classified by their main activity into different categories of industries according to the NACE classification, is processed and provided by statistical offices. However, supply, use and input-output tables are necessary in order to assess the product-specific contribution, which originates from supplying one specific product. Hence, while the first refers to indicators of companies, which often produce more than just one product, the latter refers to GVA and employment directly contributable to one specific product. Moreover, while industry-specific information is available for German federal states, the latter can only be retrieved from the compiled (multi-)regional supply and use tables. The assessment of the product-specific health economy in German federal states therefore contributes to a better understanding of the different characteristics and dynamics caused by supplying goods and services of the health economy to the domestic and foreign population. It consequently becomes possible to identify regions of Germany with major emphases on services, compared to manufacturing, R&D or wholesale and trade in the context of health products. Due to the compilation of the MRHA for a period of ten years, we also manage to examine certain developments. This information can be used for assessing past political decision making or to evaluate areas eligible for future initiatives.

Chapter 5 adds a further component to the analysis of the health economy in German federal states by evaluating the indirect output effects from certain categories of the health economy. Accordingly, it becomes possible to investigate the interdependencies of the regional health economy to other industries and federal states. Due to the lack of official multiregional input-output tables, such evaluations become only possible by modelling respective tables. The corresponding analysis on the health economy is unprecedented and can be perceived as a useful tool for regional economic planning since it provides information on the various effects of economic activities in the context of the health economy. Of particular note in this regard is the possibility of interregional impact analyses, allowing for evaluating the indirect effects caused in the rest of the economy by activities of the health economy in one federal state.

7.3. Contribution to the debate about hospital financing in Germany

Chapter 6 takes up the matter of the current political debate on lagging investments in German hospitals, which are to a certain amount caused by the established financing structure in this context. Correspondingly, current costs are financed by the health insurance funds whilst investments are financed by the federal states. The chapter finds that there is currently no interregional compensation mechanism available, which adjusts individual budgets of federal states enabling them to come up for their varying expenses of financing hospital investments. However, there is clear evidence for the differing needs of the population in the respective federal states for Germany. This is derived from an existing compensating mechanism, the Morbi-RSA, focusing on the current costs for patient treatment. However, current costs do not involve investments for hospitals and hence budgets of federal states are unaffected by the Morbi-RSA.

However, in Germany there is one compensation mechanism, which explicitly focusses on the budgets of federal states, namely the German Federal Financial Equalization System (*Länderfinanzausgleich*). Unfortunately, this mechanism does not incorporate any health-related indicators but mainly focusses on the population number of the individual federal states as its redistribution mechanism.

This dissertation contributes to the discussion on lagging hospital investments by establishing a financial equalization scheme, which is based on the Multiregional Health Account. This approach is unprecedented in the context of both health and the German Federal Financial Equalization System. It evaluates interregional spillover effects, which are generated by patient treatment. In the case one federal state profits above average from patient treatment in another federal state, since it supplies it with i.e. medication or energy, it is obliged to participate to a larger share to an earmarked fund for hospital investments. Results indicate towards higher shares of contribution for the federal states Baden-Württemberg, Berlin, Hamburg, Hesse and Rhineland-Palatinate. The main advantage of this approach is its empirical foundation of spillover effects of the health economy compared to applying indicators unrelated to health such as the population number.

In addition, chapter 6 contributes to the debate of lagging hospital investments by pointing towards the benefits for each federal state from hospital investments made by the rest of the country. This aims to provide the federal states with arguments for spending money to the earmarked fund, since increased investments made in the rest of the country results in spillover effects in the spending economy itself. Especially Baden-Württemberg, Bavaria and North Rhine Westphalia show high domestic spillover effects per Euro of hospital investments taken in the rest of the country.

To summarize, the approach developed in chapter 6 can be perceived as both an additional alternative to the current financing structure of hospitals in Germany and an input to the discussion about the design of the German Federal Financial Equalization System (*Länderfinanzausgleich*), which could potentially profit from considering multiregional input-output analysis in its concepts.

Appendix

Figure 60: vfa member sites and their subsidiaries in 2015

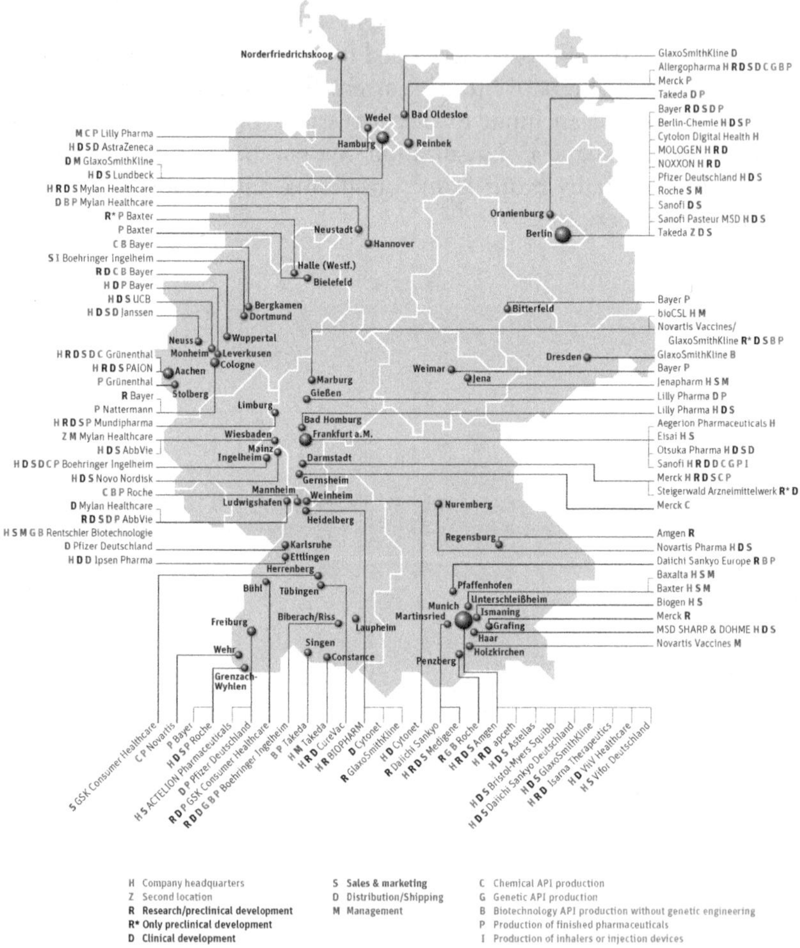

H Company headquarters
Z Second location
R Research/preclinical development
R* Only preclinical development
D Clinical development
S Sales & marketing
D Distribution/Shipping
M Management
C Chemical API production
G Genetic API production
B Biotechnology API production without genetic engineering
P Production of finished pharmaceuticals
I Production of inhalers or injection devices

Source: Verband Forschender Arzneimittelhersteller (vfa) (2015).

References

AG GGRdL. 2016. "Wertschöpfungs-Erwerbstätigenansatz nach WZ 2008. Berechnungsstand Juli 2016." Statistisches Landesamt des Freistaates Sachsen.

AGCO GmbH. 2017. "Sich selbst neu erfinden: Der Fendt Werksverbund." Available at: https://www.fendt.com/de/14819.html [Accessed April 10, 2017].

Ahlert, G., and I. An der Heiden. 2015. "Die ökonomische Bedeutung des Sports in Deutschland - Ergebnisse des Sportsatellitenkontos 2010 und erste Schätzungen für 2012." GWS Themenreport 15/1 Available at: http://papers.gws-os.com/gws-themenreport15-1.pdf [Accessed October 6, 2017].

Allergopharma GmbH & Co. KG. 2014. "Allergopharma feiert Richtfest." Available at: https://www.allergopharma.de/de/aktuelles/newsarchiv/details/?tx_ttnews%5Btt_news%5D=29&cHash=42163e12d399352e38b25d77c146de35 [Accessed April 7, 2017].

Amt für Statistik Berlin-Brandenburg. 2017. "Statistischer Bericht. E IV 4 - j /14. Energie- und CO2-Bilanz im Land Brandenburg 2014." Available at: https://www.statistik-berlin-brandenburg.de/publikationen/stat_berichte/2017/SB_E04-04-00_2014j01_BB.pdf [Accessed April 10, 2017].

Armstrong, A.G. 1975. "Technology assumptions in the construction of United Kingdom Input-Output tables." In *Estimating and Updating Input–Output Coefficients, Edited by: Allen, R. I.G. and Gossling, W. F.* Input–Output Pub. Co. Chap. 5. London, pp. 68–93.

AstraZeneca GmbH. 2012. "AstraZeneca Annual Report and Form 20-F Information 2011." Available at: https://www.astrazeneca.com/content/dam/az/Investor_Relations/annual-reports-homepage/2011-Annual-report-English.pdf [Accessed April 7, 2017].

Augurzky, B., C. Hentschker, S. Krolop, A. Pilny, and C. Schmidt. 2014. *Krankenhaus Rating Report 2014 - Mangelware Kapitel: Wege aus der Investitionsfalle*. Heidelberg: medhochzwei Verlag.

Augurzky, B., S. Krolop, C. Hentschker, A. Pilny, and C.M. Schmidt. 2015. "Krankenhaus Rating Report 2015. ‚Bad Bank' für Krankenhäuser – Krankenhausausstieg vor der Tür?" Rheinisch-Westfälisches Institut für Wirtschaftsforschung (RWI).

Baden-Württemberg International. 2017. "Gesundheitsindustrie in Baden-Württemberg." Gesellschaft für internationale wirtschaftliche und wissenschaftliche Zusammenarbeit mbH. Available at: http://www.bw-invest.de/fileadmin/user_upload/bw-invest/downloads/Branchen_Cluster/Branchenuebersicht_Gesundheitsindustrie_Jul2017_DE.pdf [Accessed December 21, 2017].

BASYS, and GÖZ. 2012. "Gesundheitswirtschaft Sachsen, Gutachten Im Auftrag des Sächsischen Staatsministeriums für Soziales und Verbraucherschutz."

Bayer AG. 2017a. "Aktivitäten und Anfahrtsbeschreibungen der deutschen Standorte." Available at: https://www.bayer.de/de/deutsche-standorte.aspx [Accessed April 7, 2017].

Bayer AG. 2007. "Bayer-Nachhaltigkeitsbericht 2006." Available at: https://www.bayer.de/de/nachhaltigkeitsbericht-2006.pdfx?forced=false?forced=true [Accessed April 8, 2017].

Bayer AG. 2012. "Geschäftsbericht 2011." Available at: https://www.bayer.de/de/gb-2011.pdfx [Accessed April 7, 2017].

Bayer AG. 2016. "Geschäftsbericht 2015." Available at: http://www.geschaeftsbericht2015.bayer.de/lagebericht-ergaenzungen/grundlagen-des-konzerns/bayer-auf-einen-blick/konzernstruktur.html [Accessed August 10, 2017].

Bayer AG. 2017b. "Supply Center Bitterfeld." Available at: http://bitterfeld.bayer.de/de/der-standort/einblicke/betriebe/herstellung-von-medikamenten/ [Accessed January 12, 2018].

BDO AG Wirtschaftsprüfungsgesellschaft, and Deutsches Krankenhausinstitut e.V. (DKI). 2015. "Investitionsfähigkeit der deutschen Krankenhäuser." Available at: https://www.dki.de/sites/default/files/downloads/2015-11_investitionsfaehigkeit_der_deutschen_krankenhaeuser_-_finale_fassung.pdf [Accessed December 21, 2017].

Berlin-Chemie AG. 2017. "BERLIN-CHEMIE und die Menarini GmbH – Arbeitgeber mit Zukunft." Available at: https://karriere.berlin-chemie.de/Was-wir-bieten/Ueber-uns [Accessed April 7, 2017].

Boehringer Ingelheim GmbH. 2015. "Bekenntnis zum Standort Deutschland." Available at: https://www.boehringer-ingelheim.de/sites/de/files/unternehmensprofil/boehringer_ingelheim_bekenntnis_zum_standort_deutschland.pdf [Accessed April 6, 2017].

Boero, R., B.K. Edwards, and M.K. Rivera. 2017. "Regional input–output tables and trade flows: an integrated and interregional non-survey approach." *Regional Studies*:1–14.

Böhm, K., C. Tesch-Römer, and T. Ziese. 2009. "Gesundheit und Krankheit im Alter." Statistisches Bundesamt, Deutsches Zentrum für Altersfragen, Robert Koch-Institut. Available at: https://www.rki.de/DE/Content/Gesundheitsmonitoring/Gesundheitsberichterstattung/GBEDownloadsB/alter_gesundheit.pdf?__blob=publicationFile [Accessed January 12, 2018].

Bonfiglio, A., and F. Chelli. 2008. "Assessing the behaviour of non-survey methods for constructing regional input–output tables through a Monte Carlo simulation." *Economic Systems Research* 20(3):243–258.

Bönte, W., and B. Lucke. 2004. "Angemessene Einwohnerveredelung im Länderfinanzausgleich – An-merkungen zu einem Quantifizierungsversuch." In *Junkernheinrich, M., (Hrsg.): Sonderbedarfe im bundesstaatlichen Finanzausgleich : Theorie - Methoden - Instrumente*. Berlin: Analytics (Forum Öffentliche Finanzen), pp. 189–206. Available at: http://www3.wiso.uni-hamburg.de/fileadmin/wiso_vwl_iwk/paper/lfaboelu.pdf [Accessed December 21, 2017].

Bowles, D., and W. Greiner. 2012. "Bevölkerungsentwicklung und Gesundheitsausgaben." G +G Wissenschaft No. Jg. 12, Heft 4/2012, Available at: https://www.wido.de/fileadmin/wido/downloads/pdf_ggw/wido_ggwaufs1_1012.pdf [Accessed December 21, 2017].

Braakmann, A., and S. Goldhammer. 2016. "Konzept zur Erfassung außenwirtschaftlicher Transaktionen in den VGR nach ESVG 2010."

Brucker, S.M., S.E. Hastings, and W.R. Latham III. 1987. "Regional Input-Output Analysis: A Comparison of Five" Ready-Made" Model Systems." *The Review of Regional Studies* 17(2):1–16.

Brucker, S.M., S.E. Hastings, and W.R. Latham III. 1990. "The variation of estimated impacts from five regional input-output models." *International Regional Science Review* 13(1–2):119–139.

Bundesagentur für Arbeit (BA). 2016a. "Der Arbeitsmarkt in Deutschland – Fachkräfteengpassanalyse." Available at: https://statistik.arbeitsagentur.de/Statischer-Content/Arbeitsmarktberichte/Fachkraeftebedarf-Stellen/Fachkraefte/BA-FK-Engpassanalyse-2016-06.pdf [Accessed November 28, 2016].

Bundesagentur für Arbeit (BA). 2016b. "Sozialversicherungspflichtig und geringfügig Beschäftigte nach Wirtschaftszweigen der WZ 2008."

Bundesärztekammer. 2015. "Vorläufige Stellungnahme der Bundesärztekammer zum Referentenentwurf des Bundesministeriums für Gesundheit (BMG); Entwurf eines Gesetzes zur Reform der Strukturen der Krankenhausversorgung (Krankenhaus-Strukturgesetz) vom 28.04.2015." Available at: http://www.bundesaerztekammer.de/fileadmin/user_upload/downloads/pdf-Ordner/Stellungnahmen/Vorl._STN_BAEK_zum_RefEntwurf_eines_Krankenhaus-Strukturgesetzes_13.05.2015.pdf [Accessed December 21, 2017].

Bundesministerium für Finanzen. 2016. "Beziehungen zwischen Bund und Ländern werden modernisiert." *Pressemitteilung des Bundesministeriums für Finanzen* Pressemitteilung 26. Available at: http://www.bundesfinanzministerium.de/Content/DE/Pressemitteilungen/Finanzpolitik/2016/12/2016-12-14-pm26-bund-laender-finanzbeziehungen.html [Accessed December 21, 2017].

Bundesministerium für Finanzen. 2017. "Vorläufige Abrechnung des Länderfinanzausgleichs für das Jahr 2016." Available at: https://www.bundesfinanzministerium.de/Content/DE/Standardartikel/Themen/Oeffentliche_Finanzen/Foederale_Finanzbeziehungen/Laenderfinanzausgleich/Vorlaeufege-Abrechnung-Laenderfinanzausgleich-2016.pdf?__blob=publicationFile&v=1 [Accessed December 21, 2017].

Bundesministerium für Wirtschaft und Energie (BMWi). 2015. "Gesundheitswirtschaft. Fakten & Zahlen, Ausgabe 2014."

Bundesministerium für Wirtschaft und Energie (BMWi). 2016. "Gesundheitswirtschaft. Fakten & Zahlen, Ausgabe 2015."

Bundesministerium für Wirtschaft und Energie (BMWi). 2017. "Gesundheitswirtschaft. Fakten & Zahlen, Ausgabe 2016."

Bundesverband der Arzneimittel-Hersteller e.V. 2017. "Der Arzneimittelmarkt in Deutschland." Available at: https://www.bah-bonn.de/index.php?eID=dumpFile&t=f&f=9614&token=394afca21e7e9be87ac0bd646f3daacd5fb53032 [Accessed June 7, 2017].

Bundesversicherungsamt. 2008. "So funktioniert der neue Risikostrukturausgleich im Gesundheitsfonds." Available at: http://www.bundesversicherungsamt.de/fileadmin/redaktion/Risikostrukturausgleich/Wie_funktioniert_Morbi_RSA.pdf [Accessed December 21, 2017].

Bund-Verlag. 2011. "Betriebsrat der Bayer Vital GmbH." Available at: http://www.bund-verlag.de/zeitschriften/arbeitsrecht-im-betrieb/deutscher-betriebsraete-preis/archiv/Preis_2015/Dokumentation-der-Projekte/Arbeitszeitgestaltung/Eintraege/Bayer-Vital_80_lang.php [Accessed April 7, 2017].

Burkert, C., and A. Garloff. 2013. "Beschäftigungsperspektiven im hessischen Finanzsektor. Finanzplatz Frankfurt." IAB Regional. Berichte und Analysen aus dem Regionalen Forschungsnetz No. 3/2013, Available at: http://doku.iab.de/regional/H/2013/regional_h_0313.pdf [Accessed December 21, 2017].

Chemieatlas. 2017. "Chemie im Ruhrgebiet." *chemieatlas.de*. Available at: https://www.chemieatlas.de/information-service/chemie-im-ruhrgebiet/ [Accessed August 4, 2017].

CLAAS KGaA mbH. 2017. "Die Gruppe – Standorte – Deutschland - Bad Saulgau." Available at: http://www.claas-gruppe.com/gruppe/standorte/deutschland/bad_saulgau [Accessed April 10, 2017].

Clade, H. 2002. "„Grauzonenfinanzierung" verzerrt Wettbewerb. Investitionsstau Störfaktor der Krankenhauswirtschaft." Deutsches Ärzteblatt(99):A327-328.

Czypionka, T., A. Schnabl, C. Sigl, J.-R. Warmuth, and B. Zucker. 2014. *Gesundheitswirtschaft Österreich: ein Gesundheitssatellitenkonto für Österreich (ÖGSK)*. Available at: https://www.bmdw.gv.at/Wirtschaftspolitik/Wirtschaftspolitik/Documents/Gesundheitssatellitenkonto%20f%C3%BCr%20%C3%96sterreich%20-%20Studie.pdf [Accessed January 12, 2018].

Dachverband Deutsche Hochschulmedizin e.V. 2015. "Gemeinsame Stellungnahme zum Entwurf eines Gesetzes zur Reform der Strukturen der Krankenversorgung (Krankenhausstrukturgesetz – KHSG)." Available at: https://www.uniklinika.de/fileadmin/user_upload/pdf/08-15-09-02_VUD-MFT-Stellungnahme_KHSG_Stand_02.09.15.pdf [Accessed December 21, 2017].

Destatis. 2016a. "Aus- und Einfuhr (Außenhandel): Bundesländer, Jahre, Wirtschaftszweigsystematik, GP2009 (2-Steller): Außenhandel."

Destatis. 2016b. "Aus- und Einfuhr (Außenhandel): Bundesländer, Jahre, Wirtschaftszweigsystematik, Warengruppen (EGW 2002: 3-Steller)."

Destatis. 2016c. "Außenhandel – Zusammenfassende Übersichten für den Außenhandel. Fachserie 7 Reihe 1."

Destatis. 2017a. "Fachserie 2, Reihe 1.6.1: Kostenstruktur bei Arzt- und Zahnarztpraxen sowie Praxen von psychologischen Psychotherapeuten. 2015." Available at: https://www.destatis.de/DE/Publikationen/Thematisch/DienstleistungenFinanzdienstleistungen/KostenStruktur/KostenstrukturAerzte2020161159005.xlsx?__blob=publicationFile [Accessed October 6, 2017].

Destatis. 2016d. “Fachserie 2 Reihe 1.6.6: Kostenstruktur bei Einrichtungen des Gesundheitswesens. 2014.” Available at: https://www.destatis.de/DE/Publikationen/Thematisch/DienstleistungenFinanzdienstleistungen/KostenStruktur/KostenstrukturGesundheitswesen2020166149005.xlsx?__blob=publicationFile [Accessed October 6, 2017].

Destatis. 2016e. “Fachserie 8 Reihe 6.2: Verkehr. Luftverkehr auf allen Flugplätzen. 2015.” Available at: https://www.destatis.de/DE/Publikationen/Thematisch/TransportVerkehr/Luftverkehr/LuftverkehrAlleFlugplaetze2080620157004.pdf?__blob=publicationFile [Accessed April 10, 2017].

Destatis. 2017b. “Fachserie 12, Reihe 6.3: Kostennachweis der Krankenhäuser.” Available at: https://www.destatis.de/DE/Publikationen/Thematisch/Gesundheit/Krankenhaeuser/KostennachweisKrankenhaeuser2120630157005.xlsx?__blob=publicationFile [Accessed October 6, 2017].

Destatis. 2017c. “Fachserie 12 Reihe 7.1.1: Gesundheit - Ausgaben 2015.” Available at: https://www.destatis.de/DE/Publikationen/Thematisch/Gesundheit/Gesundheitsausgaben/AusgabenGesundheitXLS_2120711.xls?__blob=publicationFile [Accessed October 6, 2017].

Destatis. 2017d. “Fachserie 12 Reihe 7.1.2: Gesundheit - Ausgaben 1995 bis 2015.” Available at: https://www.destatis.de/DE/Publikationen/Thematisch/Gesundheit/Gesundheitsausgaben/AusgabenGesundheitLangeReiheXLS_2120712.xls?__blob=publicationFile [Accessed October 6, 2017].

Destatis. 2017e. “Fachserie 12 Reihe 7.3.1: Gesundheit - Personal 2015.” Available at: https://www.destatis.de/DE/Publikationen/Thematisch/Gesundheit/Gesundheitspersonal/PersonalXLS_2120731.xls?__blob=publicationFile [Accessed October 6, 2017].

Destatis. 2017f. “Fachserie 12 Reihe 7.3.2: Gesundheit - Personal 2000 bis 2015.” Available at: https://www.destatis.de/DE/Publikationen/Thematisch/Gesundheit/Gesundheitspersonal/PersonalLange_ReiheXLS_2120732.xls?__blob=publicationFile [Accessed October 6, 2017].

Destatis. 2017g. “Fachserie 18 Reihe 1.4: Volkswirtschaftliche Gesamtrechnungen – Inlandsproduktberechnung Detaillierte Jahresergebnisse 2016, Veröffentlichungsstand August 2017.” Available at: https://www.destatis.de/DE/Publikationen/Thematisch/VolkswirtschaftlicheGesamtrechnungen/Inlandsprodukt/InlandsproduktsberechnungEndgueltigXLS_2180140.xlsx?__blob=publicationFile [Accessed October 6, 2017].

Destatis. 2016f. “Fachserie 18 Reihe 2. Volkswirtschaftliche Gesamtrechnungen – Input-Output-Rechnung.”

Destatis. 2018. “Gegenüberstellung der Meldenummern des GP 2009 mit den Warennummern des WA 2018.” Available at: https://www.destatis.de/DE/Publikationen/Verzeichnis/MeldeWarennummernXLS_3200220.xlsx?__blob=publicationFile [Accessed January 12, 2018].

Destatis. 2017h. "Gegenüberstellung der Warengruppen und -untergruppen der „Ernährungswirtschaft und der Gewerblichen Wirtschaft" (EGW) und der Warennummern des Warenverzeichnisses für die Außenhandelsstatistik (WA)." Available at: https://www.destatis.de/DE/Methoden/Klassifikationen/Aussenhandel/WA2007EWG.xlsx?__blob=publicationFile [Accessed January 12, 2018].

Destatis. 2011. "Gesundheitsausgabenrechnung, Methoden und Grundlagen 2008." Available at: https://www.destatis.de/DE/Methoden/Methodenpapiere/Download/Gesundheitsausgabenrechnung.pdf?__blob=publicationFile [Accessed October 6, 2017].

Destatis. 2017i. "Globalisierungsindikatoren: Unterschiede zwischen den Konzepten der VGR und der Außenhandelsstatistik." Available at: https://www.destatis.de/DE/ZahlenFakten/Indikatoren/Globalisierungsindikatoren/Indikatoren/_KonzeptvergleichVGRAH.html [Accessed January 12, 2018].

Destatis. 2010. "Input-Output-Rechnung im Überblick." Available at: https://www.destatis.de/DE/Publikationen/Thematisch/VolkswirtschaftlicheGesamtrechnungen/InputOutputRechnung/InputOutputRechnungUeberblick5815116099004.pdf?__blob=publicationFile [Accessed July 10, 2017].

Destatis. 2017j. "Kauffälle, Veräußerte Fläche, Durchschnittlicher Kaufwert für Bauland: Bundesländer, Quartale, Baulandarten, Gemeindegrößenklassen; Genesis-Destatis Code 61511-0003." Available at: https://www-genesis.destatis.de/genesis/online/data ;jsessionid=FF23E02CDE06AF556F38E6134207D395.tomcat_GO_1_3?operation=begriffsRecherche&suchanweisung_language=de&suchanweisung=61511-0003 [Accessed April 10, 2017].

Destatis. 2005. "Quality report. Sample Survey of Income and Expenditure 2003." Available at: https://www.destatis.de/EN/Publications/QualityReports/IncomeConsumptionLivingConditions/IncomeExpenditure2003.pdf?__blob=publicationFile [Accessed January 12, 2018].

Destatis. 2015. "Volkswirtschaftliche Gesamtrechnungen, Input-Output-Rechnung, Input-Output-Tabellen (ohne Weiterverarbeitung)."

Destatis. 2014. "Volkswirtschaftliche Gesamtrechnungen, Konzeptionelle Unterschiede zwischen ESVG 2010 und ESVG 1995." Available at: https://www.destatis.de/DE/ZahlenFakten/GesamtwirtschaftUmwelt/VGR/Methoden/Downloads/Revision2014_KonzeptionelleUnterschiede.pdf?__blob=publicationFile [Accessed October 6, 2017].

Deutsche Bundesbank. 2011. "Die Schuldenbremse in Deutschland - Wesentliche Inhalte und deren Umsetzung." Available at: https://www.bundesbank.de/Redaktion/DE/Downloads/Veroeffentlichungen/Monatsberichtsaufsaetze/2011/2011_10_schuldenbremse.pdf?__blob=publicationFile [Accessed December 21, 2017].

Deutsche Krankenhausgesellschaft (DKG). 2017. "Bestandsaufnahme zur Krankenhausplanung und Investitionsfinanzierung in den Bundesländern - Stand März 2017." Available at: http://www.dkgev.de/media/file/47291.Anlage_Bestandsaufnahme_Maerz_2017.pdf [Accessed December 21, 2017].

Deutsche Krankenhausgesellschaft (DKG). 2015. "Bestandsaufnahme zur Krankenhausplanung und Investitionsfinanzierung in den Bundesländern. Stand August 2015." Available at: http://www.dkgev.de/media/file/21149.Anlage_Bestandsaufnahme_August_2015.pdf [Accessed May 11, 2017].

Deutsche Krankenhausgesellschaft (DKG). 2009a. "Für eine hochwertige und flächendeckende Patientenversorgung, iinnovative Medizin und moderne Arbeitsplätze in Krankenhäusern. Positionen der Deutschen Krankenhausgesellschaft (DKG) für die 17. Legislaturperiode des Deutschen Bundestags." Available at: http://www.dkgev.de/media/file/6211.2009-07-15_DKG-Positionspapier2009.pdf [Accessed January 12, 2018].

Deutsche Krankenhausgesellschaft (DKG). 2009b. "Für eine hochwertige und flächendeckende Patientenversorgung, innovative Medizin und moderne Arbeitplätze in Krankenhäusern." Available at: http://www.dkgev.de/media/file/6214.2009-07-15_DKG-Positionspapier2009.pdf [Accessed December 21, 2017].

Deutscher Industrie- und Handelskammertag. 2010. "Der Krankenhaussektor in Deutschland - Sinnvolle Investitionsfinanzierung ist geboten." Available at: https://www.ihk-muenchen.de/ihk/documents/Branchen/Krankenhaussektor-1_DIHK-Position.pdf [Accessed December 21, 2017].

DIW Econ. 2012. "Wirtschaftsfaktor Tourismus Deutschland: Kennzahlen einer umsatzstarken Querschnittsbranche. Langfassung. Gefördert durch das BMWi." Bundesministerium für Wirtschaft und Technologie.

Drösler, S., J. Hasford, B.-M. Kurth, M. Schaefer, J. Wasem, and E. Wille. 2011. "Evaluationsbericht zum Jahresausgleich 2009 im Risikostrukturausgleich." Available at: http://www.bundesversicherungsamt.de/fileadmin/redaktion/Risikostrukturausgleich/Wissenschaftlicher_Beirat/Evaluationsbericht_zum_Jahresausgleich.pdf [Accessed December 21, 2017].

DRV Deutscher ReiseVerband e.V. 2017. "Der deutsche Reisemarkt. Zahlen und Fakten 2016." Available at: https://www.drv.de/securedl/106/0/0/1516733378/2c5d862a6efae3cbc69fa5b8f983364b80734425/fileadmin/user_upload/Fachbereiche/Statistik_und_Marktforschung/Fakten_und_Zahlen/17-08-03_Sommerausgabe_Zahlen_und_Fakten.pdf [Accessed April 10, 2017].

Dunn, A., L. Rittmueller, and B. Whitmire. 2015. "Introducing the new BEA health care satellite account. Survey of Current Business." Available at: https://www.bea.gov/scb/pdf/2015/01%20January/0115_bea_health_care_satellite_account.pdf [Accessed October 6, 2017].

Essig, H., and U.-P. Reich. 1988. "Umrisse eines Satellitensystems für das Gesundheitswesen." Satellitensystem zu den Volkswirtschaftlichen Gesamtrechnung, Band 6 der Schriftenreihe „Forum der Bundesstatistik" Kohlhammer Statistisches Bundesamt.

European Commission, International Monetary Fund, Organisation for Economic Co-operation and Development, United Nations, and World Bank. 2009. *System of National Accounts 2008*. New York. Available at: https://unstats.un.org/unsd/nationalaccount/docs/SNA2008.pdf [Accessed October 6, 2017].

Eurostat. 2017a. "Answers Questionnaire SUIOT Compilation, Update September 2017." Available at: http://ec.europa.eu/eurostat/statistics-explained/images/4/42/Answers_questionnaire_SUIOT_compilation_September2015_formatted_update_Sept_2017.xlsx [Accessed October 5, 2017].

Eurostat. 2013. "European system of accounts - ESA 2010." Publications Offi ce of the European Union, 2013. Available at: http://ec.europa.eu/eurostat/documents/3859598/5925693/KS-02-13-269-EN.PDF [Accessed January 12, 2018].

Eurostat. 1996. "European System of Accounts: ESA 1995." Office for Official Publications of the European Communities.

Eurostat. 2008a. *Eurostat Manual of Supply, Use and Input-Output Tables*. Luxemburg: Amt für amtliche Veröffentlichungen der Europäischen Gemeinschaften.

Eurostat. 2017b. "Glossary: General and special trade systems." Available at: http://ec.europa.eu/eurostat/statistics-explained/index.php/Glossary:General_and_special_trade_systems [Accessed January 12, 2018].

Eurostat. 2008b. *NACE Rev. 2. Statistical classification of economic activities in the European Community*. Luxemburg: Amt für amtliche Veröffentlichungen der Europäischen Gemeinschaften.

Eurostat. 2002. "Statistical Classification of Economic Activities in the European Community, Rev. 1.1 (2002) (NACE Rev. 1.1)." Available at: http://ec.europa.eu/eurostat/ramon/nomenclatures/index.cfm?TargetUrl=LST_NOM_DTL&StrNom=NACE_1_1&StrLanguageCode=EN&IntPcKey=&StrLayoutCode=EN [Accessed October 6, 2017].

Flegg, A.T., Y. Huang, and T. Tohmo. 2015. "Using CHARM to adjust for cross-hauling: the case of the province of Hubei, China." *Economic Systems Research* 27(3):391–413.

Forum MedTech Pharma e.V. 2015. "Branchenstruktur Medizintechnik in Bayern 2015." Available at: http://www.medtech-pharma.de/userdir/cms/docs/Studien/Branchenstruktur-Medizintechnik-Bayern_2015_web.pdf [Accessed December 21, 2017].

Fraport AG. 2017a. "LUG stärkt den Pharma-Hub FRA." Available at: https://www.frankfurt-airport.com/de/b2b/frachtstandort.detail.suffix.html/article/b2b/cargo/cargo-neuigkeiten/september2017/LUGstaerktpharma-hubFRA.html. [Accessed December 21, 2017]

Fraport AG. 2017b. "Wirtschaftsfaktor Flughafen, Unternehmensmagnet." Available at: http://www.fraport.de/content/fraport/de/konzern/flughafen-und-region/wirtschaftsfaktor-flughafen.html. [Accessed December 21, 2017]

Fuest, C., and M. Thöne. 2012. "§ 37 Der Finanzföderalismus in Deutschland und seine Reform." In I. Härtel, ed. *Handbuch Föderalismus – Föderalismus als demokratische Rechtsordnung und Rechtskultur in Deutschland, Europa und der Welt: Band II: Probleme, Reformen, Perspektiven des deutschen Föderalismus*. Berlin, Heidelberg: Springer Berlin Heidelberg, pp. 265–321. Available at: https://doi.org/10.1007/978-3-642-15523-9_12. [Accessed December 21, 2017]

Geigant, F., H.-W. Holub, and H. Schnabl. 1986. "Leistungsverflechtung und Kostenstrukturen des Gesundheitswesens in der Bundesrepublik Deutschland." Institut für Gesundheits-System-Forschung, Verflechtungsanalyse des Gesundheitswesens in der Bundesrepublik Deutschland

Gemeinsamer Bundesausschuss (G-BA). 2016. "Richtlinie über die Bedarfsplanung sowie die Maßstäbe zur Feststellung von Überversorgung und Unterversorgung in der vertragsärztlichen Versorgung. § 9 - Modifikation der Verhältniszahl durch einen Demografiefaktor." Available at: https://www.g-ba.de/downloads/62-492-1249/BPL-RL_2016-06-16_iK-2016-09-15.pdf [Accessed November 28, 2016].

GKV-Spitzenverband. 2015. "Qualität – verbessern, sichern, veröffentlichen. Geschäftsbericht 2014." Available at: https://www.gkv-spitzenverband.de/media/dokumente/presse/publikationen/geschaeftsberichte/GKV_GB2014_web_barrierefrei.pdf [Accessed January 12, 2018].

Golan, A., and S.J. Vogel. 2000. "Estimation of non-stationary social accounting matrix coefficients with supply-side information." *Economic Systems Research* 12(4):447–471.

Goldschmidt, A.J.W., and J. Hilbert eds. 2009. *Gesundheitswirtschaft in Deutschland: Die Zukunftsbranche. Beispiele über alle wichtigen Bereiche des Gesundheitswesens in Deutschland zur Gesundheitswirtschaft*. Wegscheid: Wikom.

Göpffarth, D. 2011. "Regionalmerkmale im Risikostrukturausgleich. Ein Beitrag zum funktionalen Wettbewerb und zu bedarfsgerechter Versorgung?" *BARMER GEK Gesundheitswesen aktuell 2011*:16–127.

Grünenthal GmbH. 2017. "Landesorganisationen weltweit." Available at: https://www.grunenthal.de/grt-web/136701422.jsp [Accessed April 7, 2017].

Haan, de M., and van M. Rooijen-Horsten. 2003. "Knowledge Indicators based on Satellite Accounts, Final report for NESIS-Workpackage 5.1." Statistics Netherlands, Division of Macro-economic Statistics and Dissemination Development and support department. Available at: https://www.cbs.nl/-/media/imported/documents/2003/35/knowledge-indicators-based-on-satellite-accounts-final-report-nesis.pdf [Accessed January 11, 2018].

Health Capital. 2014. "Gemeinsam Innovation Gestalten - Masterplan Gesundheitsregion Berlin Brandenburg."

Helmenstein, C., A. Kleissner, and B. Moser. 2006. "Sportwirtschaft Österreich. Eine Analyse der wirtschaftlichen Bedeutung des Sports in Österreich." SportEconAustria (SpEA). Available at: http://schasching.spoe.at/antraege2006/WKO%20Sportwirtschaft%20in%20%D6sterreich.pdf [Accessed January 11, 2018].

Hemmerling, U., P. Pascher, S. Nass, and C. Seidel. 2013. "Information zur deutschen Landwirtschaft. Zahlen, Daten, Fakten." i.m.a - information.medien.agrar e.V. Available at: http://information-medien-agrar.de/webshop/mediafiles/PDF/104-117_info-landwirtschaft.pdf [Accessed April 26, 2017].

Henke, K.-D. 2002. "Kürzer im Krankenhaus – längeres Leid? Was steckt hinter dem Fallpauschalensystem?"

Henke, K.-D., K. Neumann, M. Schneider, A. Georgi, J. Bungenstock, M. Baur, S. Ottmann, T. Krauss, and U. Hofmann. 2010. *Erstellung eines Satellitenkontos für die Gesundheitswirtschaft in Deutschland* 1. Aufl. Baden-Baden: Nomos.

Henke, K.-D., S. Troppens, G. Braeseke, B. Dreher, and M. Merda. 2011. *Volkswirtschaftliche Bedeutung der Gesundheitswirtschaft - Innovationen, Branchenverflechtung, Arbeitsmarkt* 1. Auflage. Baden-Baden: Nomos Verlagsgesellschaft mbH & Co. KG.

Hesse, S. 2013. *Input und Output der Gesundheitswirtschaft. Eine Stabilitätsanalyse der Gesundheitswirtschaft in Bezug auf die gesamtwirtschaftliche Bedeutung in den Jahren der Finanz-und Wirtschaftskrise*. Frankfurt a.M.: Peter Lang.

Hilbert, J., R. Fretschner, and A. Dülberg. 2002. "Rahmenbedingungen und Herausforderungen der Gesundheitswirtschaft." *Manuskript. Institut Arbeit und Technik. Gelsenkirchen*. Available at: http://www.iaq.uni-due.de/aktuell/veroeff/ds/hilbert02b.pdf [Accessed September 26, 2017].

IEGUS, and Rheinisch-Westfälisches Institut für Wirtschaftsforschung (RWI). 2015. "Ökonomische Herausforderungen der Altenpflegewirtschaft." Available at: http://www.rwi-essen.de/media/content/pages/publikationen/rwi-projektberichte/rwi-pb_altenpflegewirtschaft_endbericht.pdf [Accessed November 28, 2016].

IMS Health. 2015. "IMS Marktbericht. Entwicklung des deutschen Pharmaamarktes im Dezember und im Jahr 2014."

Instituto Brasileiro de Geografia e Estatística (IBGE). 2008. "Health Economics. A Macroeconomic Perspective 2000—2005."

Instituto Nacional de Estatística Portugal. 2015. "Health Satellite Account 2000-2015."

Instituto Nacional de Estatística Portugal. 2016. "Satellite Account for the Sea – 2010 – 2013, Methodological Report." Available at: https://www.ine.pt/ngt_server/attachfileu.jsp?look_parentBoui=300613867&att_display=n&att_download=y [Accessed October 6, 2017].

Janssen-Cilag GmbH. 2017. "Daten & Fakten." Available at: http://www.janssen.com/germany/unternehmen/daten-und-fakten [Accessed April 7, 2017].

Jensen, R.C. 1980. "The Concept of Accuracy in Regional Input-Output Models." *International Regional Science Review* 5(2):139–154.

Jensen, R.C., T.D. Mandeville, and N.D. Karunaratne. 2017. *Regional economic planning: Generation of regional input-output analysis*. Routledge.

Juszczak, J. 2016. "Medizintourismus nach Deutschland im Aufwind." Available at: https://www.h-brs.de/de/pressemitteilung/medizintourismus-nach-deutschland-im-aufwind [Accessed April 11, 2017].

Kassenärztliche Bundesvereinigung (KBV). 2016. "Ärztemangel." Available at: http://www.kbv.de/html/themen_1076.php [Accessed November 28, 2016].

Kersten, J., C. Neu, and B. Vogel. 2015. "Regionale Daseinsvorsorge. Begriff, Indikatoren, Gemeinschaftsaufgabe. Gutachten im Auftrag der Abteilung Wirtschafts- und Sozialpolitik der Friedrich-Ebert-Stiftung." Available at: http://library.fes.de/pdf-files/wiso/11182.pdf [Accessed December 21, 2017].

Klose, J., and I. Rehbein. 2015. "Ärzteatlas 2015. Daten zur Versorgungsdichte von Vertragsärzten." Wissenschaftliches Institut der AOK. Available at: http://www.wido.de/fileadmin/wido/downloads/pdf_ambulaten_versorg/wido_amb_pub-aerzteatlas2015_0615.pdf [Accessed November 29, 2016].

Kronenberg, T. 2009a. "Construction of Regional Input-Output Tables Using Non-survey Methods: The Role of Cross-Hauling." *International Regional Science Review* 32(1):40–64.

Kronenberg, T. 2011. "Demographically Induced Changes in the Structure of Final Demand and Infrastructure Use." In T. Kronenberg and W. Kuckshinrichs, eds. *Demography and Infrastructure: National and Regional Aspects of Demographic Change*. Dordrecht: Springer Netherlands, pp. 67–91. Available at: https://doi.org/10.1007/978-94-007-0458-9_4. [Accessed April 10, 2017]

Kronenberg, T. 2012. "Regional input-output models and the treatment of imports in the European System of Accounts (ESA)." *Jahrbuch für Regionalwissenschaft* 32(2):175–191.

Kronenberg, T. 2009b. "The Impact of Demographic Change on Energy Use and Greenhouse Gas Emissions in Germany." Ecological Economics, 68 (10)

Kronenberg, T., and K. Engel. 2008. "Demographischer Wandel und dessen Auswirkungen auf den Energieverbrauch in Hamburg und Mecklenburg-Vorpommern." *Zeitschrift für Energiewirtschaft* 32(4):280–290.

Kronenberg, T., S. Kühntopf, and T. Tivig. 2010. "Die Effekte von regionalen demografischen Trends auf die ökologische Dimension der Nachhaltigkeit." In *Hagemann, H. and M. von Hauff (Hrsg.), Nachhaltige Ent-wicklung – das neue Paradigma in der Ökonomie*. Marburg: Metropolis Verlag.

Kuratorium Gesundheitswirtschaft. 2005. "Ergebnisbericht „Nationale Branchenkonferenz Gesundheitswirtschaft 2005 "07./08. Dezember 2005, Rostock-Warnemünde." *URL:*< http://www. *bcv. org/hosting/bcv/website. nsf/urlnames/gw_rbbconference/$ file/Beri cht_BK_05. pdf.* [Accessed April 06, 2017]

Lahr, M.L. 1993. "A review of the literature supporting the hybrid approach to constructing regional input–output models." *Economic Systems Research* 5(3):277–293.

Laimer, P., S. Ehn-Fragner, and E. Smeral. 2014. "Ein Tourismus-Satellitenkonto für Österreich; Methodik, Ergebnisse und Prognosen für die Jahre 2000 bis 2015." WIFO Publication Available at: https://www.bmdw.gv.at/Tourismus/TourismusstudienUndPublikationen/Documents/Tourismus_Satellitenkonto_2000-2015.pdf [Accessed January 11, 2018].

Leber, W.-D. 2015. "Krankenhausreform 2015: Von der Landesplanung zur Marktregulierung."

Lenk, T. 2008. "Reform des deutschen Länderfinanzausgleichs - eine unendliche Geschichte?" *Position Liberal, Positionspapier des Liberalen Instituts der Friedrich-Naumann-Stiftung für Freiheit*. Available at: http://edoc.vifapol.de/opus/volltexte/2010/2327/pdf/56_Lenk_Laender_innen_print.pdf [Accessed January 8, 2018].

Lenk, T., and P. Glinka. 2015. "Steuerzuordnung nach der Wirtschaftskraft – gut für den bundesstaatlichen Finanzausgleich." *Wirtschaftsdienst* 95(9):619–626.

Lenk, T., and T. Starke. 2015. "Auswirkungen der demografischen Entwicklung auf die öffentlichen Finanzen." Finanzwissenschaft, No. 48 Universität Leipzig, Institut für Öffentliche Finanzen und Public Management. Available at: https://www.econstor.eu/bitstream/10419/107182/1/81797928X.pdf [Accessed December 21, 2017].

Lenzen, M., and J.M. Rueda-Cantuche. 2012. "A note on the use of supply-use tables in impact analyses." *SORT-Statistics and Operations Research Transactions* 36(2):139–152.

Lenzen, M., R. Wood, and B. Gallego. 2007. "Some Comments on the GRAS Method." *Economic Systems Research* 19(4):461–465.

Lünendonk. 2016. "Lünendonk-Liste 2016: Führende Wirtschaftsprüfungs- und Steuerberatungs-Gesellschaften in Deutschland."

Madsen, B., and C. Jensen-Butler. 1999. "Make and Use Approaches to Regional and Interregional Accounts and Models." *Economic Systems Research* 11(3):277–300.

Merck KGaA. 2012a. "Merck Geschäftsbericht 2011." Available at: https://www.merckgroup.com/content/dam/web/corporate/non-images/investors/events-and-presentations/annual-general-meeting-archive/2012/DE/auszulegende-unterlagen/4_Merck_Geschaeftsbericht_2011_de_DE.pdf [Accessed April 7, 2017].

Merck KGaA. 2012b. "Produktion fast ohne Tempolimit." Available at: http://www.magazin.emerck/de/Leben/Tabletten/Tablettenproduktion1.html [Accessed April 12, 2017].

Mielke, J. 2011. "Traditionsunternehmen in Berlin. Neuer Bayer-Chef lässt Schering verschwinden." *Der Tagesspiegel*. Available at: http://www.tagesspiegel.de/wirtschaft/traditionsunternehmen-in-berlin-neuer-bayer-chef-laesst-schering-verschwinden/3697516.html [Accessed April 8, 2017].

Miernyk, W.H. 1976. "Comments on recent developments in regional input-output analysis." *International Regional Science Review* 1(2):47–55.

Miller, R.E., and P.D. Blair. 2009. *Input-output analysis: foundations and extensions*. Cambridge University Press.

Mineralölwirtschaftsverband e.V. 2015. "Raffinerien bewegen Menschen und Märkte." Available at: https://www.mwv.de/wp-content/uploads/2016/07/mwv-raffinerien-bewegen-menschen-und-maerkte-2015.pdf [Accessed April 10, 2017].

Mortsiefer, H. 2016. "Monsanto-Deal; Bayer in Berlin ist selbstbewusst." *Der Tagesspiegel*. Available at: http://www.tagesspiegel.de/wirtschaft/monsanto-deal-bayer-in-berlin-ist-selbstbewusst/13632114.html [Accessed April 8, 2017].

Nowossadeck, E. 2012. "Demografische Alterung und Folgen für das Gesundheitswesen." GBE kompakt 3(2) Robert Koch-Institut Berlin. Available at: https://www.rki.de/DE/Content/Gesundheitsmonitoring/Gesundheitsberichterstattung/GBEDownloadsK/2012_2_Demografischer_Wandel_Alterung.pdf?__blob=publicationFile [Accessed December 21, 2017].

Organisation for Economic Co-operation and Development (OECD), World Health Organization (WHO), and Statistical Office of the European Communities (Eurostat) eds. 2011. *A system of health accounts 2011*. Paris.

Organization for Economic Co-Operation and Development (OECD). 2015. "OECD Health Statistics 2015, Focus on Health Spending." Available at: https://www.oecd.org/health/health-systems/Focus-Health-Spending-2015.pdf [Accessed October 6, 2017].

Orosz, E., and D. Morgan. 2004. "SHA-Based National Health Accounts in Thirteen. OECD Countries: A Comparative Analysis." OECD Health Working Papers No. 16 Organisation for Economic Co-operation and Development. Available at: http://www.oecd.org/els/health-systems/33661480.pdf [Accessed January 12, 2018].

Ostwald, D.A., K.-D. Henke, Z.-G. Kim, D. Heeger, S. Hesse, J. Knippel, W.-D. Perlitz, S. Troppens, T. Richter, and H. Mosetter. 2014. *Weiterentwicklung des deutschen Gesundheitssatellitenkontos zu einer Gesundheitswirtschaftlichen Gesamtrechnung: Abschlussbericht* 1. Aufl. Baden-Baden: Nomos.

Ostwald, D.A., S. Hofmann, O. Acker, M. Pachmajer, and R. Friedrich. 2016. *Der Einfluss der Digitalisierung auf die Arbeitskräftesituation in Deutschland. Berufs- und branchenspezifische Analyse bis zum Jahr 2030*. Frankfurt am Main: PwC.

Ostwald, D.A., B. Legler, and M.C. Schwärzler. 2014. "Ökonomischer Fußabdruck der Gesundheitswirtschaft in Thüringen unter besonderer Berücksichtigung der industriellen Gesundheitswirtschaft."

Ostwald, D.A., B. Legler, M.C. Schwärzler, J. Gerlach, A. Haaf, S. Tetzner, M. Schneider, T. Krauss, and A. Köse. 2017. "Regionalisierung der Gesundheitswirtschaftlichen Gesamtrechnung." Available at: http://www.bmwi.de/Redaktion/DE/Publikationen/Studien/regionalisierung-der-gesundheitswirtschaftlichen-gesamtrechnung.pdf?__blob=publicationFile&v=6 [Accessed August 3, 2017].

Ostwald, D.A., B. Legler, M.C. Schwärzler, C. Plaul, and S. Tetzner. 2015. "Der ökonomische Fußabdruck der industriellen Gesundheitswirtschaft in Baden-Württemberg."

Ostwald, D.A., B. Legler, M.C. Schwärzler, and S. Tetzner. 2015a. "Der ökonomische Fußabdruck der Gesundheitswirtschaft in Mecklenburg-Vorpommern."

Ostwald, D.A., B. Legler, M.C. Schwärzler, and S. Tetzner. 2015b. *Der ökonomische Fußabdruck der Gesundheitswirtschaft in Mecklenburg-Vorpommern*. Darmstadt.

Ostwald, D.A., and M.C. Schwärzler. 2015. "Gesundheitsindustrie regional denken." *GesundheitsWirtschaft* 9(1):44–47.

Ostwald, D.A., K. Zubrzycki, and B. Legler. 2015. "Der ökonomische Fußabdruck von Bayer HealthCare in Deutschland."

Pavel, F., L. Handrich, A. Mattes, and K. Peter. 2015. *Ökonomischer Fußabdruck von Novartis Deutschland. Die Bedeutung von Novartis für den Wirtschaftsstandort und Wissenschaftsstandort Deutschland.* Berlin: Deutsches Institut für Wirtschaftsforschung. Available at: https://diw-econ.de/wp-content/uploads/2015/03/diwkompakt_2015-094_v 2.0.pdf [Accessed January 22, 2018].

Peters, M. 2009. "Wirtschaftskrise - An der Verhütung wird gespart." *Der Tagesspiegel*. Available at: http://www.tagesspiegel.de/wirtschaft/wirtschaftskrise-an-der-verhuetung-gespart/1541208.html [Accessed April 8, 2017].

Pfizer Deutschland GmbH. 2017a. "Über Pfizer – Standorte - Berlin." Available at: https://www.pfizer.de/ueber-pfizer/standorte/berlin/ [Accessed April 8, 2017].

Pfizer Deutschland GmbH. 2017b. "Über Pfizer. Standorte." Available at: https://www.pfizer.de/ueber-pfizer/standorte/ [Accessed April 7, 2017].

Pharmahauptstadt Berlin. 2017. "Wirtschaftsfakten; Die pharmazeutische Industrie – ein Schwergewicht in Berlin." Available at: http://www.pharmahauptstadt.de/themen/wirtschaftsfakten/ [Accessed April 8, 2017].

Porter, M.E., and C. Guth. 2012. "Leistungserbringer im Gesundheitswesen." In M. E. Porter and C. Guth, eds. *Chancen für das deutsche Gesundheitssystem: Von Partikularinteressen zu mehr Patientennutzen*. Berlin, Heidelberg: Springer Berlin Heidelberg, pp. 129–183. Available at: https://doi.org/10.1007/978-3-642-25683-7_6. [Accessed April 8, 2017]

Prütz, F., A. Rommel, L.E. Kroll, and T. Lampert. 2014. "25 Jahre nach dem Fall der Mauer: Regionale Unterschiede in der Gesundheit." *GBE kompakt* 5(3).

Raa, ten, T., and J.M. Rueda-Cantuche. 2013. "The problem of negatives generated by the commodity technology model in input-output analysis: A review of solutions." Journal of Economic Structures, 2(5), DOI 10.1186/2193-2409-2-5 Available at: https://link.springer.com/content/pdf/10.1186%2F2193-2409-2-5.pdf [Accessed October 6, 2017].

Ranscht, A. 2009. *Quantifizierung regionaler Wachstums- und Beschäftigungseffekte der Gesundheitswirtschaft - am Beispiel ausgewählter Metropolregionen*. Berlin: Med. Wiss. Verl.-Ges.

Rehborn, M., and H. Thomae. 2015. "Krankenhausplanung, Krankenhausfinanzierung, Versorgungsverträge." In *Ratzel, R. & Luxenburger, B. (Hrsg.): Handbuch Medizinrecht*. Heidelberg: Deutscher AnwaltVerlag, pp. 1329–1418.

Rheinisch-Westfälisches Institut für Wirtschaftsforschung (RWI). 2014. "Krankenhaus Rating Report 2014. Mangelware Kapital: Wege aus der Investitionsfalle."

Roche Pharma AG. 2017. "Standort Grenzach." Available at: https://www.roche.de/about/standorte/grenzach/index.html [Accessed April 7, 2017].

Rösel, F. 2013. "Kränkelnde Krankenhäuser – Ursachen und Auswirkungen des Rückgangs der Krankenhausinvestitionen der Länder." *ifo Dresden berichtet* (20):3–15.

Rürup, B., M. Albrecht, C. Igel, and B. Häussler. 2008. "Umstellung auf eine monistische Finanzierung von Krankenhäusern. Expertise im Auftrag des Bundesministeriums für Gesundheit." Technische Universität Darmstadt. Available at: http://www.sozialpolitik-aktuell.de/tl_files/sozialpolitik-aktuell/_Politikfelder/Gesundheitswesen/Dokumente/Krankenhaus_Gutachten_Ruerup.pdf [Accessed December 21, 2017].

Sachverständigenrat zur Begutachtung der Entwicklung im Gesundheitswesen. 2007. "Cooperation and Responsibility; Prerequisites for Target-Oriented Health Care."

Sachverständigenrat zur Begutachtung der Entwicklung im Gesundheitswesen. 1998. *Gesundheitswesen in Deutschland. Kostenfaktor und Zukunftsbranche. Band II: Fortschritt, Wachstumsmärkte, Finanzierung und Vergütung.* Baden-Baden.

Sachverständigenrat zur Begutachtung der Entwicklung im Gesundheitswesen (SVR). 2014. "Bedarfsgerechte Versorgung – Perspektiven für ländliche Regionen und ausgewählte Leistungsbereiche."

Sachverständigenrat zur Begutachtung der gesamtwirtschaftlichen Entwicklung, and Statistisches Bundesamt. 2014. *Mehr Vertrauen in Marktprozesse, Jahresgutachten*. Wiesbaden: Bonifatius GmbH Buch-Druck-Verlag. Available at: https://www.sachverstaendigenrat-wirtschaft.de/fileadmin/dateiablage/gutachten/jg201415/JG14_ges.pdf [Accessed December 21, 2017].

Sachverständigenrat zur Begutachtung der gesamtwirtschaftlichen Entwicklung, and Statistisches Bundesamt. 2012. *Stabile Architektur für Europa – Handlungsbedarf im Inland. Jahresgutachten 2012/13*. Wiesbaden: Bonifatius GmbH Buch-Druck-Verlag. Available at: https://www.sachverstaendigenrat-wirtschaft.de/fileadmin/dateiablage/gutachten/ga201213/ga12_ges.pdf [Accessed December 21, 2017].

Salutas Pharma GmbH. 2015. “Salutas Pharma GmbH.” Available at: https://www.sandoz.de/ueber-uns/standorte-deutschland/barleben-magdeburg-und-osterweddingen [Accessed April 7, 2017].

Salz, J. 2010. “Pharmabranche – Der Stellenabbau bei Bayer ist unvermeidlich.” *WirtschaftsWoche*. Available at: http://www.wiwo.de/unternehmen/pharmabranche-der-stellenabbau-bei-bayer-ist-unvermeidlich/5230584.html [Accessed April 8, 2017].

Sanofi-Aventis Deutschland GmbH. 2017a. “Produktion & Fertigung – Die industrielle Dimension – Industrial Affairs.” Available at: http://www.sanofi.de/l/de/de/layout.jsp?scat=969531AE-D9AC-4555-9E1A-A62737D84A71 [Accessed April 12, 2017].

Sanofi-Aventis Deutschland GmbH. 2017b. “Standorte von Sanofi in Deutschland.” Available at: http://www.sanofi.de/l/de/de/layout.jsp?scat=85A29727-1642-4374-9C68-63D17F083ABC [Accessed April 7, 2017].

Sarrazin, H.T. 1992. “Ein Satellitensystem für das Gesundheitswesen zu den Volkswirtschaftlichen Gesamtrechnungen. Endbericht im Auftrag des Bundesministeriums für Arbeit und Sozialordnung.” Statistisches Bundesamt.

Schäuble, W. 2017. “Neuregelung des bundesstaatlichen Finanzauslgeichs.” Available at: http://www.bundesfinanzministerium.de/Content/DE/Reden/2017/2017-02-16-bundestag-bund-laender-finanzausgleich-textfassung.html [Accessed April 24, 2017].

Schmid, T., K. Stadler, and G. Zipperlen. 2016. “Investitionsbewertungsrelationen (IBR) finanzielle Folgen für das einzelne Krankenhaus.” *das Krankenhaus*:375–378.

Schneider, M. 2013. “Die gesundheitswirtschaftliche Bedeutung der Pharmazeutischen Industrie in Bayern.” BASYS.

Schneider, M. 2014. “Zwischen Kostendämpfung und Wachstum. Die Pharmazeutische Industrie in Bayern – 2008 bis 2012.” *Recht und Politik im Gesundheitswesen* 22(3):77–96.

Schneider, M., P. Biene-Dietrich, and U. Hofmann. 2000a. “Gesundheitsökonomische Basisdaten für Nordrhein-Westfalen - Berichtsjahr 1997 - Gutachten für das Ministerium für Frauen, Jugend, Familie und Gesundheit des Landes Nordrhein-Westfalen.”

Schneider, M., P. Biene-Dietrich, and U. Hofmann. 2000b. "Gesundheitsökonomische Basisdaten für Sachsen - Berichtsjahr 1997 - Gutachten für das Sächsische Staatsministerium für Soziales, Gesundheit, Jugend und Familie."

Schneider, M., P. Biene-Dietrich, U. Hofmann, A. Köse, and D. Mill. 1998. "Gesundheitsökonomische Basisdaten Rheinland-Pfalz." Schriftenreihe: Gesundheitswesen / Gesundheitsberichterstattung Ministerium für Arbeit, Soziales und Gesundheit, Rheinland-Pfalz.

Schneider, M., U. Hofmann, P. Biene-Dietrich, A. Köse, and O. Krawczyk. 2003. "Entwicklungspotenziale der Gesundheitswirtschaft in Niedersachsen, Gutachten für das Niedersächsische Ministerium für Wirtschaft, Arbeit und Verkehr." BASYS, NIW.

Schneider, M., U. Hofmann, A. Köse, and P. Biene-Dietrich. 2002. "Gesundheitsökonomische Indikatoren für Rheinland-Pfalz 1995-2000. Untersuchung für das Ministerium für Arbeit, Soziales, Familie und Gesundheit Rheinland-Pfalz." BASYS.

Schneider, M., T. Krauss, U. Hofmann, A. Köse, D.A. Ostwald, A. Gandjour, S. Hofmann, B. Karmann, B. Legler, S. Schubert, M.C. Schwärzler, A. Karmann, C. Plaul, K.-D. Henke, S. Troppens, G. Braeseke, and T. Richter. 2016. *Gesundheitswirtschaftliche Gesamtrechnung 2000-2014: Gutachten für das Bundesministerium für Wirtschaft und Energie* 1. Aufl. Baden-Baden: Nomos.

Schröder, A., and K. Zimmermann. 2014. "Erstellung regionaler Input-Output-Tabellen; Ein Vergleich existierender Ansätze und ihre Anwendung für die deutsche Ostseeküstenregion." RADOST-Berichtsreihe, Bericht Nr. 33, ISSN: 2192-3140 Institut für ökologische Wirtschaftsforschung, Technische Universität Berlin.

Schwärzler, M.C., and T. Kronenberg. 2017a. "Application of the Multiregional Health Account for Germany-A financial equalization scheme to cope with lagging investments in German hospitals." No. 80720, Available at: https://mpra.ub.uni-muenchen.de/80720/ [Accessed September 21, 2017].

Schwärzler, M.C., and T. Kronenberg. 2017b. "Basic Results of the Multiregional Health Account for Germany - Validation of Direct Effects of the Health Economy." No. 80717, Available at: https://mpra.ub.uni-muenchen.de/80717/ [Accessed September 21, 2017].

Schwärzler, M.C., and T. Kronenberg. 2017c. "Basic Results of the Multiregional Health Account for Germany - Validation of Indirect Effects of the Health Economy." No. 80719, Available at: https://mpra.ub.uni-muenchen.de/80719/ [Accessed September 21, 2017].

Schwärzler, M.C., and T. Kronenberg. 2017d. "Methodology of the Multiregional Health Account for Germany - An Iterative Algorithm-Based Multiregionalization Approach of Supply and Use Tables with Emphasis on Health." MPRA Paper Available at: https://mpra.ub.uni-muenchen.de/80712/ [Accessed September 21, 2017].

Schwärzler, M.C., and T. Kronenberg. 2016. "Methodology of the National Health Account for Germany - Database, compilation and results." No. 73561, Available at: https://mpra.ub.uni-muenchen.de/73561/ [Accessed September 27, 2016].

Schwärzler, M.C., and B. Legler. 2017. "Der ökonomische Fußabdruck der Gesundheitswirtschaft in Deutschland nach ESVG 2010."

Semerák, V., K. Zigic, E. Loizou, and A. Golemanova-Kuharova. 2010. "Regional input-output analysis: Ap-plication on rural regions in Germany, the Czech Republic and Greece." Available at: https://ageconsearch.umn.edu/bitstream/94904/2/Paper_conference_version_Semerak_v 2.pdf [Accessed April 26, 2017].

Statistische Ämter des Bundes und der Länder. 2016. "Volkswirtschaftliche Gesamtrechnungen der Länder, Reihe 1, Länderergebnisse Band 1. Bruttoinlandsprodukt, Bruttowertschöpfung in den Ländern der Bundesrepublik Deutschland 1991 bis 2015, Berechnungsstand: August 2015/Februar 2016."

Statistische Ämter des Bundes und der Länder. 2017. "Volkswirtschaftliche Gesamtrechnungen der Länder, Reihe 1, Länderergebnisse Band 1. Bruttoinlandsprodukt Bruttowertschöpfung in den Ländern der Bundesrepublik Deutschland 1991 bis 2016, Berechnungsstand: November 2016/Februar 2017." Available at: http://vgrdl.de/VGRdL/tbls/RV2014/R1B1.zip [Accessed January 12, 2018].

Statistisches Amt für Hamburg und Schleswig-Holstein. 2016. "Starke Umsatzrückgänge in der Mineralölverarbeitung." No. Presseinformation Nr. 29/2016,

Statistisches Bundesamt. 2011a. "Demografischer Wandel in Deutschland, Heft 1, Bevölkerungs- und Haushaltsentwicklung im Bund und in den Ländern." Available at: https://www.destatis.de/GPStatistik/servlets/MCRFileNodeServlet/DEHeft_derivate_00012505/5871101119004.pdf [Accessed December 21, 2017].

Statistisches Bundesamt. 2010. "Demografischer Wandel in Deutschland, Heft 2, Auswirkungen auf Krankenhausbehandlungen und Pflegebedürftige im Bund und in den Ländern." Available at: https://www.destatis.de/GPStatistik/servlets/MCRFileNodeServlet/DEHeft_derivate_00012508/Demografischer_Wandel_Heft2.pdf;jsessionid=8A4BB0D186A6BF1C74B437B5477C8CDB [Accessed December 21, 2017].

Statistisches Bundesamt. 2011b. "Gesundheitsausgabenrechnung - Methoden und Grundlagen 2008." Available at: http://www.gbe-bund.de/pdf/GAR_methodik.pdf [Accessed July 31, 2017].

Steeg, van de, A.M. 2009. "Accounting for Tourism, The Tourism Satellite Account (TSA) in Perspective." Statistics Netherlands. Available at: http://citeseerx.ist.psu.edu/viewdoc/download?doi=10.1.1.608.8801&rep=rep1&type=pdf [Accessed October 10, 2017].

Steibadler, T. 2012. "Pfizer-Werk in Illertissen steht vor Verkauf." *Südwest Presse*. Available at: https://www.swp.de/suedwesten/landkreise/kreis-neu-ulm-bayern/pfizer-werk-in-illertissen-steht-vor-verkauf-21951445.html [Accessed April 7, 2017].

Szent-Ivanyi, T. 2014. "Bayer-Manager Andreas Fibig „Wir fragen uns auch, warum das Image nicht besser ist"." *Berliner Zeitung*. Available at: https://www.berliner-zeitung.de/wirtschaft/bayer-manager-andreas-fibig--wir-fragen-uns-auch--warum-das-image-nicht-besser-ist--2983120 [Accessed April 8, 2017].

Temurshoev, U., and M.P. Timmer. 2011. "Joint estimation of supply and use tables: Joint estimation of supply and use tables." *Papers in Regional Science* 90(4):863–882.

Thüringen innovativ. 2006. "Know-how-Region Thüringen, Medizintechnik."

Többen, J., and T.H. Kronenberg. 2015. "Construction of multi-regional input–output tables using the CHARM method." *Economic systems research* 27(4):487–507.

Tukker, A., and E. Dietzenbacher. 2013. "Global multiregional input–output frameworks: an introduction and outlook." *Economic Systems Research* 25(1):1–19.

Ulrich, V., and E. Wille. 2014. "Zur Berücksichtigung einer regionalen Komponente im morbiditätsorientierten Risikostrukturausgleich (Morbi-RSA)." *Bayreuth und Mannheim*. Available at: http://www.bnfi.de/download/InformationenGutachten32_Ulrich%202014-09-21-Endbericht-RSA-Bayern.pdf [Accessed October 4, 2017].

Umweltministerium NRW. 2014. "EnergieDaten.NRW 2014." Available at: https://www.umwelt.nrw.de/fileadmin/redaktion/Broschueren/energiedaten.nrw_2014.pdf [Accessed April 10, 2017].

United Nations. 2013. "International Merchandise Trade Statistics: Compilers Manual, Revision 1 (IMTS 2010-CM). Sales No. E.10.XVII.8 (edited white cover version)." Department of Economic and Social Affairs, Statistics Division. Available at: https://unstats.un.org/unsd/trade/EG-IMTS/IMTS2010-CM%20-%20white%20cover%20version.pdf [Accessed January 12, 2018].

Verband der Ersatzkassen (vdek). 2015. "Stellungnahme des Verbandes der Ersatzkassen e. V. (vdek) zum Entwurf eines Gesetzes zur Reform der Strukturen der Krankenhausversorgung (Krankenhausstrukturgesetz – KHSG) anlässlich der Anhörung vor dem Ausschuss für Gesundheit des Deutschen Bundestages am 7.9.2015." Available at: https://www.vdek.com/politik/stellungnahmen/_jcr_content/par/download_20/file.res/2015-09-02%20Stellungnahme%20vdek%20KHSG%20final.pdf [Accessed December 21, 2017].

Verband Forschender Arzneimittelhersteller (vfa). 2015. "Statistics 2015, The Pharmaceutical Industry in Germany." Available at: https://www.vfa.de/embed/statistics-2015-english.pdf [Accessed January 22, 2018].

Verband Forschender Arzneimittelhersteller (vfa), and Stifterverband für die Deutsche Wissenschaft e. V. 2016. "Forschende Pharma-Unternehmen: Mitarbeiter und Ausgaben für Forschung und Entwicklung (F&E)." Available at: https://www.vfa.de/embed/funde-mitarb-aufwend-d.pdf [Accessed April 8, 2017].

Wenz, L., S.N. Willner, A. Radebach, R. Bierkandt, J.C. Steckel, and A. Levermann. 2015. "Regional and Sectoral Disaggregation of Multi-Regional Input–Output Tables–a Flexible Algorithm." *Economic Systems Research* 27(2):194–212.

Werling, E., C. Hamelmannn, and K.-D. Henke. 2018. "Health economy reporting: a useful tool for evidence-based investments for health and sustainable development. A case review from Germany." WHO Regional Office for Europe.

Wiebe, K.S., and M. Lenzen. 2016. "To RAS or not to RAS? What is the difference in outcomes in multi-regional input–output models?" *Economic Systems Research* 28(3):383–402.

Wirtschaftsministerium Brandenburg. 2012. “Energiestrategie 2030 des Landes Brandenburg.” Ministerium für Wirtschaft und Europaangelegenheiten des Landes Brandenburg. Referat Energiepolitik und -wirtschaft. Available at: http://mwe.brandenburg.de/media/bb1.a.3814.de/Energiestrategie2030_2012.pdf [Accessed April 10, 2017].

Wirtschaftsministerum NRW, IG Metall, and Wirtschaftsvereinigung Stahl. 2015. “Stahlgipfel Nordrhein-Westfalen, Gemeinsame Erklärung.” Available at: http://www.stahl-online.de/wp-content/uploads/2015/09/20150921_NRW_Stahlgipfel_Erkl_Unterschriften.pdf [Accessed April 26, 2017].

Wissenschaftlicher Beirat beim Bundesministerium der Finanzen. 2013. “Finanzpolitische Herausforderungen des demografischen Wandels im föderativen System, Gutachten des Wissenschaftlichen Beirats beim Bundesministerium der Finanzen.” Available at: http://www.bundesfinanzministerium.de/Content/DE/Downloads/Broschueren_Bestellservice/2013-06-28-finanzpolitische-herausforderungen-demografischer-wandel-anlage.pdf?__blob=publicationFile&v=5 [Accessed December 21, 2017].

Xu, K., and P. Saksena. 2011. “The determinants of health expenditure, A country-level panel data analysis.” WHO Working Paper World Health Organization (WHO). Available at: http://www.who.int/health_financing/documents/report_en_11_deter-he.pdf?ua=1 [Accessed January 11, 2018].

Zühlsdorf, A., and A. Spiller. 2012. “Trends in der Lebensmittelvermarktung.” Agrifood Consulting GmbH. Available at: https://www.uni-goettingen.de/de/document/download/708a28c2d41d3525cbc0356b7990d9f0.pdf/Marktstudie%20-%20Trends%20in%20der%20Lebensmittelvermarktung_Studientext_final.pdf [Accessed April 10, 2017].